Echoes of Narcissus

Polygons: Cultural Diversities and Intersections
General Editor: Lieve Spaas, Professor of French Cultural Studies, Kingston University

Volume 1
Reynard the Fox: Social Engagement and Cultural Metamorphoses in the Beast Epic from the Middle Ages to the Present
Edited by Kenneth Varty

Volume 2
Echoes of Narcissus
Edited by Lieve Spaas in association with Trista Selous

Volume 3
Human Nature and the French Revolution: Communities of Faith: From the Enlightenment to the Napoleonic Code
Xavier Martin
Translated from the French by Patrick Corcoran

Volume 4
Secret Spaces, Forbidden Places: Rethinking Culture
Edited by Fran Lloyd and Catherine O'Brien

in preparation

Volume 5
Beyond Language and Culture: Communication across Boundaries
Edited by Magda Stroinska

Volume 6
Expanding Suburbia
Edited by Roger Webster

ECHOES OF NARCISSUS

Edited by Lieve Spaas

Associate Editor Trista Selous

Berghahn Books
New York • Oxford

First published in 2000 by
Berghahn Books
www.BerghahnBooks.com

Editorial offices:
604 West 115th Street, New York, NY 10025, USA
3 NewTec Place, Magdalen Road, Oxford OX4 1RE, UK

© 2000 Lieve Spaas

All rights reserved. No part of this publication may be reproduced in anyform or by any means without the written permission of Berghahn Books.

Library of Congress Cataloging-in-Publication Data
Echoes of Narcissus / edited by Lieve Spaas ; associate editor Trista Selous.
    p. cm. -- (Polygons ; v. 2)
  Papers presented at a conference held May 1997 at the Institut français de Londres, London, England
  Includes bibliographical references and index.
  ISBN 1-57181-761-1
  1. Narcissus (Greek mythology) in literature--Congresses. 2. Narcissism in literature--Congresses. I. Spaas, Lieve. II Selous, Trista, 1957– III. Series.
PN57.N33 E24 2000
809'915--dc21

                                                                         00-045496

British Library Cataloguing in Publication Data
A catalogue record for this book is available from the British Library.

Printed on acid-free paper.

ISBN 1-57181-761-1 (hardback)
ISBN 1-57181-416-6 (paperback)

Contents

List of Figures vii
Acknowledgements ix
Introduction 1
Lieve Spaas

PART I ORIGIN AND DEVELOPMENT OF THE NARCISSUS MYTH

1. Narcissus and his Double 13
   Max Andréoli
2. The Myth of Narcissus in Courtly Literature 25
   Yolande de Pontfarcy
3. *Uror Amore Mei*: Individual and Social Identity in Psychoanalytic Theory 37
   Grahame Lock

PART II MIRRORS AND SELF-REFLECTION

4. The Mirror Preface: The Case of George Sand 57
   Anna Szabó
5. Narcissus Magnified by Marguerite Duras's Echo 67
   Trista Selous
6. Egotism and Narcissism: Avatars of the Masculine Imaginary in Nineteenth-Century French Literature 77
   Jean-Jacques Hamm

PART III MIRRORS AND IMAGES

7. Caught in the Ocular: Visualising Narcissus in the Roman World — 89
   Jas' Elsner

8. Cinema on Show in the Work of the Lumière Brothers — 111
   André Gardies

9. Double Vision: Narcissus and the Silver Screen — 121
   Wendy Everett

PART IV NARCISSUS WRITTEN AND REWRITTEN

10. Narcissus and Echo: Feminine Haunting Masculine — 137
    Naomi Segal

11. Gide's Narcissism — 151
    Scott M. Sprenger

12. Reading the Glass: Fictive Solutions to the Narcissistic Quandary in Freud and Yeats — 167
    Gregory N. Eaves

13. 'The Idiosyncratic Mode of Regard': Narcissistic Narrative in the Fiction of Thomas Hardy — 179
    Roger Webster

PART V IDENTITY AND OTHERNESS

14. Gaul and Woman as Reflected in the French Revolutionary's Mirror — 193
    Xavier Martin

15. The Politics of Extreme Narcissism in the Discourse of the *Front National* — 205
    François Nectoux

16. Self-Reflection through Language — 221
    Magda Stroinska

17. Black Narcissus: Reflections on Identity in African Narrative — 235
    Patrick Corcoran

PART VI THE FATE OF NARCISSUS

18. Jouy's *Cécile* and the Narcissistic Romantic Hero — 247
    Allan H. Pasco

19. Narcissus' Attitude to Death — 263
    Tivadar Gorilovics

Notes on Contributors — 271

Select Bibliography — 275

Index — 279

List of Figures

Figure 1 Fresco of Narcissus by the pool from the House of M. Lucretius Fronto (Pompeii (V. 4 a). Third quarter of the first century AD (Photograph: courtesy of the Deutsches Archäologisches Institut, Rom, Inst. Neg. 72.3597.) 93

Figure 2 Fresco of Narcissus by the pool from the House of M. Loreius Tiburtinus, sometimes given as the House of D. Octavius Quarto (Pompeii II. 2. 2). Third quarter of the first century AD (Photograph: courtesy of the Deutsches Archäologisches Institut, Rom, Inst. Neg. 57.872.) 94

Figure 3 The context of Figure 2 after recent restoration, with the aedicula and couches of the biclinium below it (Photograph: courtesy of the Deutsches Archäologisches Institut, Rom, Inst. Neg. 72.3543.) 95

Figure 4 Fresco of Narcissus by the pool from the Casa dell' Ara Massima (Pompeii VI. 16. 15). Third quarter of the first century AD (Photograph: courtesy of the Deutsches Archäologisches Institut, Rom, Inst. Neg. 76.1276.) 95

Figure 5 Fragment of a fresco of Narcissus by the pool with Eros, from Pompeii (VII. 15. 2). Now in the Antiquarium, Pompeii. Third quarter of the first century AD (Photograph: courtesy of the Deutsches Archäologisches Institut, Rom, Inst. Neg. 77.2283.) 96

Figure 6 Stucco bas-relief of Narcissus by the pool with
         Eros, from the baths in a villa at Stabiae.
         Now in the Antiquarium, Castellamare di
         Stabia. c. AD 60 (Photograph: courtesy of the
         Deutsches Archäologisches Institut, Rom,
         Inst. Neg. 71.492.)   97
Figure 7 Fresco of Narcissus by the pool accompanied
         by Eros and by Echo, from Pompeii (provenance
         unknown). Naples, Museo Nazionale 9380.
         Third quarter of the first century AD (Photograph:
         courtesy of the Deutsches Archäologisches
         Institut, Rom, Inst. Neg. 86.420.)   97

Acknowledgements

This book arose from an International Colloquium held at the Institut Français de Londres in May 1997. It was a warm and stimulating occasion which owes its success to all those who participated. I would like to express my gratitude to the European Research Centre of Kingston University, the Cultural Services of the French Embassy and the British Academy for their generous support. Special thanks are due to Jacqueline Page for her enthusiastic and imaginative support in the preparation of the event, also to René Lacombe for his unfailing support and to Eléonore Renault for her assistance with translating the French abstracts into English. I am very grateful to the associate editor, Trista Selous, whose contribution to this book is invaluable and also to Paul Mercken, Joyce Hamilton and Christina Mercken who helped me with the revisions of the manuscript following the copy editor's work on it.

This collection of essays is the fruit of considerable editorial revision. Trista and I are most grateful to the authors who have carefully followed editorial guidelines and been open to the changes suggested.

Introduction

Ancient myths are perpetuated through cultural transmission in a variety of ways. They are written, dramatised, metamorphosed, and developed into new myths, each reflecting the culture in which they re-emerge; they reflect culture and culture, in turn, transforms and recreates them. Myths are nonhistorical stories which express selective and collective truths. They may draw upon situations of conflict, evoke dichotomies that cannot be resolved or address nontangible or incomprehensible aspects of reality. Narcissus, one of the most poignant mythical characters from antiquity, posits, in his tragic story of self-love, two profound philosophical questions: that of the distinction between illusion and reality and that between self and other. In so doing he raises fundamental issues of knowledge and identity.

In Greek mythology, the beautiful Narcissus glimpsed his own reflection in the water of a spring and fell in love with it. This scene constitutes the core of the ancient Narcissus myth, which has been retold in different versions, of which the best known are those of Ovid and Pausanius. It may be helpful to recall briefly the story's main points at the beginning of this volume of essays. Of the two versions, Ovid's is the more elaborate. According to him, Narcissus was born to the blue-water-nymph, Liriope, after she had been raped by the river-god Cephisus. When he was born, Liriope consulted the blind seer Tiresias to ask whether her son would live to a ripe old age. The seer replied ominously, 'If he never knows himself'.

Narcissus' beauty was such that boys and girls alike fell in love with him. Among those lovers was the nymph Echo, who could no longer use her voice, except in senseless repetitions of another's shout: a punishment inflicted by Hera. One day, when Narcissus went out to net stags, Echo followed him through the forest, longing to address him, but unable to speak. Realising he had strayed from his companions, Narcissus shouted 'Anyone here?' to which Echo answered 'Here'. This surprised Narcissus since no one was in sight and he called out: 'Come!' 'Come' was the reply. When Echo rushed from her hiding place to embrace Narcissus, he shook her off roughly and ran away, saying 'I will die before I offer myself to you' and she answered 'I offer myself to you'. But Narcissus had gone and Echo spent the rest of her life in lonely glens and pined away until only her voice remained and her bones took on the appearance of stones. On another occasion, after Narcissus had been hunting, he lay down near a spring. Needing to relieve his thirst, he drank, looked into the water of the spring and became captivated by his reflection. Overcome with love he reached out towards the handsome person before him: 'How many times', Ovid writes, 'did he give vain kisses to the deceitful spring!' until he came to realise that this was a reflection of himself in the water and that he was burning with love for himself. Narcissus pined away and, on the spot where he died, the white narcissus flower with its orange corolla sprang up.

The tragic story of Narcissus, in love with himself, and of Echo, the nymph in love with him, has inspired painters, writers and film-makers and has given rise to different kinds of theoretical speculations on the concept of 'narcissism' by philosophers, psychoanalysts and sociologists. Over the years, the myth has been much discussed and reinterpreted: for philosophers, water acts as a mirror opening on to the depths of oneself, a self which tends to become idealised; for psychoanalysts, the concept has led to hypotheses concerning the investment of psychic energy in the self; for sociologists, it becomes a metaphor for the situation of mankind in modern society. The Narcissus myth continues to resonate in the deepest recesses of our minds, especially in the light of the theoretical speculations that it has stimulated.

The essays in this volume, selected from the fields of humanities and social sciences, explore the Narcissus myth in its many manifestations and also address the formation of theories based on it. They broaden our understanding of this seminal story. Some explore manifest representations of the myth: variants of the different versions, works of art Narcissus has inspired, and theoretical developments which openly claim a link with it.

Others make creative use of the myth by applying it to social phenomena, literary works, or films where it is latent rather than manifest. They address such questions as: How has the original myth been reinterpreted or rewritten? Does the Narcissus myth shed light on the relationship between self and other? How meaningful is it to transfer it from an individual level to that of a collective group? Can particular works of art, periods of history, or cultural and political movements be characterised as narcissistic? To what extent is the myth gender-related?

Origin and Development of the Narcissus Myth

It is difficult to speak of an 'original' myth, since it has reached us through various versions. Any investigation of the myth must thus address the variants and then trace the developments that have followed. The main theme underlying these variants, according to Max Andréoli, is that of duplicity or the 'double'. Narcissus is always accompanied by his double; the many versions of the myth reveal different aspects of this duplicity, which inevitably exposes the gap between the self and self-awareness. Such a fundamental human trait has understandably launched a debate which has continued till this day. In all the restagings of Narcissus, the tragedy of the split, experienced by mankind, remains fundamental.

How, Yolande de Pontfarcy asks, does Narcissus emerge in French medieval courtly love? Courtly society, she argues, was founded on an ideal of the self which literature has expressed through the relationship between men and women. Drawing upon Bernard de Ventadour's *Chanson de l'Alouette* and the *Roman de la Rose* by Guillaume de Lorris and Jean de Meun, de Pontfarcy shows how the metaphors of mirror and water elicit the Narcissus theme. Writing, inspired by the absence of the beloved, functions on the principle of the mirror: through courtly literature, the myth of Narcissus serves as a mirror for the poets to reflect their own creativity.

Sigmund Freud's use of the myth in the development of his theory on 'narcissism' remains probably the major extrapolation of the story. It is also the starting point of an ongoing debate on the theory of 'narcissism'. It is therefore crucial to examine in some depth the development of this theory. Grahame Lock draws attention to the fact that Freud hardly mentions the myth and offers no comment on the story itself but, instead, uses the notion of narcissism to postulate a new stage of development, the narcissistic stage. For Jacques Lacan, on the other hand, the central elements of the Narcissus story are vital to his discussion on the so-called mirror-stage. Lacan talks, as Ovid does, about an illusion, but for the psychoanalyst, the 'illusion' is part of an identification process. Our identity formation is a product of a process in which self-love is a necessary element. Such reasonable self-love, Lock argues, now 'seems to constitute our individual and social identity, which seems to function as the link between individual and society'.

Mirrors and Self-Reflection

Narcissus' reflection in the water is often compared to one's reflection in a mirror. The mirror, as de Pontfarcy mentions, can also become the text in which authors depict themselves as they wish to be seen. Anna Szabó argues along similar lines in her study of the self-image that an author attempts to sketch when writing a preface to her own book, with particular reference to the nineteenth-century French writer George Sand. By stating Sand's intentions in writing her book and her views on reading it, the preface functions as a mirror in which the readers will perceive the writer's self-image. But a further link between Narcissus and Sand emerges from the autobiography. Is the fate of Narcissus not related to the problem of identity and, in his case, also to the absence of the father? Similarly, Sand's autobiography is a search for her origins and an attempt to recall the absent father figure.

Trista Selous also sets out from the self-image inherent in writing. She examines the work of a female writer, Marguerite Duras, and focuses, in the first instance, on *The Lover*. Although autobiography is not necessarily a manifestation of narcissism, the opening of *The Lover*, Selous notes, is explicitly imbued with narcissism and the text as a whole provides an account of the important place of narcissism in Duras's escape from her family. However, Selous suggests, beyond the manifest narcissism present in the text, its underlying formal structure can also be seen as narcissistic in the way that it invites the reader to take a place similar to that of the lover, by reconstructing an 'emotional image' of Duras that transcends the limitations of time and appearance inherent in a physical image.

Whilst both Szabó and Selous are dealing with the narcissistic impulses of female writers, Jean-Jacques Hamm turns to nineteenth-century French male writers. A different picture emerges as Hamm introduces the notion of egotism, which he considers as akin to narcissism. He sees egotism and narcissism, the seizure and loss of the self, 'as two forms of the use of an ego devoted to freedom, solitude and specular relationships.' Although contrary movements, they are interwoven. Stendhal is said to have introduced the word 'egotisme' in France in 1823; for him it means primarily self-love and a fault to beware of. Yet, Hamm argues, egotism can stimulate the psychic energy of the subject, enabling it to grasp itself. It can lead to action, whilst narcissism leads to the impossibility of wanting to act. Hamm examines various kinds of writing in which this distinction can be discerned. Egotism and narcissism are, in his words, 'opposite movements in the epiphany of the self and movements which are historically both successive and parallel.'

Mirrors and Images

With Jas' Elsner, we enter the pictorial tradition of Narcissus in antiquity and in particular the visual examples that survive from Pompeii. Narcissus, Elsner observes, was 'the inventor of painting because painting involves "embracing with art" that objectified reflection called representation'. Elsner lays the emphasis on the viewing of the spectator, which he also examines in the written versions. In Ovid, the boy in the pool looks back at Narcissus and hence casts upon him the same inducing gaze. This *looking back*, Elsner argues, is revealing with regard to the activity of viewing. He recalls a story by Lacan imagining an inanimate object *looking back*. This, Elsner explains, destabilises the subject's sense of autonomy, it 'controls as an object the viewer who looks out at it'. So, inevitably a 'triangulation breaks out of the paintings to the viewer outside the painting'. But, he says, this triangulation is necessary, since without the viewer/voyeur Narcissus' story would have no point.

This necessary presence of a viewer also emerges in André Gardies' study on early film. In the early Lumière films, Gardies shows, the cameramen and the people filmed display their presence openly, creating a situation in which cinema itself becomes the spectacle, as if it were itself on show. One can thus speak of cinema as being narcissistic in the days of the Lumières, since it sought to contemplate itself through the images that it captured: it filmed itself in the process of filming. Here too, as Elsner showed in relation to the painting of Narcissus, there is a need for a viewer, the need to be seen. This was also the case for the casual passers-by who, when filmed, would wish to see themselves on screen afterwards. The fact that the Lumière cinématograph 'inscribed the traces of its activity on the image itself', Gardies contends, has enabled us to understand what constitutes the filmic.

Wendy Everett continues the debate in her discussion of the situation in which the director adopts a role as both narrator and protagonist in the story that is narrated. As in the cases of literary autobiography, the pictures the film-maker wishes to see, and to show to himself as well as to the viewer, are narcissistic recreations of the self. The screen thus becomes a mirror at which 'he is gazing in order to reach a remembered reflection ... of his present identity. A narrative of this kind recalls the Narcissus myth, not only through its form, that is to say using a mirror/water for self-reflection and its self-love, but also because the Narcissus myth, like the screen/mirror of memory in which the adult searches, is concerned with identity.

Narcissus Written and Rewritten

The four chapters of this section deal with written texts, dividing evenly between French and English literature. Naomi Segal's feminist essay returns to her earlier book, *Narcissus and Echo*. She reminds the reader how she drew attention to the fact that the pool must recall something uncanny, Freud's *heimlich/unheimlich* of the mother's genitals, so that what Narcissus unconsciously seeks is a prenatal 'I'. Furthermore, her discussion reversed the traditional view according to which the mirror is a 'prop of female narcissism' and the voice is male. Segal's concern then was to get the woman's voice out of the man's mirror. She now pushes this point further, particularly in her analysis of André Gide's homosexual writing. Here, she argues, where eroticism is founded on the 'undesire towards women', the 'Narcissus and Echo scenario is then the masculinity that seeks to define itself against femininity'.

Scott Sprenger also focuses on Gide and, in particular, on *La Symphonie pastorale*. Sprenger refutes earlier psychoanalytical interpretations that apply the Freudian model of a narcissistic infantile stage to the theme of homoerotic love which underlies the work. He shows how, in fact, the novella subtly manipulates the Narcissus myth. He traces important water/Narcissus analogies, which he then compares with similar uses in other Gidean texts, evoking references to images of self-embrace reminiscent of Narcissus. He compares Ovid's classical version of Narcissus with Gide's modernist one and shows how, in Ovid, Narcissus 'remains forever mystified by his ideal, whereas Gide's Narcissus ultimately breaks through the mirror and destroys the illusion'.

In Gregory Eaves's essay, Freud's 'narcissistic stage' and the notion of the 'uncanny', to which the two previous authors referred, recur. Eaves sets out from Harold Bloom's view, according to which Freud's essay on 'The Uncanny' is dismissive of the Romantic poetry of the imagination as exemplified by Yeats. This poetry, according to Freud, retains traces of a repressed state of earlier narcissism which is similar to the practice of animism in primitive societies. As Sprenger did with Gide, Eaves questions the reading of Romantic poetry as expressing an infantile narcissistic stage. Using Yeats' poem 'Ego Dominus Tuus', he shows how the poetic strategy, while self-consciously specular, avoids Romantic solipsism and how the mirror of language intervenes between the specular doubles.

Ovid's Narcissus story, according to Roger Webster, is an 'open' one and it is thus not surprising that so many different themes and readings have emerged from this story. The theme Webster develops is that of 'imagining and representation'. According to Webster, Hardy's fiction displays a self-consciousness and a self-reflexivity which reflect on art itself. Not only do narcissistic themes recur in the work, but Hardy's interest in visual perception and representation underlies his creation of characters whose self-perceptions tend to display a strong visual and even painterly dimension. This leads Webster to explore Hardy's strong interest in the paintings of William Turner. Powerful pictorial evocations, reminiscent of Elsner's analysis of the 'looking back' effect, forge a link between the written and the visual as in, for example, *A Pair of Blue Eyes* in which the central character falls over a cliff and, while clinging to a branch, is looked at by inanimate eyes 'dead and turned to stone'. For Webster such an image reflected back is seen not as a narcissistic reinforcement of the subject but as a transforming process with regard to both subject and the construction of art itself.

Identity and Otherness

If identity means, in the first instance, recognising oneself, it would seem that Narcissus' failure to recognise himself denotes a lack of identity, a theme touched upon by Wendy

Everett. Moreover, the absence of the father would call for a search for identity. There is then no doubt that identity looms large in the Narcissus myth and that this refers not only to the individual self but also to the identification with ancestors, family members or fellow citizens. The essays in this section address the question of identity, individual and collective, and examine its link with narcissism.

Myths of origin constitute a vital dimension in the identification process. To belong to an illustrious family or a celebrated nation ensures narcissistic gratification. According to the 'Frankish myth', as Xavier Martin tells us, French aristocrats were assumed to be descendants of the Franks while the commoners traced their origin to the Gauls. Before the French Revolution the Franks were traditionally seen as the more refined race who had freed the country from Roman occupation. It is perhaps surprising then that, after 1789, the revolutionaries did not seek to invert the myth to stress the importance of the commoners' Gallic origins. Martin explains this by showing how the negative characteristics associated with the Gauls, primarily to do with their volatility, as noted by Julius Caesar, made such origins less inviting. Such attributes were, moreover, seen by politicians, philosophers and scientists as feminine, making the Gallic myth even less alluring or apt to satisfy the narcissistic search for illustrious ancestry.

If the French favour a national identity which boasts an ancestral mirror to enhance their self-image, this very pride, as François Nectoux shows, is used by the leader of the *Front National* (FN), Jean-Marie Le Pen, to uphold his racist beliefs through a mirroring strategy. The FN postulates a strong French identity, which 'must be defended' and requires avoiding any 'otherness', which might contaminate it. The FN stresses that eminent French people admired by the French Left, such as Jules Ferry, were racist and even pro-colonialists. Nectoux provides a critique of FN arguments, breaking them down into their rhetorical strategies to show how they exploit narcissistic identification in their attempts to thwart the anti-racist lobby.

If Le Pen rhetorically manipulates language by playing on people's narcissistic self-image, Magda Stroinska discusses the way that different languages already contain traits of self-recognition and self-reflection, but to varying extents. Some languages emphasise the status of the speaker and have a pronoun system which gives prominence to the self. Stroinska claims that this is the case for Indo-European languages which are anthropocentric and speaker-focused. She believes that Indo-European languages could be said to be narcissistic in their core grammar because they allow a strong presence of the self in speech as well as self-reflection. Stroinska goes on to postulate that this may reflect the individualism of Western societies.

Indeed, one should not forget that the Narcissus myth is a Western myth. It is precisely this point that Patrick Corcoran wishes to test in his essay which explores the positing of connections between Western myths and African cultural tradition. To what extent, Corcoran wonders, can classical myths reveal anything about African narratives? He is sceptical about the validity of attempting to trace the Narcissus theme in African narrative. Instead he focuses on the act of looking and distinguishes between the narcissistic gaze, which is self-recognition, and the gaze which observes, or imagines, difference and otherness. It is the latter gaze that characterises the vision of the whites, when looking at the blacks, and that erects the subject/object dichotomy of the colonial situation. The ambiguity of the gaze may then illuminate some of the politics of postcolonial cultures.

The Fate of Narcissus

The ultimate fate of Narcissus is death. However, this 'death' may take many forms. The pining away of the solitary Narcissus may be profound melancholia and withdrawal. Yet when the self projects his narcissistic image upon the other, a course of personal aggressivity and destruction may set in. Allan Pasco explores these two kinds of narcissism in the Romantic hero. The self-loving ones are profoundly self-absorbed and unable to form relationships; they cannot work for the fulfilment of desire, Pasco remarks, for they do not know what would give satisfaction and suspect 'that their dismal fate will never end'. The second kind of narcissists, those whose self-love is channelled through an other, are so fixated on the object of their desire that they are incapable of accepting a substitute (e.g., the psychoanalyst). Their frustration becomes permanent, as Pasco demonstrates through examples in French Romantic literature.

Death, Tivadar Gorilovics argues, is the necessary denouement of the Narcissus story. This explains, he claims, why Pausanius' version, in which Narcissus falls in love with his twin sister so that, when she dies, his self-contemplation is a mourning for her, has attracted less interest than Ovid's story. Gorilovics carefully examines the different aspects of Narcissus' death and emphasises the importance of references to death. There was the possibility of a long life, as Tiresias had stated; then there was Narcissus' own reference to death when Echo threw her arms around him: 'I'll die before I yield to you'. Gorilovics questions the visceral fear Narcissus experiences at the embrace of Echo. Like Echo, he pined away until the body Echo loved existed no longer. Still gazing at this image, he sighed: 'Alas the boy I loved in vain! ... Farewell' and Echo said 'farewell'. The scene recalls *The Portrait of Dorian Gray*, in which Gorilovics sees a modern rewriting of Narcissus. Selous mentions how Dorian Gray became 'alienated in his own youthful image' and Gorilovics shows that in wanting to destroy the portrait, Dorian destroys himself. 'The anguish which eats him and the symbolic meaning of this final act,' he writes, 'bring the myth into harmony with the mental universe of the nineteenth-century's closing years.'

Through their discussion of the Narcissus story and its ramifications, the essays in this volume reveal how this Western myth strikes a chord in the human being, how it defies historical time to reach the twentieth century and continues to remain topical and relevant as a reflection of the human condition.

Lieve Spaas

PART I
ORIGIN AND DEVELOPMENT OF THE NARCISSUS MYTH

Chapter 1

Narcissus and his Double*

Max Andréoli

In dealing with a myth as rich as that of Narcissus, it seems useful to begin with a general discussion of the various possible interpretations, without, however, attempting to catalogue them or to suggest some kind of overview of their evolution, which would inevitably be schematic. The story's many versions seem to form a diverse and indeed heteroclite group; yet the legend of Narcissus belongs to the vast family of myths of the double and touches on themes – of reflection, water, the mirror – whose multiple aspects are bound together by their obvious affinities.[1] The myth's narrative thus brings about a kind of condensation of images which find, as it were, their echo in the deepest recesses of our minds. Hence its early annexation, along with many others, by psychoanalysis which, in the late nineteenth century, gave its hero's name to a tendency which was initially defined as a perversion consisting of exclusive self-love.

Instead of carefully cataloguing the changes undergone by the Narcissus story, I have therefore chosen to concentrate on one of its characteristic elements. Implicitly or explicitly, in all the texts I have come across, there is always an identifiable splitting, disjunction or separation to be found in the story's many variants, which is for me the essential element; Narcissus, who sees and desires himself, is a dual being and this duality or duplicity can be exploited to widely differing ends,

* Translated from the French by Trista Selous.

depending on the period and the writer. (I shall concentrate here on literary works, leaving the fields of the plastic arts, music or psychiatry to their own specialists.) Narcissus is thus always accompanied by his double, which raises the question of what kind of relationship develops between the two facets of this complex character, and also of why so many authors, in so many fields, have been fascinated by this paradoxical pair, which are both two and one. As Calderón's Narcissus says, 'Two trees, with good reason, / Dress in a single bark / If they share the same heart' (1963:2,553–5).

Since the founding text is the well-known episode in Book III of Ovid's *Metamorphoses*, lines 339–510, I shall concentrate my discussion on those passages of the poem relevant to my concerns, starting with a commentary on an episode which precedes the Narcissus story. The links in the *Metamorphoses* are known for their often casual nature; in this case it is the adventure – or misadventure – of Tiresias the seer which leads into that of Narcissus, and immediately afterwards into that of Pentheus. Tiresias has the misfortune to disturb two enormous serpents mating and is, by way of what I dare not call punishment, changed from man into woman until, seven years later and this time by means of a deliberate act, he puts an end to the same serpents' effusions and returns to his original sex. Whether in the meantime he lost by the exchange I do not know, but if he did, it was certainly not on all fronts; for when called on as an arbiter by Jupiter, who was arguing with his wife over the important question of who, man or woman, feels the greater pleasure in the act of love, Tiresias' experience led him to agree with the king of the gods, who said it was undoubtedly the woman. Some have even tried to calculate the 'ratio', as the financiers call it, of the difference. I have no intention of judging the matter here, for fear of courting divine rage; for, whether from fury or humiliation, Juno struck poor Tiresias blind, though in compensation she did give him the ability to see into the future. However, it seems to me that the notions of duality and splitting can already clearly be seen in this story: the separation of the mating serpents, the man with a dual nature and the dispute between Jupiter and Juno over love are all elements that pave the way for the Narcissus story.

The first person to test out the truth of Tiresias' predictions was, as the text tells us, the nymph Liriope, an Oceanid according to some traditions, and mother of Narcissus, whose father was the river Cephisus. I should note in passing that the Narcissus of Ovid's fable is presented from the outset as having a dual nature through his mixed parentage. He is not quite divine, nor does he belong to the human race, to which he is connected primarily by his appearance, in itself as deceptive as it is seductive. Such is not always the case in the *Metamorphoses*, in which gods and demigods mingle with men and women. Moreover, by birth, Narcissus is a child of the water, just as Echo is an emanation of the air, and they continue to develop along parallel lines with the one – but capitally important – distinction that the nymph is not in love with herself. Lastly, Ovid's Narcissus is sixteen, on the threshold between two stages of life, and, line 352 tells us, 'could seem at once boy and man'. Duplicity is thus one of this character's recurrent traits.

Tiresias is thus consulted by Liriope, who wants to know if her son will enjoy long life. The seer gives the following reply, which can be described as sibylline: 'Yes, if he is not to know himself' (*si non se noverit*, line 348). Such an oracle seems nonsensical; however, like all oracles, its difficulty lies in an excess, rather than a lack of meaning. For how should the verb 'to know oneself' – in Latin the reflexive *se novere* – be understood? Narcissus comes to see and desire himself, but to say that he 'knows' himself is an abuse of vocabulary. The word begs enormous questions which have themselves given rise to entire shelves of philosophical works. I shall confine myself here to noting that Ovid's Narcissus moves through different degrees of knowledge or recognition of that mystery that is called 'me'.

First of all, the young man 'knows himself' simply by virtue of the fact that he says 'I' and 'me', thus distinguishing himself from the other ('Why do you flee me?' (383–4)). He 'knows himself', therefore, but only as an abstract subject. For the reader, however, this is the most important thing: in its very expression the Latin verb opens up a fault line, sets up a duality of the subject of 'knows' (*noverit*) and the reflexive 'himself' (*se*). Narcissus must, on pain of death, preserve his own wholeness, must 'persevere in his being' to use Spinoza's phrase (1965:236); he must not 'reflect', far less 'reflect to himself'. At first Narcissus follows this injunction to the letter: he rejects all appeals from young men, from Echo and, above all, an obscure attraction he feels emanating from himself and whose danger he senses. 'I shall die', he tells Echo, 'before you enjoy me' (391), in other words 'before you make me into something that I am not, before you alienate me in you'. For in order not to 'know himself' any more, Narcissus must not become an object, which would be an object of knowledge, but must remain a pure subject.

Even Echo, in her way, is a figure of duality and reflection, since she reflects the last words that she hears. She brings about the first disillusionment, the first crack in Narcissus' defences, since he is 'deceived by the image of the voice granted to his' (385), words later used by Ovid to show the young man 'seduced by the image of a beautiful face' (416) in the pool.[2] I do not intend to list the ever-present parallels that give the entire text its dual structure; suffice it to say that here similar words are used to refer to one and the same trap, which Narcissus first discovers, but into which he later fatally falls, led astray by higher influences.

The rest is well known: Nemesis intervenes on behalf of one of the unhappy admirers; Narcissus, tired by a long hunt – which is also an unconscious search for himself – stops to drink at a virgin spring, sheltered from the sun, and in the water he glimpses, not his image but, as we have seen, 'the image of a beautiful face'. He is filled with desire for an 'inconsistent reflection', since this son of water 'takes for a body what is only water' (416–17). The splitting thus begun, which marks another step down the path of knowledge, manifests itself in what he calls in his long lament 'this thin water', this 'very weak obstacle', which is all that separates him, or so he thinks, from the shadow to which he is drawn (the elliptical *Exigua prohibemur aqua* (450) in Ovid's words).

The use of the plural *prohibemur* ('we are separated') should be noted here. At this moment Narcissus is fully Narcissus: the reflection that he sees is, to him, someone other than himself, independent of him; only the narrator and reader know that these two are one. There is a split here, but it has not yet been internalised, separating the one in whom it occurs from himself. Nevertheless, without being fully aware of it, Narcissus is already objectified and alienated, but only into his own image. The decisive revelation, rich in possibilities, heralded and emphasised by the narrator's pleas, the questions and entreaties Narcissus addresses to his double and the proliferation of personal pronouns, comes in the form of an enlightenment in line 463: *Iste ego sum*, 'I am him' or, literally, 'this one I am'.[3]

Although this discovery, which prefigures the primary narcissism of psychoanalysis, destroys the illusion and establishes a divorce, it does not put an end to Narcissus' love: the libido turns inwards and cathects the ego, as in secondary narcissism. Narcissus now knows that he is split, that he loves not a 'beautiful face' in the spring but this double that has suddenly sprung from him. He wants to see himself whole rather than in the form of a disembodied reflection, which still fascinates him, but which he wants to see embodied in his own body: 'Oh if only I could leave my own body!' And in the now painful awareness of the paradoxical nature of his passion, he exclaims: 'A strange wish for a lover, I would like *to be separated* from what I love' (467–8, my emphasis). In order to confirm the irreversibility of the unrealisable separation that this expression of his desire nevertheless symbolically realises, the poet adds, perhaps a little humorously, that 'even after he had entered hell, Narcissus was still looking at himself in the Styx' (504–5). The hero's concentration on himself destroys Echo, who becomes useless, and in turn Narcissus himself: all that remains of him is a flower of the damp poolsides, which itself presides over another legend of separation, that of the rape of Persephone (or Proserpine), as we see in Hesiod's *Theogony*. For Narcissus' inextricable situation can end only in his death, since he now 'knows himself', and this knowledge is to him a lethal trap.

Tiresias' prediction is thus fulfilled, yet still leaves room for reflection, for it seems to go against the Delphic and Socratic injunction to 'know thyself'; the reader might then conclude that the spontaneity of passion, which remains intact, is preferable to the self-knowledge advocated by philosophy. Such a lesson in hedonism is in keeping with the poet of the *Amores* and *The Art of Love*, although Ovid, rivalling Lucretius, devoted the first book of his *Metamorphoses* to the unfolding of an authentic and poetic creation story, and Book XV to a demonstration of Pythagorean doctrine. Everything rests on the meaning attributed to the verb 'to know oneself': in his book *L'Erreur de Narcisse* the philosopher Louis Lavelle notes that Narcissus never attains an authentic knowledge of himself, since this is possible only, if at all, by leaving oneself in communication with the other. All he gains is an imperfect and superficial perception of his double, which does not in itself enrich him. As Lavelle rightly points out, Narcissus asks 'pure sight to let him enjoy his essence alone, and his tragedy is that it can give him only his appearance' (1939:8). All the same, the ordinary sight of his reflection in the water of the spring makes him aware of this duality that shatters his original unity, splitting him down the fault line of an obscure absence, through the intrusion of death into life and nothingness into being; in this restricted, but vitally important sense, one can say that he 'knows himself'.

Ovid does not seem, however, to want to turn the reader towards philosophical abstraction. Preferring *muthos* to *logos*, he keeps to the story, which is itself excellent enough, drawing from it only the morals of ancient wisdom: avoid excess, beware of appearances, do not turn in on yourself for fear of exciting the wrath of the gods, which follows, in Narcissus' case, what Ovid calls the 'righteous prayer' (406) of one of his victims. The adjective 'righteous' implies that the narrator – and author – is taking sides and passing judgement, Ovid being no doubt well placed to wish for the punishment of over-inhuman virtues. Whatever the case, the story, which was more or less created by the poet, seems to have had few antecedents unless they be in popular tradition, in the works of authors neglected or lost today, or in those of compilers such as the Greek Conon, who collected the outlines of fifty legends, the twenty-fourth of which is a story of Narcissus. To my knowledge this story was little used in antiquity; the flower is mentioned by various poets and there is an allusion to a monument dedicated to Narcissus, to Sigelius, to the Silent One in Book IX, Chapter 2 of a work by one of Ovid's contemporaries, Strabo's *Geography*.

Of more interest is the much later critical account by the geographer Pausanias in the second century AD. At this time there was still a spring dedicated to Narcissus near Thespiae in Boeotia. Pausanias mentions it in his *Description of Greece* (IX, 31, 7); more importantly, in the same work (Boeotia, XXXI, 6–9) he gives another, Boeotian version of the myth which is very different from that of Ovid. This is an euhemerist rationalisation, which precisely seeks to reject the split which characterises Ovid's narrative: 'It is said that Narcissus looked into the water and, not understanding that he was seeing his own reflection, fell in love with himself without realising and died of love by the spring'. This casual summary is accompanied by a no less cavalier refutation, based on the simplest arguments of common sense: 'But it is totally stupid to imagine that a man old enough to fall in love could be unable to tell a man from his own reflection'.

Pausanias thus prefers the version he says is commonly found in Boeotia and which explains duality in terms of twins. This story is, he admits, 'certainly less commonly known than the former, but is not without foundation'. In this version Narcissus has a twin sister who is like him not only physically, but also in tastes, habits and clothing. Narcissus falls in love with her and, when the girl dies, finds consolation in the waters of the spring, 'knowing', says Pausanias, 'that what he saw was his own reflection'. The essential feature of splitting, though very attenuated here, has not disappeared altogether, since it gives the myth its basic *raison d'être*: something of it remains in this watered down alter ego of the young man's twin sister.

Using the hierarchy of levels of interpretation developed by Dante among others, it would seem that this very rich story can be read at all the levels in the work of Ovid, while remaining at the literal level in that of Pausanias. The medieval writers took pleasure in exploiting the second, moral level, which was already clearly perceptible in Ovid's text. Guillaume de Lorris, author of the first part of the *Roman de la rose*, was one of the first wave of poets to exploit this aspect of the myth. The sixteenth-century humanists certainly perpetuated the moral interpretation; however, between this tradition and the modern variants, which are beyond the scope of this discussion, other works were written, during the Renaissance and baroque periods, which updated the Narcissus story. Of particular interest is one of Calderón's *comedia*, *Eco y Narciso*, which was staged in 1661. Adapted for the theatre in the traditional Spanish genre of the mythological 'pastoral', this story made it possible, among other things, to show the Court and its characters transfigured on stage in a manner analogous to that of the contemporary operas by Quinault and Lulli in France, or in Spenser's pageants and masques at the end of the sixteenth century, and later in those of Shirley and Milton. The baroque spirit, with its antitheses, its marriage of symmetry and fantasy, its obsession with movement, shadows and reflections, its awareness of the fragility of worldly things and the interplay of what the Spanish call *engaño* and *desengaño* – illusion and disillusion – was highly receptive to the story of Narcissus.[4] Theatrical adaptation of course required transformations in the myth's economy, if only to meet the expectations of the audience, in this case composed of aristocrats and courtiers; hence the use of choirs, sung sections and verbal contests (*sofisterías*), the presence of minor characters forming a system of couples who mirror and contrast with each other, not to mention *gracioso*, the fool, in the person of the peasant Bato in *Eco y Narciso*. Calderón also made important changes to the unfolding of the story, of which I shall concentrate on the most important, affecting the character of Narcissus himself.

In Calderón's work Narcissus' mother Liriope is given far greater importance than she has in that of Ovid – partly, no doubt, for reasons of symmetry: she counterbalances Echo. Echo herself, no longer a nymph but a 'pastoral' peasant-girl of great beauty, has become one of the two protagonists – the play's title is *Eco y Narciso*. Her echolalia is not, so to speak, congenital, but has resulted from a poison put out by Liriope, who wanted to save her child from the danger Echo represented to him. For, while in Ovid's poem Tiresias predicts a long life for Narcissus as long as 'he does not know himself', in Calderón's play Tiresias has become an astrologer and magician who, on his deathbed, makes a quite different prediction: Liriope will give birth to a very beautiful boy whom 'a voice and a beauty' both loved and hated (a typical baroque antithesis) will try to destroy. Warned by his mother, Narcissus tries, with her help, to flee the danger, but falls into another trap – and this is where he returns to the Ovid story – which is that of the beauty of his reflection, which he takes for a nymph of the spring, in association with all that remains of Echo's voice, repeating words and fragments of words, just as the oracle's words had predicted.

Here we see the restaging of a recurrent conflict in Calderón's theatre, between human free will and the omnipotence of fate – or rather Providence – which, by a kind of transcendent trick, exploits to its own ends the efforts human beings make in their own limited sphere to avoid it. Thus the play opens up philosophical discussions of problems dear to the writer and his time; it raises the fable to its allegorical and indeed symbolic, anagogic or mystical levels, exploring the depths of the soul, which it links to the immensity of the heavens, the macrocosm reflected in the microcosm. Moreover, and crucially for this discussion, it uncovers the underlying conflicts by which the soul is split and riven: not only that of a man separated from himself and the world by an illusion and whose realisation that it is an illusion kills him, but also that of essence and appearances. The importance of this latter question for Calderón is reflected in the title of his best-known play, *La vida es sueño* (*Life is a Dream*). The main character in this drama, Sigismond, is moreover closely related to Narcissus, since he is imprisoned as the result of a prediction, while Narcissus is brought up away from other people on a mountainside by his mother Liriope.

In *Eco y Narciso*, before the paradisiacal vision which immobilises the scene of the spring, the young man, in love with his deceptive reflection, laments, as he does in Ovid's poem, that he cannot remove the insubstantial and uncrossable obstacle which keeps him from it. As he says in the well-known final lines of his great monologue, 'It is only the crystal that I touch, / It is not the soul of the crystal' (2,589–90).

'The soul of the crystal' is both what Narcissus believes to be the nymph of the spring and the pure essence of being. This assimilation is a generalisation of that made by Narcissus in

Ovid's fable: perhaps, in the nostalgic negative of appearance, the character intuits a real world in which everything is complete and true, a world separated by a kind of void from human beings, who are condemned to wander among the moving shadows of the spring or the cave. The myth thus acquires a cosmic meaning which it openly acknowledges. When she meets Narcissus in the *Second Day*, Echo says, 'Narcissus and Echo come to be / a new history of the world' (1,279–80).

In this image, the split thus spreads to everything and outlines a Platonic philosophy which, like Ovid's myth, has been reworked by a Christian. Convinced by Liriope's explanations and, better still, proof that he has fallen prey to a mirage, Narcissus understands that he can never possess the beauty he has glimpsed, because it is that of the double he carries within himself (3,114–15). He nevertheless remains in love, while loathing the voice of Echo, another mirage, thus fulfilling Tiresias' prediction, since it is the double of himself that he both hates and loves: 'I want', he says, '*to escape myself*' (3,114–15, my emphasis), a desire that will be met by death.

Thus, through the split it establishes between essence and appearances, self and self-awareness, the Narcissus myth launched a debate which has continued in very different forms into the works of authors close to our own times. I shall briefly mention the French writers Gide and Valéry, who reflected on the myth at length a century ago, in the *Treatise on Narcissus* and *Fragments on Narcissus* respectively, in a period which had, like our own, grown tired of great systems and tended to favour the cult of the ego. In the work of these writers everything begins with the still calm of a kind of Eden, into which human beings (or God himself, according to Valéry's *Sketch of a Serpent*) introduce unease and movement, in other words disturbance. For the mind, unsatisfied by the monotonous sight of the Garden, wants to see what is watching this show. However, there is a reversal: instead of allowing the splitting to which he is subjected and which separates him from his being to destroy his identity, the hero strives to rebuild the unity of things and of himself. I shall confine myself here to quoting a few lines. In 'Le Cimetière marin' ('The Marine Cemetery') Valéry addresses the following sublime invocation to the Being (or Nothingness) of Midday:

> Complete head and perfect diadem
> I am in you the secret change
> You have only me to contain your fears!

> My repentance, my doubts, my constraints
> Are the flaw in your great diamond.

In 1892 Gide, in his *Treatise on Narcissus*, said that 'Truths remain behind the Symbol-Forms. Every phenomenon is the Symbol of a truth'. Later he added that the poet, having perceived 'the Idea, the secret harmonious Number of his Being [...] uninterested in the transitory form that it took in time [...], is able to give it back an eternal form, its own true, fatal, paradisiacal and crystalline Form' like the crystal that sparkled in Narcissus' spring in the 'orchard of Déduit' in the *Roman de la rose* or the 'crystal' of the spring in Calderón's play.

Many other thinkers have tried to repair the split, including Bachelard, with what he called the 'idealising narcissism' of sublimation. Perhaps, in analysing the essential functions of the human mind, the scientists and philosophers, mathematicians, logicians, epistemologists and phenomenologists are all evoking the image and mad passion of Narcissus in love with himself and desperately seeking his essence. In a more concrete field, this indefatigable quest may be reaching its end with the recent implementation of biological cloning techniques, so far reserved for Dolly the sheep. What a triumph for Narcissus to see his image embodied and no longer an evanescent reflection in the spring waters! But here, too, such a triumph would be deceptive: 'It is what I carry within me that is unknown to me which makes me me', said Valéry. If it is true that knowledge can only be of the general, then what it is permitted to know of an individual's self, of 'that purity of ourselves that we carry', which Mallarmé invoked in *Solennité*, escapes all knowledge. Only writers and poets such as Ovid, Montaigne, Mallarmé and Valéry have the power to suggest, in the rich mirror of writing, this tangible absence through which human beings are present to themselves. It would seem that once again, the soul's thin, transparent surface separates Narcissus from his double, as it always has and no doubt always will.

Notes

1. The psychoanalyst Julia Kristeva has taken Ovid's text as the basis for an interesting study on the theory of reflection in Plotinus' *Enneads* in 'Narcisse: la nouvelle démence', in *Histoires d'amour* (Paris: Denoel, 1983), 131–53.
2. *alternae deceptus imagine vocis* (385) and *visae correptus imagine formae* (416).

3. There is another version of this crucial phrase: *In te ego sum*; but this seems to me less profound. Perhaps a more exact translation would be, 'You who are here, I myself am he'.
4. For example, Shirley wrote a *Narcissus*, inspired by Shakespeare's *Venus and Adonis*.

Bibliography

Calderón (1959) *La vida es sueño* (Buenos Aires: Losada).
────── (1963) *Eco y Narciso* [1672], ed. C. Aubrun (Paris: Centre de recherches de l'Institut d'Etudes Hispaniques).
Gide, A. (1958) 'Le Traité du Narcisse', in *Romans* (Paris: Gallimard, Bibliothèque de la Pléiade).
Lavelle, L. (1939) *L'Erreur de Narcisse* (Paris: Grasset).
Mallarmé, S. (1945) 'Solennité', in *Oeuvres complètes* (Paris: Gallimard) 334.
Ovid (1966) *Metamorphoses*, ed. J. Chamonard (Paris: Garnier Flammarion).
Pausanius (1971) *Pausanius' Description of Greece*, Boeotia (London: Penguin Books).
Spinoza (1965) *Ethique*, trans. C. Appuhn (Paris: Garnier Flammarion).
Valéry, P. (1957) 'Le Cimetière marin' [1920], in *Oeuvres I* (Paris: Gallimard) 149–50.

CHAPTER 2

THE MYTH OF NARCISSUS IN COURTLY LITERATURE

Yolande de Pontfarcy

Courtly society built itself around a heightened view of man which was essentially expressed in literature through his relationship with woman. Idealised love, however, incurs the risk of being unfulfilled, leaving the lover a prisoner of his own dream of greatness. Therefore admiration sought in the eyes of the loved one not only invited the oft-used metaphor of the mirror but recalled Narcissus (Ovid, *Metamorphoses* III, 339–510). The cruel fate of the beautiful ephebe haunted the courtly poets (see Vinge 1967:42–8; Goldin 1967:69–106; Frappier 1976:149–66 and 181–98), but the myth also revealed the combined power of water and mirrors to erase the borders between reality and illusion, self and other, life and death, and open up a whole world of images. Poets therefore used this model to reflect their own difference and power to create images.[1]

The troubadours' poetic autobiographies already place their work in the realm of Narcissus (Zumthor 1973:29–48). Bernard de Ventadour, however, who lived in the middle of the twelfth century, referred more precisely to the young hero in his famous 'Song of the Lark'. He opens his *canso* with the image of the bird which flies towards the sun then lets itself fall because of the sweetness which enters its heart. He marvels that his own heart does not melt with desire (verse I). He thought that he knew love but discovers that he knows nothing, since he cannot help loving his lady, although his love will not be reciprocated. She has taken everything from him and he is left with nothing but desire and a longing heart (II). He lost all power the moment she let him look into the mirror of her eyes. But he saw his own reflection and, like Narcissus, lost himself in the pool (III). He distrusts all women since none wants to help him to win the one he loves; for him, now, all women are the same (IV). Because of his lady's fickleness he has fallen from grace, and is like a madman on a bridge or a climber on a slope which is too steep (V). No one would believe that she could be so pitiless and would let a thirsty person die (VI); but since she is without mercy and is not happy with his love, all that remains to him is to renounce love and song, leave for exile and die (VII) (see Bec 1979:130–6, or Press 1971:76–9; Vinge 1967:66–72; Goldin 1967:92–103; Frappier 1976:162–4; Huchet 1982:21–2; Kay 1983:272–85).

The structure of the *canso* plays on images of unresolved duality and repetition. It is composed of seven verses of eight octosyllabic lines, built around the same two pairs of interlaced rhymes (abab-cdcd), each of the two pairs corresponding to the two parts of the idea developed in the verse. The melodic structure, which varies with each line, makes each stand out as if isolated. But in the *tornada* of four octosyllabic lines addressed to Tristan (the hidden name of his lady), the second part of the last verse, his renunciation of the world, love and song, is repeated phonetically, musically and thematically as an echo.

The ecstasy of the lark, metaphor of fulfilled love, is contrasted with the cruelty of unsatisfied desire. The lady is the fountain at which he wishes to quench his thirst; he had hoped to pass through the mirror of her eyes just as the lark approaches the luminous source and lets itself fall in rapture; but this has been denied him. The mirror has become a screen behind which the lady has retired; he sees only his own image. Unlike Plato's positive idea that the one who loves sees himself in the loved one as in a mirror (*Phaedrus* 255 d) the troubadour's vision of himself in his lady's eye is a cruel deception (Couloubaritsis 1989:34); instead of drawing close to her as he thought, he finds himself further away; the amorous illusion kept alive by the lady has shattered on the surface of the mirror and nothing remains but the intoxication of his desire. Thus the images of Narcissus' destiny, together with a fall from a great height, reflect his own fall into nothingness or its equivalent, indifference. In his disillusion, which is also an awareness of his lady's perfidy reflected in all women, he reduces women to simple mirrors, that is to say unfeeling objects. His broken illusions isolate him forever from courtly society, which takes its dream for reality. Cut off, therefore, from the very sources of life, having seen his double in the mirror, his image leads him to reflection and an awareness of reality in all its horror. In this conceptual immersion, he rediscovers life as *logos*.[2] On the one hand his pain, sublimated in poetic song, becomes creative and, by making the lady the object of his desire and of his discourse, he regains his position as subject. At the same time, like Athena the warrior goddess, who carried the head of Medusa on her shield, he protects himself by holding up the reflection of the face of the Other, paradoxically both attractive and repulsive, of which all indifferent women and Death itself are but a single aspect.[3] Consequently his fall has been transformed into a descent;[4] no longer a desperate search for an image, like that of Narcissus looking into the waters of the Styx, but an exile from life with neither illusions nor songs.

The dangers of indifference and its dramatic consequences appear similarly in the *Lai de Narcisse* (a tale of some thousand lines, almost six times longer than Ovid's text), written around 1170 by a Franco-Norman poet (see Thiry-Stassin and Tyssens 1976; also Goldin 1967:22–48; Vinge 1967:55–66; Lefay-Toury 1979:57–82). In the prologue, the anonymous author announces the didactic function of his work and, in this way, distinguishes it from Ovid's text. He first advises readers to be careful of the snares of love (1–16). But, if a man falls madly in love with a woman, she must listen to him and not hurt him by her pride (17–28); as to the man who rejects the love of a woman, he deserves to be burnt or hanged (29–32). The realism of this text in its adaptation to medieval culture gives weight to these warnings. Narcissus is no longer the son of a water-nymph and Cephisus, the river-god, but that of a mortal lady (47) and a knight of the king of Thebes (547). Echo, the aural image of Narcissus, has been replaced by Dane, the king's daughter. Through Dane's love for Narcissus, the anonymous author also recreates the hierarchical setting of the courtly relationship between a high-born lady and a man of inferior social status; however, contrary to the *langue d'oc* theories of love, Dane is not married and it is not she who rejects the offer of love. This difference doubly justifies Narcissus' punishment: it allows the anonymous author to use Dane's experience to show both the impasse of her dependent love and her unreasonableness in loving someone who does not reciprocate her feelings (not to mention her audacity in giving her heart without her father's consent, contrary to the matrimonial laws of the time). Moreover, the parallel experience of the two young people – that of Dane heralding that of Narcissus, which repeats it as an echo (see Lefay-Toury 1979:63–5) – stresses the equality of people in love, which affects men and women and makes them suffer in equal measures. In replacing Nemesis by Venus and her son, the anonymous author personifies Love as a power with collective and social functions, which must be acknowledged and to which private feelings must submit. Thus the implicit homosexuality of Ovid's Narcissus has disappeared: the medieval Narcissus takes his image for a feminine being, blames her refusal to respond to him on pride and becomes aware of the pain endured by those he himself had rejected in the past (681–704) (see Goldin 1967:29). Through suffering, Love subjects the indifferent Narcissus to its laws, so that he resembles all those who suffer for love. Narcissus' awareness of his own indifference makes him realise that the indifferent other is in fact himself. Unlike Ovid's Narcissus, who has never a thought for Echo, the medieval Narcissus suddenly remembers Dane and wishes to give reality to the *umbre* that he fell in love with (Goldin 1967:47); but when she arrives, he is too exhausted and can only point to the pool, hold out his arms to her and die. The conclusion, which underlines the tragic end of those who behave with indifference and pride, thus echoes the warnings of the prologue.

The circular structure shows that love as a private feeling, in conflict with the social ethic of love, carries death instead of life in its centre. The myth of Narcissus gives the teaching of the anonymous author a universal value and the weight of authority. He shows the tragic consequences of unreasonable, excessive behaviour in those who persist with a hopeless love and subtly criticises the asocial character of *fin'amor* as the shadow-bound love of a shadowy image. The author gives his moralistic work an apotropaic function, so that his image of courtly society will dissuade or protect that society from its own narcissistic tendencies.

In the following century the dialectic of the relationship between self and other in terms of that between reflection and source was again examined in the *Roman de la Rose* (Lecoy 1965–70, see Strubel 1984:61–8). The part written by Guillaume de Lorris between 1225 and 1230 (ll. 1–4028) is constructed around a reference to Narcissus, who reappears and is rejected by Jean de Meun in his continuation (ll. 4,029–21,750, written between 1269 and 1278).

The protagonist (narrator-actor) relates the premonitory dream he has had some five years before and which concerns his quest for a love revealed in the fountain of Narcissus. This fountain is situated in the centre of the square, walled garden of Deduit ('lovers' games'), into which he is led by Oiseuse ('Idle'), a lovely young lady holding a mirror in her hand (495–592). After admiring the groups of young dancers and courting couples, visiting the entire garden and marvelling at its beauty and richness (629–80 and 1,283–1,422), the protagonist discovers the Fountain among the trees, beneath a magnificent pine. On its marble steps is written: 'Here died the beautiful Narcissus' (1,423–36). The young man's story is then summarised as a warning to ladies who refuse to give themselves to their lovers: before dying, rejected by Narcissus, lady Echo asked God that the young man should also know the pain of unrequited love. Consequently one day, while hunting, he arrived thirsty at the fountain, fell in love with his own shadow, lost his reason and died (1,437–1,508).

Aware of Narcissus' fate, the protagonist is apprehensive about approaching the fountain, but feels that this is unreasonable since he knows the dangers (1,509–20). On looking into it, he sees the white gravel floor through the clear water and two crystal stones which reflect everything that can be seen in one half of the garden. On walking round the fountain, the other half appears. In the sunlight the sight is superb: nature in all the tiny detail of its beauty is reflected and enhanced, as if painted in the crystals (1,521–68). However, all who look into this Perilous Mirror, says the narrator, are destined to know love, because Love has sown the 'redoutable seed' in the fountain, whence its name 'the Fountain of Love'. Proof of this comes when, although forewarned, the protagonist is fooled (1,569–612). In the crystals he sees rose bushes covered in flowers and, filled with a powerful desire, leaves the fountain and moves towards them. Among the flowers he finds a rosebud which intoxicates him with its beauty and perfume (1,614–72). But, just as he is about to pick it, Love, who has been hunting him down since he first entered the garden (1,418–22), fires five arrows into his heart (1,673–878). The vanquished young man submits entirely and pays homage to the god (1,879–2,008). After Love has recited the ten commandments of Love (2,009–762), the narrator tells the story of the quest for the Rose, his wonder at its beauty, his rapture at obtaining a kiss from it and his renewed quest when Jealousy has a fortress built around the flower (2,763–4,028).

As the site of images and love, the writing uses an interplay of mirrors, reflections and *mise en abyme*. Ovid, Macrobius, the courtly songs and Chrétien de Troyes' romances form the intertextual context of Guillaume de Lorris's work. The long description of the garden, with the fountain under the pine at its centre, superimposes representations of the Earthly Paradise, the *locus amoenus* of the poetry of the troubadours and the courtly romances (Köhler 1963:86–103 or Fourrier 1964; Frappier 1976:187–8; also Robertson 1951; Fleming 1983), like a mirror reflecting different and similar manifestations of the 'Centre of the World', the sacred space of primordial revelations (Eliade 1975:paras 143, 145, 146). This technique of reflection is pushed to the extreme: the dreamer's view of himself, when relating the story years later, sets a distance between dream and reality (Pickens 1974), past (memory) and present, present and future (premonition), the actor (in the dream) and the narrator (of the dream) (Strohm 1968; Vitz 1973) and the image (dream, symbol, allegory, metaphor, reflection) and its source, in order to reveal a multifaceted truth completely contained in the Fountain of Narcissus, which is also the Fountain of Love. The effect of the mirror is caused not by the water but by the two crystals, so that the Fountain of Love and the Perilous Mirror are both united and disassociated, in the same way that on the one hand the source, love and life and on the other the object, the image and danger (death) are both opposed and intrinsically united (see Strubel 1984:31, 42–4; Hult 1981:147). One inside the other under the magnificent tree, they repeat this image of coinciding opposites, the intimate union of container and contained as symbols of the interconnection and dynamism of the vital forces of becoming (Durand 1969:225–30), the space of all metamorphosis, where the Dreamer-Walker, who believed himself protected by his knowledge, was transformed into a Lover despite himself. He did not linger to admire himself, nor did he see the Rose; he admired only Nature in its full beauty suffused with light. But the fall, which the downwards look symbolises, has been turned into a descent towards the centre, where the onlooker discovers an inner universe, a transformed reflection of the outer world. Transfigured reality has become an artistic creation, since every detail appears as if painted in the crystals (Huchet 1990:180). A vision larger than reality is revealed, as the protagonist discovers at the same time what is behind and above him. The totality of the universe is therefore contained in this mirror/look into the depths of the fountain (the crystals are also referred to in the singular, lines 1,541–68) (Hillman 1980; Hult 1981:38, n.17), but the protagonist cannot see it in one glance – he is not God; he must look for it and walk round the fountain.

This discovery of an inner truth, bringing a new view of the world, is revealed by the rose bush, which he had not noticed when he walked round the garden, but which he saw in the fountain and which led him beyond it. To the stasis of Narcissus' fascination with his image the poet thus contrasts the dynamism of the quest (Kessler 1982), which draws the protagonist towards an unconsciously desired goal: Rose, woman, dream. The image retains all its richness of meanings. These are superimposed and nourish the reality of life, the dynamism of a quest renewed by a constantly reborn desire. For this reason the section written by Guillaume de Lorris is open-ended and seems both finished and unfinished, like Chrétien de Troyes' romance of the quest for the grail (Ribard 1995:97–103).

The story of the myth of Narcissus was aimed at ladies in order to encourage them to give themselves to their lovers instead of turning inwards and letting themselves be caught in the trap of their own image. It exposes the anguish of the courtly man who, having given woman the power to refuse herself to him, is tortured by the idea that she might take him at his word and leave him dying of unrequited love. On the one hand the story of Narcissus thus aims to protect men by showing women a sad image of what their future holds if they should fall in love with their own image as reflected in the mirror offered to them by courtly poets and, on the other, it sets up an opposition between the old Narcissus and the ideal courtly man – an enlightened Narcissus, who is praised.

In his part of the story Jean de Meun rejects both his predecessor's ideal conception of woman as source of all men's virtues (Friedman 1959–60) and his idealised eroticism, akin to mysticism (Kamenetz 1984; Ribard 1995:315–25), for a realistic expression of creation of which, among other things, the hammer, stiletto and plough are instruments (19,475–774) (Méla 1983:73). He also contrasts the square garden of Deduit, with its Fountain of Love and Perilous Mirror in which the beautiful Narcissus met his death, with the round garden of Celestial Paradise where the Fountain of Life murmurs, in whose depths lie a carbuncle with three facets (20,237–566) (Notz 1978). He also replaces the myth of Narcissus with that of Pygmalion (*Metamorphoses* X, 235–300), for whom Venus changed the ivory statue that he had sculpted and fallen in love with into a real woman (20,787–21,184) (Poirion 1970; Dragonetti 1978; Thut 1982). Although Pygmalion thinks himself less foolish than Narcissus, since he can take the statue in his arms and kiss it (20,840-58) without the intervention of the goddess, its icy beauty has no more presence than that given by its creator's desire (Braet 1995:248). Through this myth, Jean de Meun shows that, whatever the artistic power of man, the ultimate sources of life come from God, reiterating his distinction between the ideal artistic universe, which remains human, and the sacred, which belongs to the divine. In consequence the story of Pygmalion and Venus, which precedes that of the brutal deflowering of the Rose which ends the romance, sets artistic creation, the sexual act and the birth of the book all in the sphere of human creativity, while at the same time leaving to God alone the sacred mystery of the origins of life.[5]

In conclusion, throughout courtly literature the myth of Narcissus served as a mirror in which poets reflected their own creativity. Bernard de Ventadour and the anonymous author of the *Lai de Narcisse* exploited the narcissistic vision as an apotropaic means of exorcising the dangers of repetition and affirming their originality as authors. On the other hand, Guillaume de Lorris created an enlightened Narcissus in his protagonist and made the image rich in signs, through which appearances lead to the real and the temporal to the spiritual in an endless play of reflections. Meanwhile Jean de Meun rejected this new Narcissus with his idealised eroticism, together with the power of revelation given to the image and what he may have felt to be a vulgarisation of the sacred, preferring a robust expression of creation and the production of forms. In his work carnal union, knowledge and know-how, aided by divine intervention, give reality and substance to dreams and conjure up the anguish of virginity, the blank page and unfinished work.

Notes

1. Clair (1989:173) sees modernity as condemning Narcissus and his reflection to death; but see Dubois (1990:134–41; I am indebted to my colleague Dr Johnnie Gratton for having brought this book to my attention). See also Wunenburger (1995).
2. Goldin writes that Narcissus' power to articulate his self-knowledge reminds one of St Augustine's idea (*De Trinitate* xiv, x, 13): 'The mind', says Augustine, 'always loves itself and always knows itself – but not always consciously. When, impelled by self-love, the mind comes to know itself consciously, its act is the utterance of a "word" that defines its own identity and becomes an image of it' (1967:43–5).

3. According to Ovid, 'Medusa was once renowned for her loveliness and roused jealous hopes in the hearts of many suitors' (*Metamorphoses* IV, 790–803). See also Clair, who describes Athena thus: 'Divine protectress of that which is most human in human beings, the faculty of reason, she holds out the very thing from which she protects herself, the shield bearing the face of the Other, which provokes blindness and madness' (1989:42).
4. See Durand (1969:229) on the euphemisation of the fall.
5. For another interpretation, see Huchet 1990:191–2: 'Possession of the object sets the seal on the coming of the Book, bearing all the knowledge that establishes the possibility of a literature devoted to describing a union which can overcome the impasse of sexual difference'.

Bibliography

Bec, P. (ed. and trans.) (1979) *'Quan vei la lauzeta mover': Anthologie des troubadours* (Paris: Union Générale des Editeurs).

Braet, H. (1995) 'Narcisse et Pygmalion: mythe et intertexte dans le *Roman de la Rose*, in *Mediaevalia Antiquity* (Leuven: University Press) 237–54.

Clair, J. (1989) *Méduse* (Paris: Gallimard).

Couloubaritsis, L. (1989) 'Le schème du miroir chez les philosophes Grecs', in *Figures. Miroirs et Reflets. Cahier du Centre de Recherche sur l'Image, le Symbole et le Mythe* 4 (Dijon: Université de Bourgogne) 21–45.

Dragonetti, R. (1978) 'Pygmalion ou les pièges de la fiction dans le *Roman de la Rose*', in G. Güntert, M.-R. Jung and K. Ringger (eds) 1978:89–111.

Dubois, P. (1990) *L'Acte Photographique et autres essais* (Paris: Nathan).

Dufournet, J. (1984) *G. de Lorris, Etudes sur le Roman de la Rose* (Paris: Champion).

Durand, G. (1969) *Les Structures anthropologiques de l'imaginaire* (Paris: Bordas).

Eliade, M. (1975) *Traité d'Histoire des Religions* (Paris: Payot).

Fleming, J.V. (1983) 'The Garden of the *Roman de la Rose*: Vision of landscape or landscape of vision?', in E. B. Mac Dougall (ed.), *Medieval Gardens* (Washington: Dumbarton Oaks) 201–34.

Fourrier, A. (ed.) (1964) *L'humanisme médiéval dans les littératures romanes* (Paris, Klincksieck).

Frappier, J. (1976) *Histoire, Mythes et Symboles* (Geneva: Droz).

Friedman, L.J. (1959–60) 'Jean de Meun, antifeminism and bourgeois realism', in *Modern Philology* 57:13–73.

Goldin, F. (1967) *The Mirror of Narcissus in the Courtly Love Lyric* (Ithaca, NY: Cornell University Press).

Güntert, G., M.-R. Jung and K. Ringger (eds) (1978) *Orbis Mediaevalis: mélanges de langue et de littérature médiévales offerts à Reto Raduolf Bezzola à l'occasion de son quatre-vingtième anniversaire* (Berne: A. Franke).

Hillman, L. (1980) 'Another look into the mirror perilous. The role of the crystals in the *Roman de la Rose*', in *Romania* 101:225–38.
Huchet, J.-C. (1982) 'La Dame et le Troubadour. Fin'amors et mystique chez Bernard de Ventadorn', in *Littérature* 47:12–40.
——— (1990) *Littérature médiévale et psychanalyse* (Paris: Presses Universitaires de France).
Hult, D. (1981) 'The Allegorical Fountain: Narcisse in the *Roman de la Rose*', in *Romanic Review* 72:125–248.
Kamenetz, G. (1984) 'La promenade d'Amant comme expérience mystique', in Dufournet 1984:83–104.
Kay, S. (1983) 'Love in a Mirror: an aspect of the imagery of Bernart de Ventadorn', in *Medium Aevum* lii.
Kessler, J. (1982) 'La quête amoureuse et poétique : la Fontaine de Narcisse dans le *Roman de la Rose*', in *Romanic Review* 73:133–46.
Köhler, E. (1963) 'Narcisse, la Fontaine d'Amour et Guillaume de Lorris', in *Journal des Savants* and in Fourrier 1964:147–66.
Lecoy, F. (ed.) (1965–70) *Le Roman de la Rose* (Paris: Champion).
Lefay-Toury, M.-N. (1979) *La Tentation du suicide dans le roman français du XIIe siècle* (Paris: Champion).
Méla, C. (1983) 'Le Miroir périlleux ou l'alchimie de la Rose', in *Europe* 654:72–83.
Notz, M.-F. (1978) 'Hortus Conclusus', in *Mélanges J. Lods* 1 (Paris: Ecole Normale Supérieure de Jeunes Filles) 459–72.
Ovid (1985) *Metamorphoses* Book 1–4, ed. with translation and notes by D.E. Hill (Warminster: Arris and Phillips).
Pickens, R.T. (1974) '*Somnium* and interpretation in Guillaume de Lorris', in *Symposium* 28:175–86.
Poirion, D. (1970) 'Narcisse et Pygmalion dans le *Roman de La Rose*', in *Studies in the Romance Languages and Literatures*, 92:158–65.
Press, A. (ed. and trans.) (1971) *Anthology of Troubadour Poetry* (Edinburgh: Edinburgh University Press).
Ribard, J. (1995) 'De Chrétien de Troyes à Guillaume de Lorris : ces quêtes qu'on dit inachevées' [1976] and 'Introduction à une étude polysémique du *Roman de la Rose* de Guillaume de Lorris' [1973], in *Du Mythe au Mystique* (Paris: Champion).
Robertson, D.W. (1951) 'The Doctrine of Charity in Mediaeval Literary Gardens: a topical approach through symbolism and allegory', in *Speculum* 26:24–49.
St Augustine (1970) *The Trinity*, trans. S. Mc Kenna (Washington DC: Catholic University of America Press).
Strohm, P. (1968) 'Guillaume as narrator and lover in the *Roman de la Rose*', in *Romanic Review* 59:3–9.
Strubel, A. (1984) 'Le *Roman de la Rose* de Guillaume de Lorris et Jean de Meun', in *Etudes Littéraires* 4.
Thiry-Stassin, M. and M. Tyssens (eds) (1976) *Narcisse. Conte ovidien français du XIIe siècle* (Paris: Les Belles Lettres).
Thut, M. (1982) 'Narcisse versus Pygmalion. Une lecture du *Roman de la Rose*', in *Vox Romanica* xli:104–32.

Vinge, L. (1967) *Narcissus Theme in Western European Literature up to the early 19th century*, trans. R. Dewsnap and N. Reeves (Lund: Gleerups).

Vitz, E.B. (1973) 'The I of the *Roman de la Rose*', in *Genre* 6:49–75.

Wunenburger, J.-J. (1995) *La Vie des Images* (Strasbourg: Presses Universitaires de Strasbourg).

Zumthor, P. (1973) 'Autobiography in the Middle Ages', in *Genre* 6:29–48.

CHAPTER 3

UROR AMORE MEI:

INDIVIDUAL AND SOCIAL IDENTITY IN PSYCHOANALYTIC THEORY

Grahame Lock

Narcissus, in Ovid's account in *Metamorphoses*, tells us: I am 'on fire' (*uror*) 'with love of myself' (*amore mei*). How did that come about? Is it a simple mistake, Narcissus taking a reflection of himself to be someone else's body?[1] Or is it, on the contrary, precisely the fact that the body is his own that has stirred his passions?

Narcissus is in flames. Not much later he dies, worn and wasted with love. The wood nymphs prepare 'the pyre, the tossing torches, and the bier'. They want to cremate him, to burn a body that was already in another kind of blaze. But, Ovid tells us, the body is nowhere to be found; instead there is only a flower. At this moment – too late, of course, for him – Narcissus moves into the symbolic realm. There will be no pyre: the body has disappeared, to be replaced by an emblem.

In Freud's account of narcissism, the narcissist is moved by instinctual drives which 'represent' the body at the level of the psyche. These drives mould his character, 'in spite of himself', for they help to bring that self into existence. The child passing through the phase of primary narcissism has not yet entered civilised – that is to say, law-governed – life, though he is on his way. The fire which is prone to take hold of him is not yet under control. Freud writes that among the first acts of civilisation was the 'gaining of control over fire'; this indeed stands out as 'a quite extraordinary and unexampled achievement' (Freud 1961a:90). Is something similar true of the fire of narcissistic desire?

Some psychoanalytic theory still makes extensive use of the developmental and clinical concept of narcissism, as we shall see. This concept was introduced by Freud in 1914 (Freud 1957a). But Freud's treatment seems not to have much to do with the Narcissus myth itself. He hardly mentions Narcissus, nor does he essay a study of the meaning of the myth.

In contrast, the terms of Jacques Lacan's discussion of the so-called 'mirror stage' in the constitution of the human individual seem more directly to recall central elements in the Narcissus story. Narcissus is enchanted by a reflection and falls in love with himself. At first, he does not know what it is that he is looking at, but is excited by the image. Finally he grasps the fact that the image is of himself. In Lacan's story too, someone – the child – catches sight of its own image in a mirror and thus comes to identify with the image or, as Lacan puts it, triumphantly to 'assume' it (Lacan 1973a:1–7).

In Freudian terms, the mirror stage corresponds to the period of the onset of primary narcissism (Laplanche and Pontalis 1973:250–1).[2] But Lacan's account does not, as his readers will have realised, quite follow the Narcissus myth. Lacan talks, as Ovid does, about an illusion. But while in Ovid the illusion consists in a false belief on Narcissus' part, that he is looking at (while apparently desiring) someone else – a belief which is later corrected – in Lacan the illusion rather follows on from and is indeed a consequence of the identification with the mirror image. In other words, in Lacan there is a structural illusion: the cognitive flaw is not contingent but a necessary effect. We love ourselves not by mistake, nor even as an unfortunate but temporary result of the passage through a human developmental stage; on the contrary, our bodily unity and indeed our ego, therefore our identity, are products of a process in which self-love is an indispensable and an ineliminable element.

It is, according to Lacan, a process with its own 'libidinal dynamism'. But there is, he adds, an opposition

> between this libido and the sexual libido, which the first analysts tried to define when they invoked destructive and, indeed, death instincts, in order to explain the evident connection between the

narcissistic libido and the alienating function of the I, the aggressivity it releases in any relation to the other, even in a relation involving the most Samaritan of aid. (1973a:6)

Thus for Lacan the matter is more complex than it might appear at first sight. Narcissism, we might say, is in his optic not so much self-desire as the condition of the emergence and existence of a 'self-aggressive' self. But this formulation would need to be qualified in the light of our understanding of human desire, which – on the later Freudian account – must be defined in its relation to the death drive. Narcissus, having grasped the truth about the object of his desire, pines away and dies, 'worn and wasted away with love'. The Freudian narcissist in contrast survives, but scarred: turning his death instinct, at least in part, against the external world, he may become a sadist. Thus, for many psychoanalysts, aggressivity became a core notion for the interpretation and understanding of narcissism.

Let us, however, before turning to these matters, briefly consider more closely Freud's own treatment of the topic. He seems to have borrowed the term, ready-made, from others.[3] In his originally published 1914 article he notes that

> the term narcissism is derived from clinical description and was chosen by Paul Näcke in 1899 to denote the attitude of a person who treats his own body in the same way in which the body of a sexual object is ordinarily treated – who looks at it, that is to say, strokes it and fondles it till he obtains complete satisfaction through these activities. (Freud 1957a)

Later, he corrected this statement: it was not Näcke but Havelock Ellis who had invented the term. But it seems that, after all, the credit should go to Näcke, though Ellis had certainly on the one hand described a 'narcissus-like' psychological attitude and on the other hand had made a study of 'auto-erotism'. Henri Ellenberger remarks in this connection that the interest among psychiatrists in narcissistic phenomena can be understood, at least in part, in terms of a broader movement, the rise of fin de siècle neo-romanticism, its worship of the individual and consequent celebration of Narcissus: 'never, in the history of literature, did poets celebrate Narcissus and narcissistic heroes to such an extent. ... The Narcissus figure was a general symbol and incarnation of the spirit of that time' (Ellenberger 1970:279, 505).

In Freud, moreover, Ellenberger continues, 'the theory of narcissism was to be the prelude to a complete restructuration of the framework of psychoanalytical theory'. This, it seems to me, is a correct assessment. With the notion of narcissism, emphasis is shifted away from the opposition between conscious and unconscious, and the way is cleared for the introduction of a concept of the superego – which first makes its appearance, in somewhat different form, as the ego-ideal. Thus the ground for the so-called second theory of the psychical apparatus is prepared: the ego/id/superego topography.[4] It is true, however, that Freud later allowed the concept of narcissism to drop out of sight. It was resurrected, long after his death, by a new generation of psychoanalysts: especially by Heinz Kohut and Otto Kernberg in the United States, by Béla Grunberger, by André Green and, of course, by Jacques Lacan in France. Green argues that analysts are divided into two camps in respect of the doctrine of narcissism. There are those who want to maintain and develop the notion; and those who ignore or reject it. It is typical of the second camp to consider narcissism as itself an illusion or myth, to whose enticements Freud for some time fell prey (Green 1983:36–7).

Freud's own account in *On Narcissism* manages to combine discussion of a number of important aspects of psychoanalytic theory, thus throwing new light on each. From the developmental point of view, Freud describes narcissism in the following way. In the early infantile life of human beings there develop – before the emergence of narcissism proper – forms of auto-erotic behaviour; that is to say, forms of behaviour involving the satisfaction of instinctual demands without recourse to external objects. The first auto-erotic sexual satisfactions, Freud says, 'are experienced in connection with vital functions which serve the purpose of self-preservation' (Freud 1957a:87). So it is impossible at the outset to make a distinction between the sexual instincts on the one side and the so-called ego-instincts – that is, the self-preservative instincts – on the other. It is only later that these two kinds of instinct become differentiated. Indeed, even after differentiation has taken place, sexual activity remains marked by an entirely primitive attachment, in the sense that the first sexual object is precisely that person who was in the first instance concerned with the child's feeding, care and protection: the mother. Object-choice based on this model Freud calls the 'attachment' type (otherwise known as the 'anaclitic' type or *Anlehnungstypus*).[5] This will become, so to speak, the 'normal' kind of choice. But there is also a narcissistic type of object-choice, where someone takes as his model not his mother but himself.

The existence of narcissistic object-choice was for Freud a clinical discovery. Not, however, he says, that we should conclude that each human being just makes a choice of the one kind or the other. Rather, each originally has two objects, 'himself and the woman who nurses him'. Moreover, we all continue to display a degree of 'primary narcissism', though only in some of us does this primary narcissism come to dominate our later object-choice – as 'secondary narcissism'. More generally, narcissism can be characterised, in the words of André Green, as a result of the libidinisation of the ego instincts, which previously had been directed to self-preservation (Green 1983:10).

In order to understand how these processes work, we need, according to Freud, to understand their relation to what are called (in English translation) the libidinal cathexes. The libido, as we know, is Freud's name for a kind of 'psychical energy' characterised by its sexual character, as contrasted with the energy associated with the instincts of self-preservation. Libido becomes manifest when it fixes on an object, or migrates from one object to another. This attachment of libidinal energy to an object is called a libidinal cathexis (in German *Besetzung*: literally, 'occupation'). A contrast with the self-preservative drives – sometimes called the ego instincts – is drawn by Freud quite early in his career.[6] These self-preservative drives, for their part, can only be satisfied in reality, unlike the sexual drives, which can achieve satisfaction in phantasy: thus there is a potential tension between the two kinds of drives, linked to the tension opposing the reality principle on the one hand and the pleasure principle on the other.

Primary narcissism, an early state 'in which the child cathects its own self with the whole of its libido', as J. Laplanche and J.-B. Pontalis put it, follows on from the phase of primitive auto-erotism, and differs from this latter in that it is 'contemporaneous with the first emergence of a unified subject – in other words, of an ego' (Laplanche and Pontalis 1973:337).[7] For the ego which is libidinally cathected has 'first' to be constituted. Freud thus also needed to produce an adequate account of the ego.

Let us try to establish the connection between the new theory of narcissism and the new concept of the ego. Freud says that in secondary narcissism the libido that has been withdrawn from the external world has been redirected to the ego. What, in primary narcissism, is associated with the magical attitude of the 'omnipotence of thoughts' is, in secondary narcissism, expressed as megalomania. Of course, these two narcissisms have the same roots. But in the case of the child, there is not a redirection of libido to the ego but an 'original libidinal cathexis of the ego, from which some is later given off to objects'. Freud also distinguishes between ego-libido on the one side and object-libido on the other. Originally, it seems, there is only ego-libido; or rather: 'not until there is object-cathexis is it possible to discriminate a sexual energy – the libido – from an energy of the ego-instincts' (Freud 1957a:76). But recall that the ego-instincts were conceived of by Freud as opposed to the sexual instincts, which seek to realise their respective aims in a different way. Freud now seems to argue that this opposition, indeed the very distinction between the two kinds of drive, emerges only when object-cathexis emerges. In the auto-erotic stage, the ego has yet to be formed. So it is not yet possible for the child to operate in the mode of the reality principle; for there is not yet any 'reality-ego', as Freud calls it, to 'strive for what is useful and guard itself against damage'. Here the contrast is with the pleasure-ego (Freud 1958:223). The pleasure-ego is transformed, Freud suggests in this text of 1911, into a reality-ego, which safeguards the former's longer-term interests. But four years later he makes the opposite suggestion: that the pleasure-ego emerges from an original reality-ego: 'In so far as the ego is auto-erotic', he writes, 'it has no need of the external world, but, in consequence of experiences undergone by the instincts of self-preservation, it acquires objects from that world'. Then, 'in so far as the objects which are presented to it are sources of pleasure, it takes them into itself, "introjects" them'; on the other hand, 'it expels whatever within itself becomes a cause of unpleasure. ... Thus the reality-ego, which distinguished internal and external by means of a sound objective criterion, changes into a purified "pleasure-ego", which places the characteristic of pleasure above all others.' Now, Freud concludes, the two polarities coincide once again: the ego-subject with pleasure and the external world with unpleasure (Freud 1957b:135–6).

Note that the ego is at this stage the ego-subject. In narcissism it becomes the ego-object. That is to say, the subject takes 'itself' as object: it splits. A split ego is – in this radical sense – a new idea for Freud. With the theory of narcissism the ego had also to become an object. The question then is: what kind of object? And how can such an object – an ego – be an object of desire for a subject – again, the ego – that had been understood by Freud as 'the agency which opposes itself to desire'? (Laplanche and Pontalis 1973:136).

As long as the ego is conceived of as subject, it is, so to speak, just the principle of self-preservation as this functions in the case of a given human individual. That is why the ego 'opposes itself to desire': for it resists the blind satisfaction of libidinal impulses; it prefers a sober adaptation to reality.

But there is, of course, a prior condition of the ego's successful operation in this sense: namely, that it should have come into existence, and as a unity. Yet 'a unity comparable to the ego cannot exist in the individual from the start' (Freud 1957a:77). So there is something like a process of unification.

One thing that happens in this process is the organising of the component drives or instincts. To the extent that such an instinct functions autonomously, its satisfaction is assured by a part-object. But just to the degree that the organisation of these instincts is achieved, the part-objects recede, to be replaced by a love-object: it is now a matter of a relation between a 'total ego' and its object of election. The matter is even more complicated, on account of the above-mentioned distinction between self-preservative and libidinal instincts. For 'we do not say of objects which serve the interests of self-preservation that we *love* them; we emphasise the fact that we *need* them' (Freud 1957b:137).

Such a love-object, as opposed to a part-object, is likely to be (though it need not be) a person.[8] That is to say: the account just proposed of what it is that the ego desires when it desires itself needs to be modified to allow for the fact that, in Freud's theory, the ego's object of desire is not merely or purely corporeal, nor is the satisfaction which is sought for.[9]

The ego which is the libidinal object in narcissism is a unity, but an imaginary unity. That is to say, it is a unity produced by way of the production of an imaginary scene, a phantasy. For phantasy is itself a product of desire: and the ego desires itself. It might be said that it comes to put itself in the place of desire via a process of incorporative phantasy.[10] Freud talks in this connection about a distinction between object-choice and identification. Libido can, as we know, be withdrawn not just from a particular object but from objects in general: that is to say, withdrawn into the ego. There then takes place an identification of the ego with the abandoned object. This is possible when the object-choice has been effected on a narcissistic basis; or in other words, when this object-choice is a narcissistic identification.[11] But, from the developmental point of view, such narcissistic identification is a normal 'preliminary stage of object-choice': it is 'the first way ... in which the ego picks out an object'. For 'the ego wants to incorporate this object into itself' (Freud 1957c:249). Thus narcissism is indeed linked, via identification, to incorporative phantasy.

The idea of identification is important for Freud's account of narcissism. He calls it the original form of emotional tie with an object. Later it can, in regression, become a 'substitute for a libidinal object-tie, as it were by means of introjection of the object into the ego'. And finally, it may occur between people who are not libidinal objects for one another, but who share some common quality which represents the basis of a mutual bond (Freud 1955). This mutual bond is analysed by Freud in terms, as we also know, of a set of common links to some person (or object or ideal) which comes to occupy the place of their own ego-ideal.

But the important point here is that in regressive identification the ego may be 'remoulded', in respect of its sexual character, on the model of the object from which it has detached itself. Freud's example is that of a young man who has long been 'Oedipally' fixated on his mother. Rather than replacing her with an appropriate alternative object-choice – with some woman – he establishes an identification with his mother, 'transforms himself into her', wants to be loved like her – so by a man. He wants to find an object which will substitute not for her but for his own ego; an object – a man – whom he can love as his mother loved him.

A notion close to that of narcissism had been developed by Karl Abraham in 1908 in his discussion of dementia praecox (schizophrenia), which he takes to be characterised by the patient's transferring 'on to himself alone as his only sexual object the whole of the libido which the healthy person turns upon all living and inanimate objects in his environment'.[12] Freud however, as we saw, introduced a distinction, not found in Abraham, between auto-erotism and narcissism, a distinction which, as we also noted, is closely linked to the theory of the ego. Moreover, Freud made a number of ingenious applications of the new concept. Thus he discusses the relation between narcissism and organic disease. Whoever is physically ill and in pain will, says Freud, surrender much of his interest in the things and persons of the external world, including his libidinal interest in his love-objects. But the same is true of the sleepy individual! He wants to withdraw from the world and thus he too redirects his libido onto his own self. Yet another example of temporary narcissism is provided by the hypochondriac, who suffers from a condition that brings with it the same consequences for the distribution of libido as organic disease: 'the hypochondriac withdraws both interest and libido – the latter especially markedly – from the objects of the external world and concentrates both of them upon the organ that is engaging his attention'. Looking at the matter the other way around, we can, according to Freud, say that we must love in order not to fall ill – and that if we are unable to love, we are bound to fall ill (Freud 1957a:82–3).

But the theory is capable of an even broader application. Thus Freud draws a picture in which two possible clinical deviations from normality are to be found among patients. First, there are cases of detachment of libido from its objects, leading to 'megalomania, hypochondria, affective disturbance and every kind of regression'. Second, there are cases in which there is a re-attachment to objects, but 'after the manner of a hysteria ... or of an obsessional neurosis' (Freud 1957a:86–7).

In the normal individual, the stage of primary narcissism is followed by a reorientation of libidinal energy in the direction of object-love. The Oedipus complex is destined to play a key role in guiding this choice. But there are people (see above) whose libidinal development has been disturbed: 'in their later choice of love-objects they have taken as a model not their mother but their own selves. They are', Freud remarks, 'plainly seeking themselves as a love-object, and are exhibiting a type of object-choice which must be termed "narcissistic"' (Freud 1957a:88).

Freud distinguishes between men and women in respect of the developmental story. A more or less complete overcoming of the narcissistic tendency, that is to say, the making of an object-choice on the attachment or anaclitic model, he considers to be characteristic of the male sex: the original narcissism is transferred to the sexual object. In the case of the female sex, things happen differently. With the onset of puberty there typically occurs an intensification of original narcissism, something which does not favour the development of a 'true object-choice' – especially not in cases where the woman is good-looking. Such women love themselves, says Freud, with an intensity comparable to that of men's love for them: and indeed, to an extent this is what makes them lovable, somewhat in the manner in which a child is lovable. Narcissism is only displaced by a kind of object-love when the woman bears a child, that is, when a part of her own body becomes part of the external world (Freud 1957a:89–90).

Narcissism produces a clinical problem for the psychoanalyst. A narcissist is incapable of that transference of unconscious wishes onto the analyst (that is, of the transformation of the clinical neurosis into a transference neurosis) which is a precondition of psychoanalytic treatment. In the narcissistic neuroses, Freud remarks, the resistance on the part of the patient seems to be 'unconquerable'.

The problem to which Freud here alludes is closely connected to that of the psychoanalytic treatment of the psychoses; indeed, the field of what used to be called the narcissistic neuroses may now be regarded as more or less identical with that of the functional psychoses.[13] Sufferers from narcissistic neuroses, he notes, since they have little capacity for transference, reject the analyst, not with hostility but with indifference. So the analyst can do very little with them. Their own attempts at recovery, on the other hand, tend to produce 'pathological results': that is to say, to lead to psychotic disorders. This is because, in such attempts at a recovery of the object, what is in effect recovered is rather the 'shadow' of such an object – its 'word-presentation'. And it is this latter, rather than some object, to which libidinal desire is reconnected. Roughly: there is reconnection in the conscious mind, but not in the Unconscious (Freud 1963:447; 1957d:201). Freud also remarks on the fact that in *paranoia persecutoria*, which is the other side of megalomania ('the patient, who [...] believes that he is being persecuted, infers from his persecution that he must be someone of quite particular importance'), there is an essential element of defence against a homosexual impulse. When the homosexual impulse is strong, the path back to narcissism is an easy one. Or, to put the matter the other way around: 'a strong libidinal fixation to the narcissistic type of object-choice is to be included in the predisposition to manifest homosexuality'. That is to say: the homosexual, as we saw, takes as the model of his love-object not his mother but himself; he loves bodies that are like his own.

If we compare melancholia with persecution paranoia, we discover that, while in the former there is a withdrawal of libido from the object, this object has, by a process of narcissistic identification, been relocated 'in the ego itself'. Thus the ego becomes at one and the same time the primary object of libidinal desire, but also the object of the kind of reproaches typical of the melancholic personality – reproaches which we call, and which seem to be, a form of self-aggression, just because their true external object has been relocated in the ego. So the ego becomes at one and the same time an object of love and of hatred; of what Freud calls ambivalence (Freud 1963:424–7).

The mirror stage is the topic of an early (1936) paper by Lacan which, in a much revised version, was published in 1949 and became one of his best-known contributions to psychoanalytic theory.[14] The mirror stage is, on the one hand, a developmental phase, which Lacan locates at the age of six months or a little later. On the other hand it is a kind of mould of the emergent ego. It is the moment of the advent of subjectivity, a moment at which the body, which up to that time is experienced only as a 'fragmented body-image', takes on a unitary form. The idea is that the mirror presents the child with an imago of itself, in which it for the first time experiences itself, recognises itself, identifies with itself: thus does an ego, its ego, come into being.[15] And so the ego, as Freud suggested, is indeed, from the moment of its inception, a bodily ego, at least in the sense that it is a product not of introspection but of the perception – from the 'outside' – of the body, via the specular image; the body is given 'in exteriority', says Lacan. But the identity thus constituted, he adds, is just for that reason 'alienating'. The ego's unity is created – a familiar point by now – only at the cost of (indeed by way of the operation of) a division: between self and image, between 'inside' and 'outside', between, we could say, 'mind' and 'body'. The process of recognition is indeed at the same time a process of misrecognition; for it produces an 'illusion of autonomy', the illusion proper to the ego. The image in the mirror 'obeys' the will of its owner. Anika Lemaire remarks in this connection that, by the end of the mirror phase, the child 'realises not only that the reflection is an image, but that the image is his own and is different from the image of the other. He manifests his intense joy in the classic game of the registration of the movements of his own body in the mirror' (Lemaire 1977:177).

Yet the autonomy turns out to be deceptive: I depend for my (more than biological) existence on others. But in Lacan's account we all owe our specifically human existence to language. It is not we who created language; on the contrary, language creates us. And the entry into the imaginary sphere which takes place in the mirror stage is, he says, followed by an entry into the linguistic sphere, or the sphere of the symbolic. The ego which emerges at the mirror stage is thus no more than a rough version. Lacan writes that the child's assumption of his specular image is a primordial form of the symbolic matrix which will later take the objective form of a 'dialectic of identification with the other', when 'language restores to it in the universal mode its function as a subject' (Lacan 1973a:2).

For all these reasons, he adds, the ego is from the beginning an 'ideal ego': what in *On Narcissism* Freud called the *Idealich*. But Lacan, unlike Freud, distinguishes between on the one hand the ideal ego – a 'narcissistic construct of the imaginary order' – and on the other hand the ego ideal, which belongs to the symbolic order, the Oedipal order of the paternal law.[16] The important point, however, is that the story of the constitution of the ego at the mirror stage is a story of primary narcissism, of 'the notion of an aggressivity linked to the narcissistic relation and to the structures of systematic *méconnaissance* and objectification that characterise the formation of the ego'. Or, to put the matter in much simpler terms: there is no ego without narcissism, and this narcissism never disappears as an element in the human psychic economy. The subsequent Oedipal crisis produces, it is true, a 'blind supersession' of the individual in favour of the species, that is to say, a series of 'sublimating effects'. But the narcissistic structure is as 'irreducible' as aggressive tension is constant in all moral life involving subjection to this structure (Lacan 1973b:21, 24). Narcissism is not then, in Lacan's account, just a stage in sexual development or, in the secondary form, a regression to self-love, but one of the basic structuring principles of the ego.

Lacan was of the opinion that, in his account of the mirror stage, he had moved close to certain aspects of the work of Melanie Klein.[17] It is certainly true that Klein problematises the concept of the ego in a way in which neither her rival Anna Freud nor the ego psychologists were prepared to do. The Kleinian Hanna Segal notes that, in Klein's view, 'the infant, from the beginning of life, introjects the desired breast, both in phantasy and in real feeding, and, desiring its goodness', identifies with it. This introjection, she adds, 'is not only a function of the ego but an important root of its formation'. Here too, then, we have an account of the constitution of the ego, and one which involves a rectification of Freud's position. For Klein supposes that such introjection of the breast – thus of an 'external' object – begins very early in the child's life, as does the 'growth' of the ego. For Freud, in contrast, such early life is characterised first by auto-erotism and then by narcissism, where the latter is understood not in terms of the introjection of a part-object (part of the mother) but, as we know, of an original libidinal cathexis of the ego itself. Segal remarks indeed that, in Klein's account, even auto-erotism is to be explained by the introjection of a good breast, but that 'in narcissism the situation is more complicated. Narcissism is a later condition, more hostile to the external world and involving a greater perception of frustration.' The turning against a bad external object is in this optic more important in narcissism than the turning to a good internal object; and 'Melanie Klein was to extend this view in her later work' (Segal 1979:105).

In his paper on 'Aggressivity in Psychoanalysis', Lacan draws on Melanie Klein's notion of the bad internal object in his discussion of the 'subjective function of identification'. He discusses the 'paranoiac structure of the ego', and in particular the manner in which 'certain imaginary personae' may produce a fragmenting effect on the imago of the original identification. These ideas constitute an addition to the mirror stage theory. There are clinical consequences to be drawn from the notion of the ego as a creation and a creator of *méconnaissances*: that it must be approached in treatment in a 'roundabout manner', which 'amounts in fact to inducing in the subject a controlled paranoia'. It is in this connection that Lacan remarks that

> it is one of the aspects of analytic activity to operate the projection of what Melanie Klein calls bad internal objects, a paranoiac mechanism certainly, but one that is here [i.e. in analysis] properly systematised, filtered in a certain sense and carefully controlled. (Lacan 1973b:15, 21)

At least, we hope so.

None of this discussion should cause us to forget that Klein herself had little use for the concept of narcissism. Her work, 'which was entirely centred on Freud's final theory of the drives', André Green notes, 'takes no account of narcissism. Only H. Rosenfeld among the Kleinians tried to integrate it into Kleinian conceptions'. Winnicott's work 'hardly gives it more attention' (Green 1983:12). In taking this position, these thinkers follow, as we have seen, the final phase of Freud's thinking.

Narcissus, as we know, was 'burning with love for himself'. But what, for Lacan, is love? Or, to pose the question, in Freudian terms, what is libido? And what is the relation between libido and desire? We are familiar with the idea that 'in so far as the sexual instinct lies on the borderline between the somatic and the psychical, libido represents the mental side' (Laplanche and

Pontalis 1973:239). For Lacan, libido is instinct; it is canalised by the delimitation of the erogenous zone, which transforms it into 'partial instinct'. Thus something 'biological' – the pure biological energy of the pre-imaginary and pre-symbolic domains – is lost to man, Lacan suggests. This loss can only be represented in the imaginary mode, and in particular in the images of anatomical apertures (of lips, slits, gaps in the body) – of objects which are 'themselves imaginary', because they merge in their primitive manner with lived experience. This state of affairs is characteristic of primary narcissism (Lemaire 1977:127–8). Thus we come to understand just what has become of biology for Lacan; why he, so to speak, expels it from his theory. The reason is that biology, rather like Kant's thing-in-itself, is beyond all symbolisation: it is 'part of the unknown dimension of truth' which 'cannot be the object of any knowledge'.

Psychoanalytic theory, in the Lacanian version, prefers to centre itself on concepts like those of demand and of desire. The former has its roots in the imaginary, the latter in the symbolic order. Lacan's idea seems to be that desire is the symbolic transformation of instinct, or its 'alienation' in the signifying chains of language. It is therefore language which makes desire possible. That is why desire is 'desire of the Other'. For it now – following the child's entry into the symbolic sphere – emerges ensnared in the web not just of language, but, through it, of the paternal law, which indeed Lacan says 'institutes desire by way of the prohibition of incest' (Lacan 1966b:852).

Desire, he says, is 'desire of the Other', in the sense of subjective determination; 'namely that it is *qua* Other that [man] desires'. But this means that the subject is alienated: he has transferred his desire 'to an ego that is [...] intermittent', and which even 'protects [him] from his desire' by means of these very intermittences (Lacan 1973c:312–13).

The truth about the object of Narcissus' desire is, in this light, not so much that he desires himself as that he desires – it is Ovid's own term – nothing. In Ovid, as we saw, the illusion is nothing: that is to say, it is not a thing, but a mere shadow: so there is nothing which Narcissus desires – or nothing that could satisfy his desire. In Lacan, however, Narcissus' love functions at the presymbolic level; there is no desire, but only an undifferentiated libidinal relation.

Ovid tells us that Narcissus was 'slowly consumed by the secret fire' (*tecto paulatim carpitur igni*) of love. In contrast, contemporary Western man seems to be moved by a kind of pale fire.

In this connection one is reminded of Bishop Butler's reference to a 'reasonable self-love', the goal of which is the totality of our worldly interest.[18] It is this 'reasonable' self-love that now seems to constitute our individual and social identity, which seems to function as the link between individual and society – at least in that society's approved, moderate self-image. The institutionally promoted narcissism of capitalism is indeed not normally of the extreme or spectacular variety. But the pale fire of institutional narcissism can also consume, slowly but steadily; perhaps in the end with results which would not have surprised the socially and politically pessimistic Freud.

Notes

1. Pausanias introduces his own version of the myth with the suggestion that this possibility can be excluded, for reasons of common sense.
2. Laplanche and Pontalis note that there is 'one difference' between the conceptions of Freud on the one hand and Lacan on the other; that 'Lacan sees the mirror stage as responsible, retroactively, for the emergence of the phantasy of the body-in-pieces.'
3. In Freud's German *'Narzissmus'*, following Näcke's *'Narcismus'*, rather than the commoner *'Narzissismus'*.
4. The first topography having distinguished between the conscious, preconscious and unconscious systems.
5. See Freud 1953:222: 'At a time at which the first beginnings of sexual satisfaction are still linked with the taking of nourishment, the sexual instinct has a sexual object outside the infant's own body in the shape of his mother's breast. It is only later that the instinct loses that object, just at the time, perhaps, when the child is able to form a total idea of the person to whom the organ that is giving him satisfaction belongs. As a rule the sexual instinct then becomes auto-erotic, and not until the period of latency has been passed through is the original relation restored. There are thus good reasons why a child sucking at his mother's breast has become the prototype of every relation of love. The finding of an object is in fact a refining of it.'
6. The English *Standard Edition* of Freud's works (translated by James Strachey et al.) renders the German *Trieb* as 'instinct', thus giving it a biological connotation which risks obscuring Freud's meaning (and the contrast he draws, though not systematically, between *Trieb* and – animal – *Instinkt*). Drives, in Freud's account, have an organic or somatic source, an object – real or imaginary, a person or part-object – and an aim (satisfaction of the appropriate kind).
7. But 'subsequently, with the elaboration of the second topography, Freud uses the term "primary narcissism" to mean rather a first state of life, prior even to the formation of an ego, which is epitomised by life in the womb', so that 'the distinction between auto-erotism and narcissism is eradicated' (Laplanche and Pontalis 1973:338).
8. Karl Abraham and Melanie Klein produced particularly elaborate accounts of part-objects. According to Klein, there is often in the patient's

phantasy an attribution to part-objects of features which transcend the corporeal characteristics of these part-objects: they are not simply good or bad, but are compassionate or persecutory and so on.

9. Freud talks (in Freud 1963:416) about sexual instincts which find satisfaction 'in the subject's own body', calling this auto-erotism, but adding that auto-erotism is the 'sexual activity of the narcissistic stage' (thus not clearly distinguishing the two phenomena).

10. See Wollheim (1982:131, 133): 'The two [occurrent and dispositional] fantasies essential to introjection represent themselves corporeally ... The subject [then experiences] the dispositional phantasy as a corporeal process of containing the [incorporated] figure in the very place where [that figure] is phantasized as being: that is, inside the subject's body.' Mental acts thus come to represent themselves as bodily phenomena, and to represent the ego – phenomenologically, the organised system of such mental acts – as a corporeal reality. Of course, since it is an imaginary corporeal reality, it suffers from none of the flaws of nonimaginary reality. Produced by the 'omnipotence of thought', it is itself immune from destruction: deathless.

11. Presumably an identification of the object with the ego and not of the ego with the object. The latter is more like the kind of process which Freud later studied in the framework of his 1921 essay on *Group Psychology and the Analysis of the Ego*: an original narcissistic projection produces an ego-ideal (a 'substitute for the lost narcissism of childhood'); this ego-ideal in turn is replaced in each member of a group of individuals by some external object – for instance a 'beloved leader' – to which each individual is bound by 'ties of identification'. In this way, Freud adds, the group members come to identify with each other 'in their ego' (1955).

12. Laplanche and Pontalis 1973:255 (quoting Abraham's *Selected Papers* of 1927).

13. Freud himself, however, came to make a distinction between the narcissistic neuroses and the psychoses. Thus at one point he proposes a classification according to which 'transference neuroses correspond to a conflict between the ego and the id; narcissistic neuroses, to a conflict between the ego and the super-ego; and psychoses, to one between the ego and the external world' (Freud 1961b:152).

14. It was republished in the *Ecrits* under the title 'Le stade du miroir comme formateur de la fonction du Je' (1973a).

15. As the title of the paper suggests, Lacan is concerned not just with the ego but with the 'I' (French je): he distinguishes these two concepts. The ego (moi) is the product of imaginary identification, whereas the I is what becomes a subject by becoming an object for others and so for itself. The emergence of the ego is thus a necessary condition of the precipitation of the I. It is the I or subject which, on Lacan's account, is split or alienated.

16. Lacan 1966a:677. Cf. Lacan 1979:257:

> It is ... in the field of primary narcissistic identification ... that is to be found the essential mainspring of the effects of the ego ideal. I have described elsewhere the sight in the mirror of the ego ideal. ... By clinging to the reference-point of him who looks at him in a mirror, the subject sees appearing, not his ego ideal, but his ideal ego, that point at which he desires to gratify himself in himself.

17. Some commentators agree: thus Roudinesco writes that the Kleinians' reading of Freud (on ego, id and superego) 'was the opposite of the Anna-Freudians' interpretation and close to the positions at which Lacan was to arrive' (Roudinesco 1997:193).

18. Bishop Butler, *Analogy of Religion in Works*, quoted in Hirschman 1977:35. Vladimir Nabokov's 'pale fire' is borrowed from Shakespeare's Timon of Athens, where it is a matter of thieving: it is fire stolen by the moon from the sun. In the present context, we might better think in terms of parasitism. That is, 'respectable' desire is parasitic on the deeper, 'unspeakable' variety.

Bibliography

Abraham, K. (1927) *A Short Study of the Development of the Libido, Viewed in the Light of Mental Disorders* (London: Hogarth Press).

Ellenberger, H.F. (1970) *The Discovery of the Unconscious* (New York: Basic Books).

Freud, S. (1953–74) *The Standard Edition of the Complete Psychological Works of Sigmund Freud in XXIV Volumes*, trans. J. Strachey et al. (London: The Hogarth Press).

Green, A. (1983) *Narcissisme de vie, narcissisme de mort* (Paris: Minuit).

Hirschman, Albert O. (1977) *The Passions and the Interests* (Princeton, NJ: Princeton University Press).

Klein, M. (1975) 'A Contribution to the Psychogenesis of Manic-Depressive States', in *The Writings of Melanie Klein*, Vol. 1. (London: Hogarth Press).

Lacan, J. (1966a) 'Remarque sur la rapport de Daniel Lagache', in *Ecrits* (Paris: Editions du Seuil).

—— (1966b) 'Du Trieb de Freud et du désir du psychanalyste', in *Ecrits* (Paris: Editions du Seuil).

—— (1973a) 'The Mirror Stage as Formative of the Function of the I as Revealed in the Psychoanalytic Experience', in *Ecrits* (London: Tavistock Publications).

—— (1973b) 'Aggressivity in Psychoanalysis', in *Ecrits* (London: Tavistock Publications).

—— (1973c) 'The Subversion of the Subject and the Dialectic of Desire in the Freudian Unconscious', in *Ecrits* (London: Tavistock Publications).

—— (1979) *The Four Fundamental Concepts of Psycho-analysis* (Harmondsworth: Penguin Books).

Laplanche J. and J.-B. Pontalis (1973) *The Language of Psycho-analysis* (London: Hogarth Press).

Lemaire, A. (1977) *Jacques Lacan* (London: Routledge and Kegan Paul).

Roudinesco, E. (1997) *Jacques Lacan* (Cambridge: Polity Press).

Segal, H. (1979) *Klein* (London: Fontana).

Wollheim, R. (1982) 'The Bodily Ego', in R. Wollheim and J. Hopkins (eds), *Philosophical Essays on Freud* (Cambridge: Cambridge University Press).

PART II
MIRRORS AND SELF-REFLECTION

Chapter 4

THE MIRROR PREFACE: THE CASE OF GEORGE SAND*

Anna Szabó

Narcissism involves not only the subject's identification with an image of him- or herself but also that subject's relationship with the Other, with the surrounding world. By explaining his or her intentions as an author and suggesting the 'right way to read' the work, the preface-writer sketches a self-image in which he or she would like to be recognised. This image, created for the reader, also functions as a mirror in which the preface-writing author chooses to be reflected. Following the rules of the genre, codified long ago, the preface contains the same ambiguity of truth and lies characteristic of the aesthetic function of the mirror, that enigmatic object.

The preface as a genre is a type of discourse whose aim is to explain, persuade and, particularly in the novel, to legitimise both itself as a 'bastard' genre and the author's place in a genealogy which he or she wants to claim for him- or herself. In this sense the preface is also part of the search for origins.

In 1871, towards the end of her career, George Sand spoke of herself as follows:

> The external world has always acted on me more than I have been able to act on it. I have become a mirror from which my own reflection has disappeared, since it is so filled with the

---

* Translated from the French by Trista Selous.

intermingling reflections of faces and objects. When I try to look at myself in this mirror, I see, passing before my eyes, plants, insects, landscapes, water, the silhouettes of mountains, clouds and extraordinary light falling over everything; and, among it all, excellent and splendid people. (1873:43)[1]

Leaving aside the incoherence of this use of the image of the mirror, it is clear that this is both a moral and intellectual self-portrait, a metaphorical account of inner development, in which the self's disappearance seems to be the end point of a long process of depersonalisation, suggestive not so much of a fusion with the surrounding world as the world's gradual invasion of the self. This invasion is, however, perceived not as failure (although it does contain traces of a vague sense of regret at the incapacity to act on the world) or an attack on the integrity of personality, but rather as a gentle, benevolent, and fecund conquest which meets some secret desire and brings a soothing sense of plenitude.[2]

In another passage from *Impressions et souvenirs* we read:

There are times when I escape myself, I live in a plant or I feel I am grass, a bird, a treetop, a cloud, running water, the horizon, colour, form and sensations all changing, mobile, undefined; moments when I run, fly, swim, drink the dew, when I open out to the sun, sleep under the leaves, glide with the larks, creep with the lizards, shine in the stars and glow-worms, in other words when I experience in everything that exists the mid-point of an evolution which is like the dilation of my being. (1873:8–9)

As with magic mirrors, this interior landscape, with its cosmic elements taking shape in the self-mirror, seems to reveal a supreme secret: the secret of the novelist who has reached old age and whose serenity has become almost legendary. We can interpret this hard-won inner equilibrium as the result of a harmonious marriage of what are called narcissistic and anti-narcissistic cathexes. In this mirror Sand resembles Bachelard's Narcissus: 'He is no longer alone, the universe is reflected with him and envelopes him in return, its soul is the very soul of Narcissus' (Bachelard 1942:35).

Although George Sand constantly stresses that she does not like telling her readers about herself, this does not mean she is not given to introspection. In 1847, when she began her autobiography, she thought she was 'fulfilling a [painful] duty', since she could think of 'nothing more difficult than defining oneself'.

'However, I shall fulfil this duty', she wrote in 1855 at the beginning of *Histoire de ma vie*, in the chapter which functions as a preface, entitled 'Why this book?': 'I have always promised myself not to die without having done what I have always advised others to do for themselves: a sincere study of my own nature and a careful examination of my own existence.'

To do this, she must first conquer her 'mortal disgust' at speaking about herself and then try not to 'boast', even if this is 'a natural law of the human mind, which cannot help embellishing and exalting the object of its contemplation'. She relegates 'enthusiasm for oneself', with its 'leaps towards the sky', to the realm of poetry, where it has a 'special and sacred privilege'. Although she judges the 'subtle balm' of poetic idealisation to be 'useful and life-giving', she also finds that it lacks 'reality'. Thus, she proposes to try to 'descend into the prose of [her] subject' (1970, 1:5–7), telling primarily 'the story of her own mind and heart' with the aim of 'fraternal teaching' intended to help others to know themselves; for without self-knowledge a person's life remains 'incomplete and morally barren for the rest of humanity' (1970, 1:9).[3] Distancing herself from Rousseau, she says that she does not want either to accuse or to justify herself for her mistakes and faults.[4] In this spirit she refuses to speak about her private life: 'let no scandal-lover rejoice, I am not writing for them'(1970, 1:13).

Sand returns to these ideas many years later, at the point when, in her autobiography, she has reached the story of her new, independent life in Paris (1970, 2:110–14). She states that she wants to keep silent rather than '*rearrange* or *disguise* many circumstances of [her] life' (1970, 2:110). In fact, she offers almost no anecdotal information relating to her private life, particularly her love affairs, and her explanations of the underlying causes of this almost complete silence imply that she is acting primarily out of consideration for others.[5]

Sand's approach to autobiography corresponds perfectly to her thoughts on history: 'Everything contributes to history, *everything is history*', she wrote (1970, 1:78). Individuality in itself cannot have either significance or importance, since it acquires meaning only when it becomes a 'part of general life'. This view sees history as an effort of interpretation which is both global and unitary, aiming to unify that which is divided (a very Romantic idea), be it individuals and social classes, the living and the dead, or different historical periods. It is the 'gregarious' instinct, as René Girard would call it (1961:330), which drives Sand towards the Other.

The real drive behind the autobiography was no less than to understand what Sand calls her 'mystery', in other words her identity. To do this, she starts with a detailed investigation of her father's life, in accordance with her belief in the continuity of history and the solidarity between generations. From this perspective her father's history is also her own. As Roland Barthes said, to recount is to search for one's origins and relate one's brushes with the Law.[6] In the recounting of the myth of the father, words and images are used to fill the gap caused by his brutal defection and to recreate the absent paternal figure. Above all, Sand wants to resuscitate the Father's word to give herself at least the illusion of a spiritual father. Despite appearances (reinforced by the tenacious 'legend' with which she was surrounded), she has a great need for order and it is in the name of this need – and to legitimise her emotional and spiritual filiation – that she creates a paternal imago for herself, endowed with seductive, juvenile powers and strongly idealised. In this reconstituted paternal image, somewhat 'cleaned up' and embellished, her autobiography looks at itself: leaning over the mirror of the past, it seeks out its own face, whose outlines gradually come into focus through the distant reflections of the faces of her parents, above all her father. Sand-Narcissus is thus not alone. She is her parents' daughter and if she looks beautiful, it is because they were beautiful.

Yet the woman who is looking at herself in the mirror is in fact wearing a mask: she prefers to talk about herself indirectly or through others. Is this modesty or false modesty? Readers must decide for themselves. What seems clear is that, despite a certain obvious narcissism, which nevertheless remains within the limits of the natural, Sand does not get carried away with her own image. Here we glimpse her main concern as an autobiographer and novelist: to show the extent to which general life influences the life of an individual.

A tendency to idealise – which Sand openly recognises and indeed often champions – was an integral part of her poetics and her vision of the world. However, there is nothing exclusive or egocentric about her narcissism. We can say with Bachelard that narcissism is not always neurotic. It can play a positive part, notably in aesthetic works, as a form of sublimation for an ideal. Sand's narcissism can be interpreted in this light.

The role of the prefaces in the elaboration of the image in which the novelist thought she recognised herself towards the end of her life is, of course, only part of the question. However, we should ask whether this very specific discourse functions purely as a distorting, and thus deceitful, mirror, or as a mirror which only distorts to the extent that it highlights the virtual, but no less real traits of the individual rather than the banality of the visible.

Despite its conventionality, Sand's discursive strategy is fairly complex and original, particularly because of the role-play and *personae* characteristic of her prefaces. It could be said that the two distinct roles that she adopts in the preface – those of preface-writer and author – are further split through the use of the masculine in most of the prefaces, which lends a certain dichotomy to her language in the context of the accepted masculine and feminine roles of the time. Although the masculine at first appears to be simply the result of her choice of pseudonym, from the outset it nonetheless signifies a detachment from the young woman Sand was in 1832 (suffering constraints and prey to all kinds of anxiety), and above all it signifies a specific figure giving voice to a 'second existence', both literary and private, which she managed to forge for herself.[7] The masculine continues to fulfil this function and eventually becomes the natural expression of the deeply internalised consequences of using a pseudonym, marking her writings in a manner that is both personal and universalising.[8] The continual coming and going between different roles is characteristic of the language of any preface. It is clear, however, that, in its more diverse changes of role, Sand's language acquires certain particular traits that have some influence over the image of herself that the novelist creates and over her entire strategy in the prefaces.

Sand explains to herself several times why, in her youth, she had this imperative need for a mask. On *Lettres d'un voyageur* she writes,

> I was certainly allowed to philosophise in my way about the difficulties of life and to speak as if I had drunk my fill of them, but not to set myself up, me, a woman still young ... as a tried and tested thinker or as a particular victim of fate. ... So I followed my pen, giving myself over entirely to fancy, creating a fantastical self who was very old, very experienced and thus very despairing. ... In a word, I wanted to write my own novel of my life and not to be the real character but the character who thought and analysed it. (1971, 2:299)

As Gorilovics notes, 'as a young woman and young author she was trying to attain a higher viewpoint or knowledge which would allow her to look at both herself and at the world and life with a philosopher's eye' (1996:254). He adds, 'the role of the narrator is that of a supreme, just authority.' The need for justice remains a constant in Sand's attitude, a familiar one among the Romantics for whom the paradigmatic just individual of modern times was none other than the artist. In *Lettres d'un voyageur* Sand writes:

> I made this word just into a whole moral world and ... I had fashioned its portrait according to my dreams. ... The just person has no moral sex, being man or woman as God chooses; ... the just person has no social status, being beggar, traveller or prince of the world, as God chooses. The goal, the profession of this person is to be just. (1971:134)

This attitude of being above the represented universe, characteristic of Sand's narrators, is also found in the preface-writer, who is the supreme authority in the preface.

Until the early 1850s, Sand expressed herself almost always in the masculine. This period, when she was writing her autobiography, was also, not coincidentally, the time when she was mastering her identity as a woman writer, openly and unselfconsciously acknowledging this status. It was not until the *General Preface* of 1851 that Sand the preface-writer finally expressed herself in the feminine, without, however, abandoning the masculine completely.

While the preface is primarily a literary discourse, it also reflects the history of the work, from its origins to the way in which it was conceived, written and structured. It also relates to the author's life story, with its pleasures, fears, intellectual preoccupations and, sometimes, its everyday concerns. Reflections on literature mingle with reflections on life. The image of the author, revealed in the 'preface-mirror', does not entirely correspond to the one that we have of her through 'objective' documents; this apparently distorted image nevertheless reflects the same author, as she saw herself or as she wanted herself to be seen at a given moment.

Thus, the preface becomes a place for self-reflection in which an idealised and reassuring image of the author comes to life. Even the earliest prefaces reveal a wide range of canonical strategies to win the reader's good will or complicity. Amongst them is also the image of an author who, in 1842, in the preface to the *Lettres d'un voyageur*, declares: 'I am like you, men of bad faith'.

Timidity, modesty, docility, submission to literary criticism, and a total rejection of ambition: these principal traits of the double reflected in the mirror-preface seem to contradict any self-assurance of the person to whose image they contribute. In most cases, however, the defensive strategy inherent in the prefaces and which is largely responsible for the image of the author they create, is paradoxically valorising, tending to produce a rather deceptive discourse, which generally fools no one. Therefore, we shall perhaps not be accused of bad faith for finding in it the signs of an idealisation in the common sense of the term: the author is shown as a person like any other, one of the brotherhood of men, belonging not to any particular literary school, but, in the first place, to Humanity, which here fulfils the function of the paternal figure, reassuring and legitimising. Here we should note that concrete 'genealogical' references to this or that writer (Scott, Rousseau, or Balzac) are comparatively rare in Sand's prefaces – which may have something to do with her status as a woman. Thus, identity is acquired, not through some concrete spiritual father-figure, but rather from the collective spiritual 'parent' who delegates his authority to the preface-writer. In Sand's work narcissism appears 'eminently dialectical'[9] in its double orientation, being both centripetal and centrifugal. The principle of union (life principle), in the name of which she seems to give up a part of herself in order to be enriched by other people, is so strong that Eros finally kills Thanatos: the 'very strong feeling' of her former lives,[10] her belief in metempsychosis and her deep conviction that human beings are immortal in Humanity are all pillars of her thought and work. To find oneself one must first lose oneself: her 'flights from myself' (Didier 1981:189), so apparent in both the autobiography and the prefaces (and even in her correspondence), are closely linked to the search for her own identity, which she fully developed in her forties. Sand's later progression, which was in total accord with her fundamental idealism, was a constant struggle to reach perfection, the Ideal, and the re-establishment of a lost wholeness. In her testament-preface of 1875 she addressed her critics who claimed that she had idealised her characters too much:

> I did not do it deliberately. They came to me as I depicted them, perhaps the world in which I lived with them was too much of a paradise. I gave myself up to the sweetness of this dear company which formed itself around me; I may also have met too many beautiful souls in real life, and I believed in rightness, strength, friendship and disinterestedness, in everything that results from a well-spent life and the goal of a well-developed awareness. (*La Revue de Paris*, 15/1/1896)

In the same preface, surrounded by a spring landscape, she ponders on death: 'Should I say that everything dies because I am nearing the end of my own life?' If she rejects the idea of eternal death, it is because she has found support in 'eternal freshness' and 'the incommensurable power of universal life'; 'hope is infinite' she writes; 'and those who have it feel that everything will survive their death and that as a consequence they will outlive themselves in the inexhaustible vitality of the universe'.

Her faith in immortality is inseparable from her faith in the perpetuity of the artist's words. In 1839, in the preface to *Lélia*, she repeatedly expresses the belief that the 'clamour' of those looking for truth 'will not fall back into the silence of eternal night: it will have called up echoes'. Other prefaces also contain the image of a better educated and more understanding future audience. Even in her moments of discouragement, as in the preface to *Petite Fadette* of 1848, knowing that 'faith counts in centuries' she has the courage to state that 'the future is ours, I know it'. This future, with its 'responsive understanding' on which Sand calls so often in her prefaces, is the guarantee of the artist's immortality.

Notes

1. Similar ideas can be found in her correspondence, particularly in letters to Flaubert, especially in those of 14 June 1867 and 25 October 1871. In the latter she speaks of 'the broad feeling of self-love, of the horror of *me alone*' (1987:595).
2. On the subject of depersonalisation, Béatrice Didier aptly notes that Sand's entire work and life reveal 'a gradual dispossession of self' (1996:56).
3. The idea of the 'pedagogic' objective, which alone can justify 'entirely personal sentiments', had already appeared in the first version of the preface to *Lettres d'un voyageur* (1836), a work which prefigures the autobiography.
4. She proceeds in this way because 'there are no isolated faults', 'no mistake for which no one has been cause or accomplice' and because the 'public consists of both. To show oneself worse than one is, to touch or please them is to court them a little too much' (1:13). In public life, however, she accepts the existence of situations in which it is necessary 'to prove one's excellence' or to dismiss a calumny, on the condition that one has 'some serious project to bring to fruition'. She does this herself, responding to crude attacks, in the preface to *Romans et nouvelles* (1834), in her letter to Nisard (*Lettres d'un voyageur*) and in the foreword to *Jean de la Roche* (1859) on the *Elle et lui* affair.
5. 'When made public in literature, certain personal confidences, whether confessions or justifications, become attacks on the consciousness, the reputations of others; or else they are incomplete, which makes them untrue' (1970, 2:114).
6. Cited in Berthier (1992:203).

7. Let us take two examples from her correspondence: in July 1832 she wrote to a woman friend, 'In Paris Mme Dudevant is dead. But George Sand is known as a hearty fellow' (1966:120). A few years later, on 18 July 1836, she wrote to Scipion du Roure:

> Madame Sand told M. George how kind and sympathetic you are towards him. Madame Sand is a beast I shall not require you to meet and who would bore you to death; but George is an excellent lad, full of love and gratitude for those who are willing to love him. He would be happy to shake the hand of an unknown friend and, as he has a fairly good opinion of himself, he is quite ready to believe that those who accept him as he is are perfect'. (1967:490–1)

8. See Tivadar Gorilovics (1996:251). Françoise van Rossum-Guyon's observations on the prefaces to *Indiana* (1832, 1842) can be applied to the entire corpus: 'the utterer is not always the same. Sometimes it is the concrete person, Aurore, George? sometimes the novelist, witness, storyteller, entertainer, moralist? sometimes the Writer entrusted with a serious mission' (van Rossum-Guyon 1983:9).
9. Béla Grunberger cited in Dessuant (1994:23).
10. In her letter of 1 October 1866 to Flaubert she writes, 'but if one remembers nothing distinct, one has a very strong feeling of one's own renewal in eternity ... I believe that I was a plant or a stone. I am not always sure that I exist completely and, at other times, I feel a great accumulated tiredness from having existed too much' (1985:136).

Bibliography

Bachelard, G. (1942) *L'Eau et les rêves* (Paris: Corti).
Berthier, Ph. (1992) 'Barbey d'Aurevilly, La question du père', in *Figures du Phantasme* (Toulouse: Presses Universitaires du Mirail).
Dessuant, P. (1994) *Le Narcissisme* (Paris: Presses Universitaires de France).
Didier, B. (1981) *L'Ecriture-femme* (Paris: Presses Universitaires de France).
——— (1996) 'George Sand écrivain réaliste?', in *George Sand et l'écriture du roman* (Montreal: Paragraphes).
Girard, R. (1961) *Mensonge romantique et vérité romanesque* (Paris: Grasset).
Gorilovics, T. (1996) 'Un regard d'homme: le narrateur sandien', in *George Sand et l'écriture du roman* (Montreal: Paragraphes).
Rossum-Guyon, F. van (1983) 'Les enjeux d'*Indiana* I, Métadiscours et réception critique', in *CRIN* 6–7.
Sand, G. (1873) *Impressions et souvenirs* (Paris: Michel Lévy).
——— (1966) *Correspondance 2*, ed. G. Lubin (Paris: Garnier).
——— (1967) *Correspondance 3*, ed. G. Lubin (Paris: Garnier).
——— (1970) *Histoire de ma vie* and *Manière de préface à une nouvelle phase de mon récit*, in G. Lubin (ed.) *Oeuvres autobiographiques* 1 and 2.

——— (1971) *Lettres d'un voyageur* (Paris: Garnier-Flammarion).
——— (1985) *Correspondance* 20, ed. G. Lubin (Paris: Garnier).
——— (1987) *Correspondance* 22, ed. G. Lubin (Paris: Garnier).

CHAPTER 5

NARCISSUS MAGNIFIED BY MARGUERITE DURAS'S ECHO

Trista Selous

There is one thing that every Narcissus needs to fulfil his self-loving destiny, and that is a mirror. However, the beloved image the mirror reflects is treacherous: it changes with time and has no substance – it cannot return love. Ovid's Narcissus avoided the former problem and illustrated the latter by drowning; Oscar Wilde's Dorian Gray temporarily solved both by becoming alienated in his own youthful image; for flesh-and-blood narcissists, however, such solutions are not necessarily appropriate. I want here to consider Marguerite Duras's writing, and particularly *The Lover*, in its capacity as a narcissistic response to the problem of both the inconstancy and ultimate insubstantiality of the image of the self.

That Duras herself was not unaware of the potential of writing as a vehicle of narcissism is clear from her own use of autobiography. Autobiography can, of course, take many different forms and is not inevitably an expression of narcissism; however, Duras's most overtly autobiographical work, *The Lover*, opens in classically narcissistic style with the narrator's contemplation of her own image:

> One day, I was already old, in the entrance of a public place a man came up to me. He introduced himself and said, 'I've known you for years. Everyone says you were beautiful when you were young, but I want to tell you that I think you're more

beautiful now than then. Rather than your face as a young woman, I prefer your face as it is now. Ravaged'.
　　I often think of the image only I can see now, and of which I've never spoken. It's always there, in the same silence, amazing. It's the only image of myself I like, the only one in which I recognise myself, in which I delight. (1993:1)

This opening is indicative of what is to follow, on a number of counts. First, as an open manifestation of narcissism, almost to the point of overstatement, it undercuts any potential criticism of the autobiographical project on these grounds; second, it articulates the power of appearance, which will recur throughout the text, and questions – while reinforcing – the intangible notion of beauty; third, it raises the interconnected problems of time, loss, change and transcendent singularity: the beautiful young face is gone, yet in some way young woman and old are the same; fourth, it demonstrates the power of the imaginary image as created by words, describing Duras contemplating her own image in the words of her admirer;[1] lastly, it provides a guarantee of the beauty, the amazing, delightful mystery and thus implicitly the interest value of the woman in whom the reader is being invited to invest attention, suggesting that being a celebrated author is not, in itself, quite enough.

However, its significance as a framing moment notwithstanding, this particular scene and its accompanying image are never again returned to in the text. Instead the crucial image of *The Lover* is that of Duras at fifteen, a white girl in Indo-China, crossing the Mekong river on the ferry the locals use, dressed in her man's hat, faded silk dress and golden sandals, as she is first seen by the man who is to become her first lover. Like Ovid's Narcissus, the adolescent Duras is both woman and child, and the image the reader is invited to contemplate ('On the ferry, look, I've still got my hair. Fifteen-and-a-half' (15)) is, like the moment that defines Narcissus, that of the point when she explicitly becomes an object of overpowering, taboo-breaking sexual desire. Of course, in Duras's case, there is another person involved, the lover of the title; however, she will later explain, 'You didn't have to attract desire. Either it was in the woman who aroused it or it didn't exist. … It was in the instant knowledge of sexual relationship or it was nothing' (18). The desire incited by the image of the adolescent on the ferry is her own for herself as object of desire. It is just that, unlike Narcissus, she wants that desire to pass through another person before returning to her, so that she can both emit and receive it as both subject and object; she wants a man as mirror.

For Narcissus, apprehension of himself as object is direct and fatal; for the narrator of *The Lover* the same realisation, mediated through the desire of another, is salvation. Until this point her entire emotional life has been bound up with her troubled family – mother and two brothers – in an entanglement of irreconcilable love and hate that ensnares them all, preventing the distance and separation necessary to individual existence. The volatile mother has nothing to live for but her children, binding them to her with an intense mixture of fierce love and, where her daughter is concerned, callousness. The brothers, towards whom the mother seems less ambivalent, never escape to independence; the younger dies, while the elder becomes a gambler and petty criminal, financially dependent on his mother to the end. The daughter is enabled to separate, however; while ostensibly condemning it, the mother seems implicitly to encourage what Duras describes as her own prostitution as a way out of poverty, while the mother's manifest preference for her sons provides a space which the daughter can reclaim for herself through narcissism.[2] This separation through narcissism is thus the process that makes possible the narrator's adult destiny as a woman who escapes the destructive confines of her family to a life which allows her other loves and, crucially, a career as a writer. As such it is of primary importance to an understanding of Duras the author and explicitly forms the central theme of *The Lover*.

At the same time, and in a way which may at first seem incompatible with any manifestation of narcissism, in form *The Lover* is a highly fragmented text, from the chronology it follows through to the shifts in narratorial perspective which may occur within a single paragraph or indeed a single sentence. If, following both Ovid and Lacan, we take the quintessential narcissistic moment as one where the subject falls in love with, or identifies with, a unified self-image, then *The Lover*'s formal fragmentation would seem to counteract the importance given by the narrator to the crystallisation of her narcissism in the image of the fifteen-year-old on the ferry. For a start, this image of the narrator is no longer current, as we have known from the opening paragraph. 'Very early in my life', she goes on to tell us, 'it was too late' (1), meaning that her face began ageing early on its journey to the 'ravaged' state. Furthermore, the image does not exist except in words, and never has. So the archetypal narcissistic moment, when the adolescent first sees her image mirrored in her lover's eyes, is doubly absent. Yet its presence in the text suggests that the importance of that moment, and the need it meets, remain. Something more durable, therefore, must replace it and this is, as Duras herself explains, a word portrait that replaces the 'photo [that] might have been taken' and which, precisely because no actual image exists, she tells us, 'has the virtue of representing, of being the creator of, an absolute' (8–9). It seems that the loss of the moment that epitomises Duras's escape to herself through narcissism has required her to formulate another, ultimately more effective strategy and that what we are witnessing here is the linguistic echo of a kind of transcendent Narcissus who can be reconstructed from the fragments or ripples left behind after the image in the pool has gone.

The Lover is written in short, distinct sections, some no longer than two or three lines, the longest two or three pages, separated by blank spaces. Sometimes one section follows on from the previous one, either chronologically or thematically, but often it does not, or else the link is not immediately apparent. This way of proceeding is reminiscent of the visual storytelling strategies of cinema and television, in the way that a film may take us from one scene to another, very different scene with a simple cut no more marked in itself than the cuts between related shots in the same scene. The connection between individual shots or scenes may not always be immediately apparent but, as consumers of audio-visual media, we have learned not to let this bother us, confident in the belief that everything we are shown is shown for a reason and understanding that the image itself cannot tell us why it is there, it can only show us something, which we must then link to all that we have seen and will see before and after it.

So it seems that Duras draws on and trusts to the conventions of the audio-visual media, and particularly cinema, to construct *The Lover*. However, *The Lover* is of course a text, whose constraints and possibilities in the matter of expression and the construction of meanings are very different from those of a piece of film or video tape. Of these the most crucial difference for the subject of my discussion centres around the notion of 'voice'. A film or television programme may be said to have a style and, indeed, a 'visual language'; it may be made in such a way that we sense the intelligence of the director/editor/director of photography in the way the images are constructed and/or assembled; yet, actors and other on-screen human participants aside, there is always a distance between the human agents responsible for the production of an audio-visual drama or documentary and the images themselves, which are the result of mechanical, chemical and possibly electronic processes.[3] A text, on the other hand, is made of words which speak in our heads as we read them; it talks to us as one human being to another in a language which refers to the external world but does not directly bear its traces. On the contrary, the traces it bears are those of the linguistic unconscious of the narrator, writer, genre, culture and/or species, in endlessly varied combination. In *The Lover*, while the text certainly exploits a certain willingness on the part of the audio-visually-trained late twentieth-century reader to absorb information in short chunks and to wait for connections to form, the ends to which it exploits these attitudes are entirely text- and language-based. So from this perspective also I would suggest that, at the formal level, our familiarity with images, their limitations and connections, is being exploited and replaced by something akin to their linguistic echo, which is, however, conveying more than just images themselves, as I hope now to show with an analysis of the text.

Pages 20–1 are taken up with a comparatively long section describing the adolescent Duras's experience of crossing the Mekong river on her way to the *pension* in Saigon, where she stays while attending school. I shall quote the end of this section and the following paragraph:

> [The river] carries everything along, straw huts, forests, burned-out fires, dead birds, dead dogs, drowned tigers and buffaloes, drowned men, bait, islands of water hyacinths all stuck together. Everything flows towards the Pacific, no time for anything to sink, all is swept along by the deep and head-long storm of the inner current, suspended on the surface of the river's strength.
>
> I answered that what I wanted more than anything else in the world was to write, nothing else but that, nothing. Jealous. She's jealous. No answer, just a quick glance immediately averted, a slight shrug, unforgettable. I'll be the first to leave. There are still a few years to wait before she loses me, loses this one of her children. For the sons there's nothing to fear. But this one, she knows one day she'll go, she'll manage to escape. Top in French. The headmaster of the high school tells her, your daughter's top in French, Madame. My mother says nothing, nothing, she's cross because it's not her sons who are top in French. The beast, my mother, my love, asks: what about maths? Answer: not yet, but it will come. My mother asks: When? Answer: When she makes up her mind to it, Madame. (21–2)

This transition from one paragraph to the next is typical of *The Lover*. The reader is taken from a visual description of the Mekong river – with its possible symbolic interpretations – to the middle of a conversation, a reply to an unidentified 'she'. Such a scene change is easy to imagine in a film and would be simpler to follow: we would at once see who was talking, to whom and where. The written text requires a far greater attentiveness on the part of the reader, a willingness to follow where the narration goes and to make the effort of interpretation, of reconstruction, in the mind's eye, of what is happening. We are asked to match the thought-processes of the narrator/author; the text operates on the assumption that we will plunge from the immediacy of one scene to the next, understanding and 'seeing' who the protagonists of the conversation are without having to be told, because we have come to identify with our narrator and her world. Thus the fact that the 'she' of the conversation is not named until the scene shifts to the mother's own conversation with the headmaster of the high school (although the English version has already mentioned 'her children', this is expressed without the possessive in the French) has the effect of demonstrating and adding to the emotional weight of the relationship between narrator and mother: the unreferenced use of 'her' and 'she' implies that there is no need to explain who the narrator's interlocutor is, because who else could it be but her mother? No other female character in the text is important enough to spring to mind unnamed and unexplained.

A similar process is at work in the shift to and back from the brief distancing of the description of the mother's reaction to the daughter's words: 'No answer, just a quick glance immediately averted, a slight shrug, unforgettable', with its sting in the tail that suddenly casts everything back into the past, to the use of free indirect style to convey the mother's understanding of the situation: 'I'll be the first to leave', which then moves further to the mother's point of view with the shift of pronoun in 'before she loses me, loses this one of her children'. This movement continues with the rendering of the mother's conversation with the headmaster, at which the daughter may or may not have been present, which may or may not be imagined, but in which she at any rate is not included; however, while the daughter seems physically absent from the conversation, her attitude is brought back into focus with 'The beast, my mother, my love'.

The text thus flows from point of view to point of view, in a linguistic transposition that reflects, through its use of pronouns and focalisation, both the closeness of the relationship between mother and daughter and the daughter's brief, abrupt distancing in her description of the mother's reaction to her desire to write and her qualification of the mother as 'The beast, my mother, my love'. It thus provides the linguistic echoes of emotion in a way analogous to that in which objects leave their traces in light, whether on film or a reflective surface such as a mirror or pool of water, except that here the narrator is mirrored emotionally rather than physically, in a way that transcends the temporal and spatial specificity of physical images to allow for a simultaneous presence of different times and perspectives.

Seen in this light the fragmentation of the narrative, with its constant shifting between a kaleidoscope of moments, scenes, places and points of view, is not so much a counter-indication of any textual manifestation of narcissism, as a vital component in the expression of a kind of narcissism that goes beyond the physical image and seeks to construct an 'emotional image' of the narrator/author. After providing the reader with an initial paradox concerning Duras's appearance – her face is more beautiful in its old, 'ravaged' state than it was when she was young and generally considered beautiful – *The Lover* sets out to explain this paradox by exploring what it is that lies behind this face and gives it its power of beauty. Like the unexpected assemblage of man's hat, faded dress and gold lamé shoes with which the fifteen-year-old Duras invites the desire of a man who will reflect back to her an image made unique by love, so the combination of elements in the text and the gaps between them invite another form of desire, in the shape of the reader's emotional identification with the narrator/author. The 'image' of the author/narrator thus constructed transcends appearance and time, producing a Duras whose textual skeleton, once fleshed with the reader's affective intelligence, integrates elements from a lifetime in a centripetal movement which seeks to link and understand them all in relation to the unified source signified by the single author's name on the cover: Marguerite Duras.

In this way *The Lover* not only describes a process by which the young Duras escapes into life by means of her own narcissism, it is itself also a manifestation of that narcissism, or rather a kind of post-narcissism, the aftermath of narcissistic revelation, where the power of the image has been replaced by the different power of the word. Now that the days of the narcissism of appearance are over, the reader is invited to act as lover by reconstructing, from the text of fragmentary echoes left behind, an ur-Duras who both includes and transcends the image of the fifteen-year-old.

That an overtly autobiographical work should be a manifestation of narcissism, or of post-narcissistic echoes, is perhaps not surprising, although, as I said above, neither is it inevitable. In the case of Duras's fiction, however, I would suggest that, particularly in her more experimental texts, starting with the publication of *Moderato Cantabile* in 1958, it is possible to identify a similar narcissistic mode of writing in narratives which are not directly autobiographical. In these works also, Duras uses the mechanism of 'gaps' or 'blanks' where the reader must infer a connection between elements which remains at the unarticulated, emotional level, thus aligning her- or himself with what appears to be the narrator/author's own emotions in order to give the text meaning and continue reading. The conflation of author and narrator is also important here and is maintained across Duras's work through a great consistency in both form and content.

In style Duras's texts vary little, either internally or in comparison to each other, no matter who is ostensibly speaking; from unnamed narrators to the ambassador's wife Anne-Marie Stretter of *The Vice-Consul* or the unemployed dockyard worker Chauvin of *Moderato Cantabile*, all use the same clear, standard French with the same kinds of sentence structure. Why should this be? The answer is, I think, because these different texts are seeking to communicate not character, contingency, particularity, diversity or individuality within the worlds they create, but that which lies behind their production: the emotional energy that gave rise to the existence of the text. As such the ultimate meaning of Duras's texts is always located beyond the narrative itself, or perhaps before it, in the energy source which is the person of the narrator/author. Because of the similarity of style across the different texts, and the recurrence of certain stories or characters, such as those of Anne-Marie Stretter or Lol V. Stein, each individual text's construction of a narrative voice is largely eclipsed by the sense that the voice is in fact that of Duras, whose name is on the cover of her thematically interconnected and stylistically unified oeuvre.[4]

As such, like the disparate elements of her fifteen-year-old image or the montage of echoes that is *The Lover*, Duras's individual works, and indeed her films, nonfiction and public pronouncements, can all be understood as so many elements in the construction, via her audience, of the persona 'Marguerite Duras', which Duras pursued throughout her life as a writer.[5] As Leslie Hill (1993) has said, 'Duras's critical and political remarks need to be read not as constituting a theoretical discourse existing apart from her creative writing, but, more modestly, and perhaps more interestingly, as a wayward yet integral part of that writing'.[6]

This is not to suggest that either Duras's public persona or her writing can or should be summed up as purely '(post-)narcissistic'; the fact that her texts succeed in harnessing their readers' emotions demonstrates that they have a power extending far beyond their relationship to their author alone. Duras writes about various fundamental aspects of human experience in a way that, to a greater or lesser extent depending on text and circumstance, resonates with the other human beings that are her readers. That narcissism should play a vital part in that process is not, however, surprising. The way that narcissism manifests itself in Duras's work may well echo the structurally important place identified by psychoanalysts in the construction of the human psyche; at the very least it is bound to resonate with inhabitants of our image-bound late twentieth-century Western culture.

Notes

1. For a detailed discussion of this and other word-images in *The Lover*, see Solomon (1997).
2. This process of separation through narcissism, as depicted in *The Lover*, is very close to what psychoanalyst Béla Grunberger describes in relation to female sexuality and narcissism. According to Grunberger, the fact that mother and daughter are of the same sex means that the relationship between them will always entail a degree of frustration: 'The pregenital stages are much more frustrating for the girl because the maternal object is only a substitute for a *truly adequate sexual object*' (1970:72). The effect of this, Grunberger continues, is to incite girls to give themselves their own narcissistic confirmation at an earlier age and more extensively than is the case for boys: 'Much doll play, for example, is a way of taking over the mother's role and achieving by use of the doll (with which the girl also identifies herself) a narcissistic confirmation which is otherwise the mother's responsibility'(*ibid.*).
3. For a more detailed discussion of the place of an 'author' in Duras's films and film in general, see Selous (1997).
4. In this context it is interesting to compare Duras's style with that of Samuel Beckett, a writer whose work may, superficially at least, share certain characteristics with hers, notably in terms of a certain thematic and stylistic unity, its concern with the silence within and around language and the recurrent theme of death. However, Beckett's approach to language is very

different from that of Duras in the way that he plays on and with linguistic incongruities, giving the signifier an often amusing opacity that it seldom if ever has in Duras's more deliberately 'transparent' language. Beckett's stress on the signifier tends to locate the emotional weight of the text within language itself, in terms of both failures and excesses of meaning, rather than in some prelinguistic elsewhere, as Duras's does.

5. Perhaps the most striking example of this in Duras's cinema, relevant here because of the 'unvisual' nature of the film itself, is *Le Camion*. This film consists largely of shots of Duras who, in response to Gérard Depardieu's questions, describes the actions of a woman hitchhiker in a film that she has imagined but not actually made. Of all her films it is this one in which Duras's own very particular form of narcissism finds its most overt expression, since in it we both see and hear Duras herself playing herself as author of the unmade film, with Depardieu playing the part of the interested interlocutor/interviewer. Not that Duras seems particularly interested in her own image as such: she simply sits in a chair and reads her script; however, what this film is about, on one level at least, is Duras, beyond or behind her image, as source of the film her descriptions invite us to imagine.

6. Hill (1993) gives a fulsome and perceptive account of Duras's construction of her own persona through journalism and media interviews. Sankey (1997) also provides a useful account of the 'Duras phenomenon' as a media construction.

Bibliography

Duras, M. (1993) *The Lover*, trans. B. Bray (London: Bloomsbury).

Grunberger, B. (1970) 'Narcissism in Female Sexuality', in J. Chasseguet-Smirgel (ed.) *Female Sexuality* (London: Maresfield) 68–83.

Hill, L. (1993) *Marguerite Duras Apocalyptic Desires* (London: Routledge).

Sankey, M. (1997) 'The Duras Phenomenon', in *Australian Journal of French Studies* 34, 1:60–76.

Selous, T. (1997) 'Imaginary pictures in *Le Vice-consul* and *India Song*', in *Australian Journal of French Studies* 34, 1:77–87.

Solomon, J. (1997) '"J'ai un visage détruit": Pleasures of Self-Portraiture in Marguerite Duras's *L'Amant*', in *Australian Journal of French Studies* 34, 1:100–14.

CHAPTER 6

EGOTISM AND NARCISSISM: AVATARS OF THE MASCULINE IMAGERY IN NINETEENTH-CENTURY FRENCH LITERATURE*

Jean-Jacques Hamm

From the Renaissance to the pre-Romantics, the representation of secular man tended to show him in the context of his social relationships. Michel de Montaigne, living alone 'in the bosom of the learned virgins' (1948:15), wrote a book addressed to his friends and relatives, but which does not exclude the reader; this book states that, beyond the individual adventure of a life, 'each man carries the complete form of the human condition' (1948:900) and constantly weaves links with human beings from books and history, both distant and contemporary. Classical solitude was never total separation. Furthermore, in Court society, solitude could even be a desirable commodity, as reflected in this quotation from the dream of an 'inhabitant of the Mogol': 'If I might dare to add to what the interpreter says, / I would take this chance to encourage a love of retirement. / This offers its lovers a pure, unencumbering wealth, / a gift of heaven, that appears beneath their feet, / and solitude, which brings me a secret sweetness' (La Fontaine XI, 4).[1]

---

* Translated from the French by Trista Selous.

To these words can be contrasted the following: 'I am shaping an undertaking which has never had a model and whose execution will have no imitators ... Myself alone. I feel my heart and I know men. I am not made like any of those I have seen; I dare to think that I am not made like any that exist' (Rousseau 1964:5). Elsewhere the same author says, 'So now I am alone on earth, with no brother, family, friend or company but myself' (Rousseau 1964:995). Jean-Jacques Rousseau's words and those of the *Fragment du Narcisse* a century and a half later outline a way of being whose very centre is solitude:

> I am alone...
> ....
> But I, beloved Narcissus, am curious
>   About nothing but my essence;
> For me any other's heart is mysterious
>   Any other is only absence.
> Oh sovereign wealth, my body dear, you are all I have!
> Himself alone is all the most beautiful mortal can love...
>   (Valéry 1962:128)[2]

These assertions of self-sufficiency, whose painfulness should not be underestimated, reveal the formation of an autarchic and indeed solipsistic masculine ego. Rousseau seems to me both revealer of the crisis and architect of the recovery that was exercising the masculine imagination in the eighteenth century. With Rousseau Romantic (or pre-Romantic) solitude, with its games and points of conflict, enters into literature. With him comes the end of Montaigne for whom we 'must reserve a back shop all our own, entirely free' (1948:177) and the eminently social *honnête homme* or decent gentleman presented by the seventeenth-century moralists. Michelle Coquillat has detailed the changes brought about for women by the Rousseauist position inherited by the nineteenth century in *La Poétique du mâle* (1982).

Beyond what could be a study of the ideologies which become established during a historical process (such as the dialectic which forms between progress and unhappiness), my concern here is with the development of a masculine ego and imaginary and their representation in French nineteenth-century literature. I would see egotism and narcissism, in other words the seizure and loss of the self, as two forms of the use of an ego devoted to freedom, solitude and specular relationships. Though egotism and narcissism are contrary movements, we shall see how much they are interwoven. Egotism as a concept appeared in France during the Restoration, in the context of a conflict between the familialist theses of the ultras and the individualism inherited from the French Revolution. Narcissus as a character and subject of poems or texts came later. Generally speaking, egotism and narcissism formed around different moments of the century's cultural and intellectual history and the choices they manifest can be read as signs of the increasing alienation of the artist and poet: the passage from the July Monarchy to the Second Empire led to the internal or external exile of writers who had been politically active (Hugo, Lamartine, Sand). We should note, however, that this is a haphazard division; there were no clean breaks, only continuities and rifts, slippages and tectonic superpositions. We should also note that the artist's isolation and alienation were invested in many other archetypes, mythical characters, themes and images, such as Moses, Prometheus, Icarus, Orpheus, Don Juan, the Albatross, the swan, the androgyne, the Baudelairean stranger or the 'infanta in her ceremonial dress', alone at the top of her tower, in Albert Samain's poetry (1913:7).

This bad-tempered century opened with a turning inwards: works expressing proscription, endings and exile. Let us cite a few titles of novels: Chateaubriand's *Atala* and *René*, Mme de Staël's *Delphine*, Charles Nodier's *Les Proscrits* and his later *Jean Shogar*, *Adolphe* by Benjamin Constant and *Ourika* and *Edouard* by Mme de Duras. A more secret, underground and specular solitude was expressing itself in a new, as yet uncodified genre, in which fears and dreams, sickness and poverty, suffering and happiness were articulated away from prying eyes; this was the private journal. The earliest diarists include Henry Beyle, Maine de Biran, Benjamin Constant, Eugène Delacroix and Alfred de Vigny. The *Robert* French dictionary defines egotism as:

1. The tendency to talk about oneself, to make detailed analyses of one's physical and moral character;
2. A way of understanding and behaving which makes the self the most important reference point;
3. A tendency to refer all one's mental life to oneself: the cult of the self, an over-exclusive pursuit of one's personal development. *Smug egotism* → Narcissism.

In eighteenth-century England Addison used the word to translate the French *egoïsme* (in sense 1 above). In the early nineteenth century 'egotism' and 'egotist' entered into common parlance.³ In 1824 William Hazlitt wrote an essay 'On Egotism', in which he shows the ill effects of arrogance, such as the painter Salvator Rosa declaring himself to be the equal of Michelangelo.

The word was introduced into French by Stendhal in 1823, in his essay on laughter. Here is the context in which it appears:

> Many things make us laugh, when we see them, which, when recounted merely make us exclaim, 'that wasn't worth telling'; for example, everyday misfortunes: people falling over in the mud; a husband discovering, for the first time, a love-letter written by his faithful wife; our soap that leaps out of our hand and under the bed to cover itself in dust when we are shaving. ... When someone recounts these little misfortunes to us, we call it *egotism*. (Cited by del Litto in Stendhal 1970:viii)

For Stendhal the word means, primarily, excessive self-love. Egotism is systematically denigrated in his work, a little too much, it might be said. In 1826, when he was writing a new preface to *De l'Amour* – a work which had had no success – he noted apropos of the use of the first person singular, 'The form I have chosen could be criticised for its *egotism*' (1980:334). The real or simulated fear of being accused of egotism often returns in his writings and doubtless hides a *captatio benevolentiae* which is customary in Stendhal's work. In 1826, in the new edition of *Rome, Naples et Florence*, he wrote apropos of a visit to Santa Maria del Fiore: 'I was happy not to know anyone, and not to fear being obliged to speak. This medieval architecture took my whole soul over; I felt I was living with Dante ... I am ashamed of my story, which will make me seem an *egotist*' (1973:482). In the same way, in *Promenades dans Rome*, having alluded to an anecdote from his first visit to the city in 1802, he adds, 'Will I be accused of *egotism* for recounting this little incident?' (1973:597). In the *Mémoires d'un touriste*, he states from the outset, 'It is not out of *egotism* that I say *I*, it is because there is no other way to tell things quickly' (1992:3). Above all he wanted not to follow the example of Chateaubriand, whom he particularly loathed, describing him moreover as the 'king of the *egotists*' (1982:533) and, in a parody of Molière, accusing him thus: 'You repeat the offence of *I* mixed with *me*' (1982:534).⁴

Egotism is thus a fault to beware of since, as V. del Litto says, 'it is a way in which individuals grant themselves a preponderant place, making a space around them' (Stendhal 1970:xiii). Egotism may be bad because it gives rise to the games of vanity and affectation; however, it is nevertheless, though not only, to egotism that can be attributed the upsurge of psychic energy which enables the self to be grasped, allowing people threatened with dispersal or death to take hold of themselves. This is exemplified by Julien Sorel who, when threatened with misfortune, quotes Corneille's Medea: 'Surrounded by so many dangers, I still have myself' (1952:530). Triumphant egotism and the exaltation of the self, a form of pride, can thus be put at the service of a dual aim: the conquest of a world, whether physical, spiritual, social or private, and the deepening of self-awareness. Behind its ironic intention, which does not succeed in concealing its author's suffering, *Souvenirs d'egotisme* was written with such an aim in mind.

In Stendhal's work images of the egotism of conquest can be read in terms of the cult of energy; in that of other authors they may be associated with Byronism, the Sadean undercurrent which haunts the century, the Barresian cult of the self, that 'pedagogy of the self' (Moreau 1957:42), the Nietzschean construction of the superman or Lafcadio's gratuitous act in *Les Caves du Vatican*.

The egotism of knowledge, *Gnôthi seauton* or *nosce te ipsum* – 'know thyself' – the searing self-exploration which is sometimes painful and always minutely detailed, such as that carried out by Maurice de Guérin or Amiel, also appears in other places closer to the novel as a form of cerebrality. From Louis Lambert to Monsieur Teste, the nineteenth century was fascinated by cerebrality, which challenged production, sociality and, all in all, life itself. We need only think of the hero of Huysmans' *Against Nature*. The law which states that the greatest successes are those which remain unknown is a constant in this type of egotism: 'I dreamed then that the cleverest people, the wisest inventors, those who most understood thought must be strangers, misers, men who die without confessing. Their existence was revealed to me by that of the slightly less *solid* brilliant individuals' (Valéry 1946:17).

Vigny's avowed project in *La Mort du loup* was to die without confessing. Egotism uses language to state its right to silence and to singularity. Yet, by using language and in its desire to affirm its singularity, it enters the order of duality. To talk about oneself is to bring the other into being. In the poetry and prose of solitude, alienation, exaltation and poverty the double is born.

'The real,' to quote Clément Rosset, 'is that which presents itself without a double, as a singularity both ungraspable and invisible because it can have no mirror' (1979:15). Since the real is both ordinary and fortuitous, how can one enter into contact with it?

> There are two major possibilities for contact with the real: rough contact, which trips over things, getting nothing from them but an awareness of their silent presence, and the smooth, polished, mirror contact which replaces the presence of things by their appearance in images. Rough contact is contact without doubles; smooth contact exists only with the help of a double. (Rosset 1977:43)

Phrases expressing abandonment mirror that abandonment through the doubling of consciousness: 'It will be obvious that this is written only for me', notes Henri Beyle (Stendhal) in his *Journal* in 1811 (1981:736). It will be obvious I'm writing for myself. In this way a shadow play is set up. All monologue is dialogue and Narcissus haunts all introspective writing, all writing that turns in on itself.

Narcissus – 'You all know the story', says André Gide, summing it up as follows: 'Narcissus was perfectly beautiful – and that's why he was chaste; he rejected the Nymphs – because he was in love with himself. No breath troubled the spring in which, leaning calmly over, he spent all day contemplating his own image' (1958:3). Narcissus appears to us as a story, in other words a chain of cause and effect, death and rebirth. His is a story of passivity, of getting sucked in; it is a tale of looking and the clutching prison of love. Narcissus is born of the fascination and fatefulness of a single mirror. He remains a stranger to the labyrinths of the psyche whose crumbling, both positing and obscuring its origins, traces the ups and downs of pursuit and reconstitution. Narcissus is the one who wants to be one, wrestling with duplication.

I would draw a distinction between thematic narcissism, the manifest narcissism which reworks the elements of the myth from Ovid or Pausanias, and the narcissism of writing imbued with the absolute and nihilism. These two ways of proceeding both suggest and propose evanescence, annihilation and passage. They may both lead to palingenesis. The first reformulates the myth in its own way; the second eliminates it, transforming it into an absolute figure.

Let us take some examples. Valéry's Monsieur Teste as a Narcissus ceaselessly staring at himself: 'I *am* me, I answer, reflect and echo myself, I tremble at the infinity of mirrors – I am glass' (1946:73). Narcissus as a Laforgue character plays serious or ironic games: 'In brief, I was going to give myself with an "I love you" / When I saw, not without pain, / That I was not in full possession of myself' (1993:138).[5]

As Mallarmé's *Hérodiade* suggests, narcissism implies the impossibility or refusal of, and indeed a disdain for, the couple relationship. Valéry states this view in Sémiramis' invective against lovers and 'low beatitudes' (1962:94) and again in *Fragments du Narcisse*, in which Narcissus suffers from a preordained solitude which gives him his being.

> You were waiting, perhaps, for a face without tears,
> You so calm, you always all leaves and flowers
> ....
> Dream, dream of me! ... Without you, lovely springs,
> My beauty, my pain, would be uncertain things.
> I would search in vain for what is to me most dear,
> Its confused tenderness would astound my flesh,
> And my sad glances, ignorant of my charms,
> Would address their tears to someone other than me.
> (1962:122–3)[6]

At the thematic level, narcissism also expresses itself in the speaker's pleasure in and communion with himself or the world. Narcissism expresses itself in the abandonment of privileged moments: the amniotic bathing of the *Cinquième promenade*, Rimbaud's dawn swoon at the *wasserfall*, Valéry's Genoese night, Proust's immense rushes of emotion. This is a luminous aspect of narcissism which the writer allows into himself in a century devoted to unhappiness and, most often, determinism.

There is an absolute of writing that seeks and exposes itself in narcissism, in the evanescence of language, in death as rebirth. On Mallarmé's central point Maurice Blanchot wrote,

> That is the point where the performance of language coincides with its disappearance, where everything speaks to everything ... everything is speech, but where speech itself is now no more than the appearance of what has disappeared, the incessant, interminable imaginary. (1955:42)

Narcissus, haunted by his own disappearance, his own suicide through writing, is also the sublimation of both object and poet in the pure work: 'What use is the miracle of transposing a natural thing into its vibratory near-disappearance in the play of speech, however, if it is not so that from it will emanate the pure notion, unhindered by close or concrete recall?' (Mallarmé 1945:368). Narcissus the poet suddenly and knowingly absents himself. The masculine vanishes in this process of loss. 'A contradictory adventure, in which this goes down; from which that escapes' (*ibid.*:385).

Egotism, the valorisation and sometimes excessive taking of responsibility for oneself, and narcissism, which is both the valorisation and loss of self, are thus opposite movements in the epiphany of the self which are historically both successive and parallel. Egotism can in some cases lead to action; narcissism leads to the impossibility of wanting to act. Both involve the dimension of seeing, a meta-visual dimension summed up in Valéry's words: 'I am being, and seeing myself; seeing myself see' (1946:34) or those of Stendhal: 'Octave said foolish things in bad taste aloud to himself, observing with curiosity their bad taste and foolishness' (1967:112).

Egotism and narcissism can also be identified in the writer's attitude to his audience. Stendhal's self-imposed project was to select his audience of a happy few then wait to prepare for his moment; the same is true of Chateaubriand, addressing his readers from beyond the grave. Valéry seems to have refused to publish, rejecting literature as something impure; but he was not alone in his time. Masculine literature and imagination, threatened by the encroachment of the prosaic and the flattening of values, were haunted by Narcissus' silence and death. 'His ideas of hiding away, far from the world, of cocooning himself in a retreat, of deadening the rolling cacophony of inflexible life, as the road is covered in straw for some sick people, these ideas grew stronger' (Huysmans 1977:87). Thus spake Des Esseintes.

Egotism and narcissism express separation, a break. Echo and Narcissus will not form a couple. There is a lament in T.S. Eliot's *The Waste Land* which could be that of Echo, if she had any power to speak, if she had the gift of tongues; but she is condemned to repeat words from some other source, unceasingly, in a diminuendo. Narcissus, if it is he, has better things to do than to listen to echolalic speech that mimes the despair of his impossible partner: 'Speak to me. Why do you never speak. Speak. / What are you thinking of? What thinking? What? / I never know what you are thinking. Think' (1969:65). Someone speaks, repeats and is not heard. In this context writing becomes echolalia. Is this a portrait of the artist as the nymph Echo? Or Echo's revenge in twentieth-century literature? It is the revenge of the feminine at any rate, of a feminine writing. But that is another story.

Notes

1. *Si j'osais ajouter au mot de l'interprète,*
   J'inspirerais ici l'amour de la retraite:
   Elle offre à ses amants des biens sans embarras,
   Biens purs, présents du ciel, qui naissent sous les pas,
   Solitude, où je trouve une douceur secrète.
2. *Je suis seul ...*
   ....
   Mais moi, Narcisse aimé, je ne suis curieux
   Que de ma seule essence;
   Tout autre n'a pour moi qu'un coeur mystérieux
   Tout autre n'est qu'absence.
   O mon bien souverain, cher corps, je n'ai que toi!
   Le plus beau des mortels ne peut chérir que soi ...
3. On the origins of the word in French and Stendhal's contribution, see V. del Litto's preface in Stendhal (1970).
4. *De je mis avec moi tu fais la récidive.*
5. *Bref, j'allais me donner d'un 'Je vous aime'*
   Quand je m'avisai non sans peine
   Que d'abord je ne me possédais pas bien moi-même.
6. *Vous attendiez, peut-être, un visage sans pleurs,*
   Vous, calmes, vous toujours de feuilles et de fleurs,
   ....
   Rêvez, rêvez de moi!... Sans vous, belles fontaines,
   Ma beauté, ma douleur, me seraient incertaines,
   Je chercherais en vain ce que j'ai de plus cher,
   Sa tendresse confuse étonnerait ma chair,
   Et mes tristes regards, ignorants de mes charmes,
   A d'autres que moi-même adresseraient leurs larmes ...

Bibliography

Blanchot, M. (1955) *L'Espace littéraire* (Paris: Gallimard).
Coquillat, M. (1982) *La Poétique du mâle* (Paris: Gallimard).
Eliot, T.S. (1969) *The Complete Poems of T.S. Eliot* (London: Faber & Faber).
Gide, A. (1958) *Romans récits et soties. Oeuvres lyriques*, ed. Y. Davet and J.-J. Thierry (Paris: Gallimard).
Huysmans, J.-K. (1977) *A Rebours* (Paris: Folio).
La Fontaine, J. de *Fables*.
Laforgue, J. (1993) *Que la vie est quotidienne...* (Paris: La Différence).
Mallarmé, S. (1945) *Oeuvres complètes* (Paris: Pléiade).
Montaigne, M.E. de (1948) *The Complete Works of Montaigne*, trans. D.M. Frame (Stanford: Stanford University Press).
Moreau, P. (1957) *Autour du 'culte du moi'. Essai sur les origines de l'égotisme français* (Paris: Archives des Lettres Modernes).
Rosset, C. (1977) *Le Réel. Traité de l'idiotie* (Paris: Minuit).
—— (1979) *L'Objet singulier* (Paris: Minuit).

Rousseau, J.-J. (1964) *Oeuvres complètes* 1 (Paris: Pléiade).
Samain, A. (1913) *Au jardin de l'Infante* (Paris: Mercure de France).
Stendhal (1952) *Romans et nouvelles I* (Paris: Pléiade).
―――― (1967) *Armance* (Paris: Garnier Flammarion).
―――― (1970) *Souvenirs d'Egotisme* (Geneva: Le Bibliophile).
―――― (1973) *Voyages en Italie* (Paris: Pléiade).
―――― (1980) *De l'Amour* (Paris: Folio).
―――― (1982) *Oeuvres intimes II* (Paris: Pléiade).
―――― (1981) *Oeuvres intimes I* (Paris: Pléiade).
―――― (1992) *Voyages en France* (Paris: Pléiade).
Valéry, P. (1946) *Monsieur Teste* (Paris: Gallimard).
―――― (1962) *Oeuvres* 1 (Paris: Pléiade).

PART III
MIRRORS AND IMAGES

CHAPTER 7

CAUGHT IN THE OCULAR: VISUALISING NARCISSUS IN THE ROMAN WORLD

Jas' Elsner

By the river
His eyes were aware of the pointed corners of his eyes
And his hands aware of the pointed tips of his fingers.
 ('The Death of Saint Narcissus' 13–15, in Eliot 1969:605)

The body of Narcissus flows out and loses itself
In the abyss of his reflection,
Like the sand glass that will not be turned again.
 ('Metamorphosis of Narcissus' 75–7, in Dalí 1937)

Narcissus, who was changed into a flower according to the poets, was the inventor of painting. Since painting is already the flower of every art, the story of Narcissus is most to the point. What else can you call painting but a similar embracing with art of what is presented on the surface of the water in the fountain.
 (Alberti 1977:64)[1]

The story of Narcissus has proved a deep pool, reflecting multiple interpretations. Every reading, every retelling, every reworking – whether visual or verbal – is a new eddy in the waters of hermeneutic possibility steeped in and mirrored by the image of the boy who dies entranced by his own reflection (see Vinge 1967). One of the special qualities of the story is the fact that its manifold readings are mutually supportive in their highlighting of different – sometimes complementary and sometimes contradictory – facets of the problem of subjectivity, rather than being in conflict. The myth is a fundamental paradigm for the inseparability of self from representation, and for the inextricability of desire from either. Whether one emphasises issues of reflection (as did Eliot in an early poem which conflated the adolescent youth of ancient mythology with a Christian martyr) or focuses on the ebb of a self-absorbed inertia leading to death and metamorphosis (as did Dalí in a fascinating poem written to accompany his great 1937 painting of Narcissus), the problems of the theme turn on the question of self and its objectification. Narcissus sees himself as an other person sufficiently outside his own subjectivity for his subjective self then to fall in love with that fantasy. Effectively, as Alberti so rivetingly put it, Narcissus is indeed the inventor of painting not only because Narcissus became a flower and painting is the flower of the arts, but – more significantly – because, however one defines painting, it involves 'embracing with art' that objectified reflection called representation. To rephrase Alberti's specifically art-centred formulation of the myth, painting is not just the result of the artist's desire to make objective an internal vision (to embrace an object with art); it is also the focus for the viewer's desire to possess as if it were real what is no more than pigment, to embrace what is no more than a reflection writ on water. Narcissus invented painting because he is both the paradigmatic artist, in that he saw his own image and mentally turned it into an objective being, and at the same time the ideal viewer, whom all artists would wish for, the viewer who so believes the depicted image is real that he falls in love with it.[2]

My concern here is with the myth of Narcissus as conceived and portrayed by artists in the Roman Empire. No less than Alberti, or than the modern painters of the theme from Poussin and Caravaggio to Salvador Dalí (see Bann 1989:127–56), Roman artists (and I shall here mainly concentrate on anonymous fresco painters from the region around Pompeii, working in roughly the second and third quarters of the first century AD) were interpreters. To help us understand their interpretations, we have a number of texts from antiquity which deal with the myth – not just Ovid's superlative retelling in his *Metamorphoses*, finished c. AD 7, but also some later descriptions (examples of the literary genre known as ekphrasis),[3] which specifically focus on works of art representing Narcissus, by the great third-century sophistic writer Philostratus and the late third- or fourth-century rhetorician Callistratus.[4] What all the ancient retellings and visualisations of the theme have in common is an erotic context, explicit in the myth itself though sometimes only implicit in any particular version, which would have guided any reader's or viewer's response, in part at least.[5]

The story of Narcissus raises with intense clarity a particular anxiety within the panoply of erotic desire: above all it focuses on the extent to which the person a lover may profess to love (the beloved), is in fact no more than the lover's self-projection (i.e., an objectified self-imitation). In the tragic core of Ovid's narrative, it is not Echo's plaintive aural mirroring that attracts Narcissus, but rather his own ocular reflection of himself. If the view is always in danger of being a self-reflection, to what extent is the beholder looking at a work of art (or reading a poem) not also imposing his or her own idealist fantasy upon the seen, just as Narcissus turned a pool of water into a portrait of himself and then imagined that portrait to represent an other and then fell hopelessly in love ... ?

The literary versions of the myth differ significantly in several aspects. It is only Ovid who includes the Echo story (3:356–401; 494–510) as well as the episode by the pool (3:407–510). In the specific narrative of Narcissus' obsession with his reflection, the accounts of Philostratus and Callistratus turn on two crucial self-deceptions: first, Narcissus never doubts that the image in the pool (a mere representation) is in fact a real person and, second, he never perceives self-reflexively that he is himself the object reflected in the pool.[6] Ovid, by contrast, having set up the scene so that Narcissus should 'unwittingly desire himself' (3:425), then brilliantly breaks the spell when he has his Narcissus address the pool and say: 'Oh I am he! I know it, and my image does not deceive me; / I am aflame with love for myself' (3:463–4).

While Philostratus and Callistratus use the myth to explore the problems of naturalism, viewing and representation, Ovid takes a devastatingly psychological turn. For him the ultimate tragedy of the myth is not self-absorption and death, but an inner struggle between an insight that could break the deadly trance of self-absorption and a passion so overwhelming as to prevent Narcissus from acquiescing to his knowledge that the pool offers merely a reflection of self.[7]

The pictorial tradition of Narcissus in antiquity is as varied as the literary interpretations of the myth. Not surprisingly it focuses above all on the theme of reflection – both on the image wrought by the water and on Narcissus' fascination with it. Implicitly then, the ancient visualisation of the myth focuses on the art-historically interesting problem of viewing, as emphasised by Philostratus. The surviving images comprise wall-paintings and a stucco from the region around Vesuvius, floor mosaics from both the east and west of the Roman Empire, as well as a few statuettes, gems, terracottas and textiles.[8] Most belong to the Roman period, to roughly the time between Ovid's retelling of the myth in the early first century AD and Callistratus' description, which most probably dates from the late third or early fourth century. They come from the private sphere and decorated the houses and persons of the wealthy elite – though not (in the case of any surviving examples) of the most elevated aristocracy. While Narcissus occasionally appears as a hunter (sometimes in the company of nymphs or of Artemis, the goddess of the hunt), the majority of the surviving images focus – like Caravaggio's painting – on the boy rapt in intense visual dialogue with his image in the pool (see Balensiefen 1990:130–66; Frontisi-Ducroux and Vernant 1997:200–41). I shall concentrate here on the visual examples that survive from Pompeii and its surroundings, which were preserved under the lava of Vesuvius when it erupted in 79 AD.

The 'reflective Narcissus' appears under what may be divided into three principal headings: alone by the pool (for instance, Figures 1–4), by the pool in the company of Eros (Figures 5–6) and by the pool accompanied by Echo and Eros (for example, Figure 7). In every case, Narcissus is semi-nude, his cloak having fallen about his legs, usually to reveal his genitals as well as his torso. Normally, he carries a spear – the mark of his huntsman's profession (as in Philostratus 1. 23. 4). This signals more than a mere attribute. In being a hunter, Narcissus is aligned (like Hippolytus in Euripides' play) with the world of Artemis and hence with chastity, as is implied by his rejection of Echo in Ovid's version (*Met.* 3:352–5). But, as a hunter, he was also implicitly a figure of erotic desire – his game always potentially a sexual pursuit (see Schnapp 1997:318–54). This is suggested visually by the way Eros holds Narcissus' spear for him, just as Narcissus himself cradles Eros in Figure 4.[9] In all the images, therefore, there is an ambivalence between eroticism and chastity which reflects the myth's double focus between one who rejects the passion of Echo and yet who falls passionately in love with himself. This ambivalence is itself aligned with the

Figure 1 *Fresco of Narcissus by the pool from the House of M. Lucretius Fronto (Pompeii V. 4 a). Third quarter of the first century AD (Photograph: courtesy of the Deutsches Archäologisches Institut, Rom, Inst. Neg. 72.3597.)*

age at which Narcissus is represented – in Ovid's words, 'when he might seem either a boy or a man', and at a moment when 'many youths and many girls desired him' (*Met.* 3:352–3).[10] Like the texts, the images all cast the subject within what was, in antiquity, the charged erotic landscape of pastoral (see Ovid, *Met.* 3:356; 407–12; Philostratus, 1. 23. 1–2; Callistratus, 5. 1).

Before examining the images, it is worth remarking on their context. None would have been displayed in isolation in antiquity – though many have been removed from their archaeological find-spot (and from the other images with which they were originally connected) in the wake of modern

Figure 2 *Fresco of Narcissus by the pool from the House of M. Loreius Tiburtinus, sometimes given as the House of D. Octavius Quarto (Pompeii II. 2. 2). Third quarter of the first century* AD *(Photograph: courtesy of the Deutsches Archäologisches Institut, Rom, Inst. Neg. 57.872.)*

Visualising Narcissus in the Roman World 95

Figure 3 *The context of Figure 2 after recent restoration, with the aedicula and couches of the biclinium below it (Photograph: courtesy of the Deutsches Archäologisches Institut, Rom, Inst. Neg. 72.3543.)*

Figure 4 *Fresco of Narcissus by the pool from the Casa dell' Ara Massima (Pompeii VI. 16. 15). Third quarter of the first century AD (Photograph: courtesy of the Deutsches Archäologisches Institut, Rom, Inst. Neg. 76.1276.)*

Figure 5 *Fragment of a fresco of Narcissus by the pool with Eros, from Pompeii (VII. 15. 2). Now in the Antiquarium, Pompeii. Third quarter of the first century AD (Photograph: courtesy of the Deutsches Archäologisches Institut, Rom, Inst. Neg. 77.2283.)*

Figure 6 *Stucco bas-relief of Narcissus by the pool with Eros, from the baths in a villa at Stabiae. Now in the Antiquarium, Castellamare di Stabia. c. AD 60 (Photograph: courtesy of the Deutsches Archäologisches Institut, Rom, Inst. Neg. 71.492.)*

Figure 7 *Fresco of Narcissus by the pool accompanied by Eros and by Echo, from Pompeii (provenance unknown). Naples, Museo Nazionale 9380. Third quarter of the first century AD (Photograph: courtesy of the Deutsches Archäologisches Institut, Rom, Inst. Neg. 86.420.)*

excavation (for example Figures 5–7). In the case of those which survive *in situ*, some come from interiors and some from garden settings. Figure 1, the image from the house of M. Lucretius Fronto (Pompeii V. 4 a) comes from the north wall of what was probably a ground-floor bedroom. The wall is divided into three equal panels with a yellow ground. The Narcissus image is presented as if it were a framed painting placed on the central panel within the wall. In each of the side panels are small vignettes painted directly onto the yellow ground, showing amorini carrying a cornucopia (on the left) and a drinking cup (on the right). The opposite wall is divided in the same way, with an illustration of the story of Pero and Mycon (told in the *Memorable Deeds and Sayings* 5. 4. 7 of Valerius Maximus, a younger contemporary of Ovid) which is identified by an elegiac couplet painted on the left of the picture (see Bragantini 1991). The context isolates the painting of Narcissus (though the amorini on either side might be said to provide the company of Eros offered in other pictures, such as Figures 5 and 6) and the image seems resolutely focused on its subject's fixation with his reflection. The highly literary (and rather obscure) subject-matter of the painting of Pero giving the breast to her father Mycon as if he were her baby, while they are both in prison (see Berger-Doer 1994), may suggest that the Narcissus image is specifically alluding to the literary context of Ovid's poem. Certainly, there is a parallelism of different kinds of imprisonment and the reversal of the natural order in both themes, while the maturity of Pero combined with the simultaneous old age and babyhood of Mycon throw a particular emphasis on the adolescence of Narcissus on the opposite wall. Likewise, the very close human interaction of Pero and Mycon contrasts with the solipsism of Narcissus, who has no other company in this image than his own reflection.

The isolated Narcissus (Figure 4) from the Casa dell' Ara Massima (Pompeii VI. 16. 15) is also from an interior setting. It comes from the alcove (described as a *pseudotablinum*) off the west wall of the house's main ground-floor atrium, facing the entrance. Again the image is presented as if it were a framed panel-painting, this time rendered as if it were propped on two wooden supports with *trompe-l'oeil* shutters depicted as if they had been left open. The white wall around the picture is embellished with elaborate fantasy architecture and playful vine-scrolls showing birds, animals and winged figures (see Stemmer 1992:31–3, figs. 188–204). On the ground below the image, it appears that there was a basin on a high stand containing water, in which not only would this painted Narcissus have been reflected, but also anyone who paused to look at the fresco with any care. While Narcissus is the only image in its alcove, the painting looks into the extensively decorated main room, with what appears to be an elaborate theatre-set with statues, masks, standing figures and a central landscape on the wall directly above and to either side of the alcove (Stemmer 1992:17–21, figs. 70–93). This time the Narcissus theme seems staged within a theatre – a kind of mythical performance of isolated individualism within one of the house's more public rooms, directly visible in a view across the atrium as one entered from the street.

By contrast, the Narcissus (Figure 2) from the house of M. Loreius Tiburtinus (Pompeii II. 2. 2) comes from a much less public spot within the orchestration of the Roman house – a terrace with a pool overlooking the house's long back garden with a nymphaeum, fountains and vine-covered pergola (on issues of public and private in the Roman house, see Wallace-Hadrill 1994:3–61). The north-east corner of the terrace consisted of two masonry couches (a *biclinium*) on either side of the pool, beneath an aedicula niche framed with two columns (Figure 3). On the walls behind the couches, on either side of the niche, are the paintings of Narcissus (on the viewer's left) and Pyramus and Thisbe (on the right) (See M. de Vos in *Pompeii* III 1991:102–5; Jashemski 1993:78–82; Zanker 1995:152–3). Here there is a clear parallelism intended between the diner reclining on the couch overlooking the pool and the image of Narcissus behind him. The painting has an ironic relationship with its viewer – looking askance at the role of the diner, reclining over the pool and his own reflection in the water. Even the rock on which Narcissus sits is not unlike the form of the masonry couch on which the diner beneath Narcissus would recline. The tragic deaths of Pyramus and Thisbe over the other couch may mean that both images were understood to refer specifically to Ovid (the Pyramus and Thisbe narrative follows that of Narcissus in *Met.* 4:55–166). Certainly, the figure of Pyramus – with his flowing cloak and spear – looks like a fallen Narcissus, while Thisbe might be said to echo Echo!

The emphasis on the viewing context is significant because the Narcissus images foreground the theme of viewing in what might seem the artificial ambience of an idyllic pastoral setting. The images can be viewed as one visual narrative within a whole pattern of connected stories (as in Ovid's *Metamorphoses*), where it is up to the viewer to construct his or her own meanings in relation to Narcissus' juxtaposition with Pyramus and Thisbe or Pero and Mycon (see Brilliant 1984:53–89). Alternatively, they may be seen as isolated scenes, set individually within the visual space defined by their painted frames (like the paintings individually described and never overtly compared in the text of Philostratus). A viewer may not directly relate them to the images nearby, and yet there may be certain tantalising parallels. In the case of Philostratus' gallery, the image of Olympus (I. 21), described before that of Narcissus (I. 23) and with only one painting intervening, clearly anticipates many of its themes:

> I do not understand why you take delight in the pool of water by the rock and gaze into it. What interest have you in it? ... As far as the breast the water pictures you, as you bend down over it from the rock; but if it pictured you full length, it would not have shown you as comely from the breast down; for reflections in the water are but on the surface, imperfect because stature is foreshortened in them. (Philostratus, *Imagines* I. 21. 1 and 3)[11]

This pattern, whereby the image is presented to be viewed either as an isolated narrative in its own right, or as an item within the broader interconnections of mythological subject-matter, is repeated in the surviving floor mosaics. Those from the east – including four examples from Antioch on the Orontes (the main metropolis in Roman Syria) and one from Paphos in Cyprus – have a single square or oblong panel depicting the scene by the pool, set within a design of geometrical ornament which covers the rest of the floor.[12] Of course, we cannot know how this floor decoration married with any images painted on the walls of the rooms concerned. By contrast, the impressive octagonal medallion from Orbe in Switzerland figures as one of thirteen mythological or religious scenes set in an elaborate floor (see von Gonzenbach 1961:184–92 (esp. 189–90), pls. 60–7). Other subjects depicted include Ganymede, Venus, Mercury, Mars, Saturn, Jupiter and various sea deities. Moreover, the formal type used to depict Narcissus in the Pompeiian images (as a youth slouching diagonally and holding a spear) is one which appears in other mythological subjects – for example, to render Ganymede, Cyparissus or Endymion (see the examples illustrated by Rizzo 1929:pl. 105a (Ganymede), pl. 107b (Cyparissus), pl. 125 (Endymion)). Again, this subject might spark the viewer to relate Narcissus to visually parallel images, even if nothing in their subject-matter immediately suggested this.

Yet the focus on the viewing context is complicated. Is Narcissus alone, self-immersed in his own reflection (as in Figure 1, for instance), or is he accompanied – alone, as it were, with Eros (Figures 5 and 6) and with the reflected self whom Eros is seducing him into loving? The boy in the pool looks back at Narcissus and casts him within the same entrancing gaze as he himself directs to the water (Ovid, *Met.* 3:450–62; Philostratus, I. 23. 3). Effectively this poses a crisis of visuality: Narcissus perishes in part because the sovereignty of subjecthood in looking out and controlling the world of the seen becomes inverted in a kind of paranoiac catastrophe in which the seen looks back and controls as an object the viewer who looks out at it. Inevitably, this subject has its relevance for viewers looking at works of art – especially at works depicting the tragedy of Narcissus.

Interestingly this scenario, where the viewer finds himself watched (which has been called the 'paranoid or terrorist coloration [of] the Gaze' in association with 'menace' and 'persecution'), is at the centre of Jacques Lacan's influential formulation of the psychological dynamics of the gaze.[13] In *The Four Fundamental Concepts of Psycho-Analysis*, Lacan tells the story of the sardine can. As a young man he went sailing and one day a fisherman, Petit-Jean, pointed out a sardine can floating on the waters and glittering in the sun. The fisherman tells Lacan: 'You see that can? Do you see it? Well it doesn't see you!' This appears to be an ironic joke, yet for Lacan, the affirmation that the can could not see him was deeply disquieting:

> To begin with, if what Petit-Jean said to me, namely that the can did not see me, had any meaning, it was because, in a sense, it was looking at me, all the same. It was looking at me at the level of the point of light, the point at which everything that looks at me is situated. (Lacan 1977:95–6, with Bryson's commentary in Bryson 1988:91)

Unlike the can in Petit-Jean's formulation, but very like Lacan's own fears, Narcissus' reflection does look back at its viewer out of the waters. Whether Lacan was deliberately alluding to the tale of Narcissus in setting his story (which he claims to be true) in the dangerous context of the reflective waters, its point about the destabilising of the subject's sense of autonomy and of his reversal into an object under the gaze of an inanimate other is strikingly parallel to the dynamic of Narcissus at the pool.

Yet in looking at the paintings of Narcissus, the problem of viewing is more complex still. For how can we know that our observation of his tragedy is always preserved within the safety of voyeurism, within that inalienable line which demarcates the represented as utterly separate from its viewer? What if the viewer's presence, intruding on the peculiar privacy of Narcissus' self-obsession, raises the spectre of a response from the painting, just as the pool responds to Narcissus in the myth – whereby we who watch may ourselves be observed by him? This is, in fact, precisely the problem suggested in Philostratus' account, which opens: 'The pool paints Narcissus, and the painting represents both the pool and the whole story of Narcissus'.

If the painting within the painting (the painted pool which is Narcissus' portrait) should have the effects on Narcissus described in the story, then what guarantee have we that the image described by Philostratus (or the frescoes from Pompeii) will not have similar entrancing effects on us? Unlike the reader of Lacan's sardine story, who is safely excluded from the potential gaze of the can because he or she is only reading about it, viewers of a painting of Narcissus are exposed both to the gaze of the reflection in the pool and to the possible gaze of the figure of Narcissus himself.

In Figure 2, is Narcissus glancing up so as to see if we are watching him? Or are his up-turned eyes simply dazed with the engrossing power of his own self-love? Another Pompeiian Narcissus in the same pose (now preserved in the Naples Museum) does appear to gaze straight out at the viewer, challenging us with the thought that Narcissus (and his story) may be our own self-reflection, and turning our environment (in the context of the Roman house) into an extension of the mythical world of pastoral where metamorphic tragedies, like that of Narcissus, can take place.[14] The context of some of the Pompeiian paintings, in relation to water and reflections (for instance, Figures 2 and 4) hardly makes it easier for the viewer. In effect, these paintings set up visually the pattern so consummately elaborated by Philostratus, where the subject-matter of the work of art becomes a sign for the viewer's own relationship with the image he is looking at.

But the paintings take the challenge to the viewer further than this. They propose a triangulation of viewing which breaks out, beyond the engrossment of Narcissus in his own reflection, to the viewer outside the painting. If the painting reflects us, as the pool reflects Narcissus, then in what sense does it do this? Are we reflected in the painted pool? Or in the image of Narcissus? Or is our visual relationship with the painting mirrored in his relationship with the reflection in the pool? Is it our viewing, or (perhaps more disturbingly) our desire, which the paintings mirror? Is our relation with what we look at, what we think about, what we may engage in narrative fantasies about, always a version of Narcissistic self-absorption, such as these images represent?

Philostratus, in particular, is aware of the problem of triangulation. He plunges into an imagined discussion with Narcissus about the image in the pool:

> As for you, however, Narcissus, it is no painting that has deceived you, nor are you engrossed in a thing of pigments or wax; but you do not realise that the water represents you exactly as you are when you gaze upon it, nor do you see through the artifice of the pool, though to do so you have only to nod your head or change your expression or slightly move your hand, instead of standing in the same attitude; but acting as though you had met a companion you wait for some move on his part. Do you then expect the pool to enter into conversation with you? Nay this youth does not hear anything we say, but he is immersed, eyes and ears alike, in the water ... (I. 23. 3)

By stepping so boldly over the boundary which separates viewer from image, Philostratus immediately casts the spectator within the net of Narcissian desire – and brilliantly includes not only himself (the speaker who addresses Narcissus as 'you') but also his readers (the 'we' of the imagined dialogue between Philostratus and us). In effect, Narcissus is only self-absorbed in his reflection (whether in a text or in an image) because we are there to witness it. His tragic self-engrossment cannot be separated from its triangulation with our voyeuristic desire to observe his predicament, just as Lacan's story about the sardine can would have no point if there were no one to listen to it or read it.

Figure 2 adds a particular frisson to these issues; for the reflected face of Narcissus, upside down at the bottom-centre of the visual field, seems to resemble not so much the slender youth as a Gorgon's head. Since the Gorgon's head turned anyone who looked at it into stone, this is a particularly appropriate characterisation of the reflection which petrified Narcissus. But does its power extend outside the fresco to its non-painted viewers? Certainly the suggestion of turning Narcissus to stone picks up a series of images in the texts – from Ovid's reference to the youth 'motionless, like a statue carved from Parian marble' (*Met.* 3:418–9) to the motionlessness of Philostratus' painted addressee to the marble statue described by Callistratus, which is so life-like as to be almost real. In Dalí's painting of 1937, the surrealist does in fact have his Narcissus turned into a vast stone hand (complete with ancient cracks) that holds an egg from which the Narcissus flower emerges.

These consummate visual interrogations of viewing and voyeurism become more complex as more figures intrude into the scene. In the images where Narcissus is accompanied by Eros, both he and his reflection are themselves being observed by an other (Figures 5 and 6) (see also Balensiefen 1990:taf. 26–7, 32–3). In the case of the stucco from Stabiae (Figure 6) (see Mielsch 1975:45–6 and 129), where Eros holds a flaming torch (as in a number of painted examples), the iconography may well relate the representation back to Ovid's text. In Ovid, there is not only much discussion of burning (ironic in the context of Narcissus' watery passion) but Echo is compared with the 'quick-burning' sulphur smeared on a flaming torch (*Met.* 3:371–4) (see also Stirrup 1976:100). Yet, when Echo herself intrudes into Narcissus' seclusion by the pool (Figure 7) (see Michel 1982:567–71), as she does towards the end of Ovid's account (*Met.* 3:494–510), the viewer's difficulties simply amass. Echo is Narcissus' double – repeating his every word, wasting away as he will, loving in vain as he does (Stirrup 1976:97–103; Rosati 1983:20–41). Cast in the visual form of one who watches him, she stands for the viewer who watches the image. She adds a dimension of female viewing which breaks across the insistent homosexuality of Narcissus' self-absorption, to incorporate the female spectator in the Roman house as well as the male. Yet her watching is – emphatically in Ovid's account – a version of Narcissus' own desire. Instead of being confronted with just the reflection and its hopeless spectator (Narcissus), the viewer of the painting is offered another hopeless spectator of the tragic event, whose every feeling (and every word) echoes Narcissus. Instead of just the reflection in the pool, the Echo and Narcissus paintings stage a hall of mirrors in which the viewer is challenged as the final reflection of the myth's narrative of endlessly hopeless visual desires.

For both female and male viewer outside the picture (as well as for Echo within the image), Narcissus is an inaccessible object of desire. He is incapable of reciprocating, because his love is always wrapped up in a mirror from which he has no escape. Yet love for him, the attraction of looking at him, is itself bound up with a version of his own failure. To what extent is it the self-absorption of Echo – her own set of purely self-generated fantasies – which cause her to imagine that she could ever get a response from Narcissus? To what extent is the fantasy of reciprocation in a lover not always a version of Narcissus' deranged obsession that the image in the pool is reaching out to touch him? In the spectacle of the Roman house's range of mythical imagery (not to speak, more generally, of any viewer's relation with any work of art), to what extent is our expectation that a picture relate back to us, may speak to us, not in fact simply a version of narcissistic delusion or of Echo's desire?[15]

We know that Roman public culture was highly ocular – given to a complex of voyeuristic, violent and extravagant visual relationships (see Segal 1994:257–8; also Coleman 1990 and Barton 1993). In the domestic world, the context for all our images of Narcissus, this ocular culture was extended into the private sphere in several ways. First, the Roman house was itself open to a series of views and viewpoints cutting across sequences of rooms, which have been shown to form a remarkable architectonics for orchestrating the passage through the building and which helped to define relationships between those who lived in the house and those who came to visit (see, for instance, Drerup 1959:155–9; Bek 1980:181–203; Jung 1984; Elsner 1995:74–85). Second, mythological and other scenes painted onto the walls of the house as *trompe-l'oeil* panel paintings have a tendency to be dramatised both by being set in a highly theatrical staging (as in Figure 4 from the Casa dell' Ara Massima) and by including what have been called 'supernumerary' figures, who observe the main action, as does Echo in Figure 7 (see Klein 1912, and Michel 1982). Effectively, both within the space of specific paintings and within the living space of the house itself, which those paintings adorned, there was an intense visual awareness of events existing above all in the ocular dispensation of their being witnessed, of things happening always in a panopticon of spectatorship (both real and imagined).

Within this broad cultural context, where the view was staged, made self-reflexive and self-conscious, in both the public and the private domain, the subject of Narcissus had a particular bite. It challenged the culture in two ways. In one sense, Narcissus is the ultimate example of individual solipsism – someone who is always alone and enamoured of himself, even in the company of others who love him or may at least wish to observe him. The challenge and ambivalence of the viewer's triangulation with his reflection is that he may look back but he may not: it is perhaps for the viewer's own fantasy to decide. Yet that aloneness is always within the presence of others – it is constituted by (or against) the intrusive or voyeuristic gaze not only of Echo and of Eros but also of viewers as they wander through the house and its gardens. On the other hand, Narcissus challenges the myth of a public or shared world in which we may all participate. For he represents the extreme position that nothing can ever be seen beyond what the subject fantasises, imposes on or appropriates from the world he occupies. Despite the presence of Echo, of Eros, of other potential supernumerary figures, and of the Roman viewer in the house, Narcissus resolutely ignores all socialisation, all the claims of reality on his attention, and plunges ever deeper into self-absorption. Is this the fate of his spectators, whether they watch images of him, whether they watch each other, whether they watch theatrical re-enactments of myths such as his in real theatres, where real convicts in mythological garb were made to die on stage (Coleman 1990)? Is this the ultimate tragedy of 'Narcissism', as conceived by antiquity and handed down in so many recensions to the modern world?

Notes

1. On this text, see Bann (1989:105–6).
2. For further reflections on the relevance of the Narcissus theme for the problems of naturalism, see Elsner (1996a).
3. The literature on ancient ekphrasis is vast and burgeoning. Useful are Fowler (1991), and the essays collected in Goldhill and Osborne (1994), and in Elsner (1996b).
4. The ancient texts on Narcissus include Ovid, *Metamorphoses* 3:341–510; Pausanias, *Description of Greece* 9, 31:7–9; Philostratus the Elder, *Imagines* 1:23; Callistratus, *Descriptions* 5; Plotinus, *Enneads* 1, 6:8; Conon, *Diegesis* 2–4; Vatican Mythographer 2:180. For general discussion of these various versions, see Eitrem (1935); Vinge (1967:1–41); Pellizer (1986).
5. Further on issues of eroticism and viewing in antiquity, see Henderson (1991:60, 81–6); Walker (1992); Frontisi-Ducroux (1996). For a more general psychoanalytically informed discussion, see Rose (1986) and her further thoughts in Rose (1988).
6. On these self-deceptions and their relation to naturalism, see Elsner (1996a:249). For Philostratus' Narcissus, see Vinge (1967:29–32); Kalinka and Schönberger (1968:348–51); Bann (1989:108–13); Elsner (1996a:252–4); Frontisi-Ducroux and Vernant (1997:225–30). For Callistratus' Narcissus, see Elsner (1996a:250–2); Frontisi-Ducroux and Vernant (1997:231–4).
7. Ovid's account of the myth is the subject of an extensive and excellent literature. See especially Fränkel (1945:82–5); Skinner (1965); Galinsky

(1974:114–22); Stirrup (1976:97–103); Brenkman (1976); Rosati (1983:1–51); Hardie (1988); Frontisi-Ducroux and Vernant (1997:210–17); Bettini (1999:94–108).
8. On the images, the most comprehensive catalogue is Rafn (1992). Important discussions include Zanker (1966) and Balensiefen (1990:130–66).
9. In one of the second-century AD mosaic versions from Antioch (now in Baltimore: BMA 1938. 710), the spear glides down along Narcissus' arm to penetrate the pool and his reflected image beneath. See Levi (1947:pl. 10b) or Kondoleon (1995:fig. 14) for photographs.
10. Cf. Callistratus 5. 1: 'He was a boy, or rather a youth, of the same age as the Erotes'. In the context of homoeroticism, this ambivalence is interesting. In ancient, especially Athenian, male homosexuality, it was the norm for the lover (*erastês*) to be older than the beloved (*erômenos*) – hence the term *paederasty*, meaning the love of men for boys (see further Dover 1978: esp. 16–17, 85–6). By loving a youth of the same age, Narcissus was in fact inverting traditional practice (see further Elsner 1996a:248). But one might argue that the man in him (the viewer crouching by the pool) had fallen in love with the boy in him (the reflection). The ambivalence of Narcissus – and of adolescence generally, poised between boyhood and manhood – is here used to confuse not just those who might normally desire boys, but specifically the adolescent hunter, whose own subjectivity is split between manhood and boyhood and who enacts that split by objectifying one half of it. Part of the paralysis at the pool depends on the fact that Narcissus does not know whether he is the lover (of the boy in the water) or the beloved (of the man in the water) – as implied by Ovid's 'What shall I do? Shall I woo or be wooed?' (3:465). For more on this theme, see Elsner (1996a:254–5).
11. On the parallelism of this and the Narcissus, see Bann 1989:108–9.
12. The Antioch mosaics are illustrated and discussed by Levi 1947:60–6, pl. 10b (House of Narcissus); 89, pl. 14b (House of the Red Pavement); 136–7, pl. 23c (House of the Buffet Supper); 200–1, pl. 45a (House of Menander). The Paphos image, from the House of Dionysos, is discussed by Kondoleon, 1995:30–40, figs. 10–2.
13. The key passage is Lacan (1977:67–122). A useful discussion (comparing Lacan and Sartre with Oriental notions of the gaze), from which come the quotations is Bryson (1988: esp. 87–94, 104–8, quotes from 107).
14. The painting is Naples, Museo Nazionale 9388, illustrated in Balensiefen 1990:tafel 34.2.
15. The exploration of this theme is, I believe, at the heart of Philostratus' enterprise in the *Imagines* as a whole; see Elsner 1995:23–39.

Bibliography

Alberti, L.B. (1977) *On Painting* [1435], trans. J.R. Spencer (New Haven and London: Yale University Press).

Balensiefen, L. (1990) *Die Bedeutung des Spiegelbildes als ikonographisches Motiv in der antiken Kunst* (Tübingen: Ernst Wasmuth Verlag).

Bann, S. (1989) *The True Vine: On Representation and Western Tradition* (Cambridge: Cambridge University Press).

Barton, C. (1993) *The Sorrows of the Ancient Romans* (Princeton: Princeton University Press).
Bek, L. (1980) *Towards a Paradise on Earth* (Odense: Odense University Press).
Berger-Doer, G. (1994) 'Pero II', in *Lexicon Iconographicum Mythologiae Classicae* 7, 1 (Munich: Artemis Verlag) 327–9.
Bettini, M. (1999) *The Portrait of the Lover* (Berkeley: University of California Press).
Bragantini, I. (1991) 'V.4a: Casa di M. Lucretius Fronto', in *Pompeii* III:1000–8.
Brenkman, J. (1976) 'Narcissus in the Text', in *Georgia Review* 30:293–327.
Brilliant, R. (1984) *Visual Narratives: Story Telling in Etruscan and Roman Art* (Ithaca and London: Cornell University Press).
Bryson, N. (1988) 'The Gaze in the Expanded Field', in H. Foster (ed.), *Vision and Visuality* (Seattle: Bay Press) 87–114.
Coleman, K. (1990) 'Fatal Charades: Roman Executions Staged as Mythological Enactments', in *Journal of Roman Studies* 80:44–73.
Dalí, S. (1937) *Métamorphose de Narcisse* (Paris: Editions Surréalistes).
Dover, K. J. (1978) *Greek Homosexuality* (London: Gerald Duckworth).
Drerup, H. (1959) 'Bildraum und Realraum in der römischen Architektur', in *Römische Mitteilungen* 66:147–74.
Eitrem, S. (1935) 'Narkissos', in *Realencyclopädie der classischen Altertumswissenschaft* 16:1,721–33.
Eliot, T.S. (1969) *The Complete Poems and Plays of T. S. Eliot* (London: Faber and Faber).
Elsner, J. (1995) *Art and the Roman Viewer: The Transformation of Art from the Roman World to Christianity* (Cambridge: Cambridge University Press).
—— (1996a) 'Naturalism and the Erotics of the Gaze: Intimations of Narcissus', in N. B. Kampen (ed.), *Sexuality in Ancient Art* (Cambridge: Cambridge University Press) 247–61.
—— (ed.) (1996b) *Art and Text in Roman Culture* (Cambridge: Cambridge University Press).
Fowler, D. (1991) 'Narrate and Describe: The Problem of Ekphrasis', in *Journal of Roman Studies* 81:25–35.
Fränkel, H. (1945) *Ovid: A Poet Between Two Worlds* (Berkeley and Los Angeles: University of California Press).
Frontisi-Ducroux, F. (1996) 'Eros, Desire and the Gaze', in N.B. Kampen (ed.), *Sexuality in Ancient Art* (Cambridge: Cambridge University Press) 81–100.
—— and J.-P. Vernant (1997) *Dans l'oeil du miroir* (Paris: Odile Jacob).
Galinsky, K. (1974) 'Ovid's Metamorphosis of Myth', in K. Galinsky (ed.), *Perspectives of Roman Poetry* (Austin and London: University of Texas Press) 105–28.
Goldhill, S. and R. Osborne (1994) *Art and Text in Ancient Greek Culture* (Cambridge: Cambridge University Press).

Gonzenbach, V. von (1961) *Die Römischen Mosaiken der Schweitz* (Basel: Birkhaüser Verlag).
Hadot, P. (1976) 'Le mythe de Narcisse et son interprétation par Plotin', in *Nouvelle revue de psychanalyse* 13:81–108.
Hardie, P. (1988) 'Lucretius and the Delusions of Narcissus', in *Materiali e Discussioni per l'Analisi dei Testi Classici* 20–1:71–89.
Henderson, J. (1991) 'Wrapping up the Case: reading Ovid *Amores* 2. 7 (+8)', in *Materiali e Discussioni per l'Analisi dei Testi Classici* 27:37–88.
Jashemski, W. F. (1993) *The Gardens of Pompeii, Herculaneum and the Villas Destroyed by Vesuvius* II (New Rochelle, NY: A. D. Caratzas).
Jung, F. (1984) 'Gebaute Bilder', in *Antike Kunst* 27:71–122.
Kalinka, E. and O. Schönberger (1968) *Philostratos: Der Bilder* (Munich: Ernst Heimeran Verlag).
Klein, W. (1912) 'Pompejanische Bildstudien', in *Jahreshefte des Österreichischen Archäologischen Institutes in Wien* 15:143–67.
Kondoleon, C. (1995) *Domestic and Divine: Roman Mosaics in the House of Dionysos* (Ithaca and London: Cornell University Press).
Lacan, J. (1977) *The Four Fundamental Concepts of Psycho-Analysis*, trans. A. Sheridan (Harmondsworth: Penguin).
Levi, D. (1947) *Antioch Mosaic Pavements* (Princeton: Princeton University Press).
Michel, D. (1982) 'Bemerkungen über Zuschauerfiguren in pompejanischen sogenannten Tafelbildern', in *La regione sotterata dal Vesuvio: Studi e prospettive* (Naples: Università di Studi di Napoli) 537–98.
Mielsch, H. (1975) *Römische Mitteliungen Ergänzungsheft 21: Römische Stuckreliefs* (Heidelberg: Kerle Verlag).
Pellizer, E. (1986) 'Reflections, Echoes and Amorous Reciprocity: On Reading the Narcissus Story', in J. Bremmer (ed.), *Interpretations of Greek Mythology* (Totowa, N.J.: Barnes and Noble) 107–20.
Pompeii: Pitture e Mosaici, since 1990, Rome: Istituto della Enciclopedia dell' Arte Antica, Classica e Orientale.
Rafn, B. (1992) 'Narkissos', in *Lexicon Iconographicum Mythologiae Classicae* 7, 1 (Munich: Artemis Verlag) 703–11.
Rizzo, G. E. (1929) *La Pittura Ellenistico-Romana* (Milan: Fratelli Treves).
Rosati, G. (1983) *Narciso e Pigmalione: Illusione e Spettacolo nelle Metamorfosi di Ovidio* (Florence: Sansoni).
Rose, J. (1986) *Sexuality in the Field of Vision* (London: Verso).
——— (1988) 'Sexuality and Vision: Some Questions', in H. Foster (ed.), *Vision and Visuality* (Seattle: Bay Press) 115–30.
Schnapp, A. (1997) *Le chasseur et la cité: Chasse et érotique dans la Grèce ancienne* (Paris: Albin Michel).
Segal, C.P. (1994) 'Philomela's Web and the Pleasures of the Text: Reader and Violence in the Metamorphoses of Ovid', in I.J.F. de Jong and J.P. Sullivan (eds), *Modern Critical Theory and Classical Literature* (Leiden: E.J. Brill) 257–80.

Skinner, V. (1965) 'Ovid's Narcissus – An Analysis', in *Classical Bulletin* 41:59–61.
Stemmer, K. (1992) *Haüser in Pompeji 6: Casa dell' Ara Massima* (Munich: Hirmer Verlag).
Stirrup, B.E. (1976) 'Ovid's Narrative Technique: A Study in Duality', in *Latomus* 35:97–107.
Vinge, L. (1967) *The Narcissus Theme in West European Literature up to the Early Nineteenth Century* (Lund: Gleerups).
Walker, A. (1992) 'Erôs and the Eye in the *Love-Letters* of Philostratus', in *Proceedings of the Cambridge Philological Society* 38:132–48.
Wallace-Hadrill, A. (1994) *Houses and Society in Pompeii and Herculaneum* (Princeton: Princeton University Press).
Zanker, P. (1966) '"Iste ego sum". Der naive und der bewuste Narziß', in *Bonner Jarbücher* 166:152–70.
——— (1995) *Pompeji: Stadtbild und Wohngeschmack* (Main: Verlag Philipp von Zabern).

CHAPTER 8

CINEMA ON SHOW IN THE WORK OF THE LUMIÈRE BROTHERS*

André Gardies

Is the cinema screen a window on to the world or a mirror inviting us to step through it? For a long time now film-makers, philosophers and theorists have noted the magic particular to the cinematographic mechanism. Studies drawing on psychoanalysis have not failed to notice the similarities and differences between the screen and the mirror. The screen has all the characteristics of the mirror bar one, but this difference is crucial: while the screen gives us an image of the world, it never shows us our own reflection. Offered primary identification with the camera and at the same time removed from the representation, the spectator-Narcissus remains a lone voyeur in the darkness of the theatre.

In its earliest manifestations, however – and this is particularly true of the Lumière brothers' cinematographe – the cinema was more directly narcissistic, contemplating itself through the images that it captured and filming itself in the process of filming. The space of the image and that of shooting the film were as yet largely undifferentiated; it was only later that the separation between them was established, turning the space of the working camera into a taboo zone and forcing Narcissus to become a voyeur. A careful examination of the

---

* Translated from the French by Trista Selous.

Lumières' cinema may thus allow us to understand better the effects of this transformation of Narcissus.

The Cinematographe Mirrored

In scenes nos 1,008 and 1,009, *Concours d'automobiles fleuries* (*départ*) and (*retour*) ('Flower-covered car race', 'start' and 'finish'), there are two aspects to what is shown: the event announced by the title and, far more unexpectedly, the sight of a cameraman going about his business. In the foreground, by the side of the road and partly hidden by the crowd, we can distinguish the activity of a man – who may be either a photographer or camera operator – trying to photograph the vehicles' departure. In the next scene, when the cars are returning, the crowd has moved and the operator is now quite visible turning the camera handle. Thus the cinematograph is filming cinema in action. Furthermore, from the way the cameraman looks quickly over his shoulder at the very beginning of the shot before beginning to turn the handle, we can infer, if not a deliberate staging, at least an active complicity between the cameraman we can see and the one who is filming what we see. While to my knowledge this is the only example of this type of *mise en abyme* (reinforced by the similar angle of the two cameras) in the work of the Lumières, there are plenty of other ways in which the cinematograph contemplates itself. In so doing, it reveals itself through actions which, though not unconnected to a concern for publicity, also suggest a form of self-gratification. The same can be said of the two versions of the *Entrée du Cinématographe* ('Entrance of the Cinematograph'), one in London, the other in Vienna. Beneath a large and highly visible sign announcing the 'Lumière Cinématographe' we see the comings and goings in the street, just as they are mirrored in the working camera. Sometimes this ostentation is offset by humour, particularly in the comic scene, the *Colleur d'affiches* ('Bill sticker'): a poster on the wall opposite the camera praises the qualities of the 'Grand Four Cinematograph'; a little later a team of bill stickers arrives and, after some arguments, covers this poster with another displaying the words 'Lumière Cinématographe'.

Thus the new invention was quite explicitly willing to act as its own object, if not of love, then at least of its look. However, the way that the cinematograph imprinted its activity on the images it recorded was primarily implicit. In one of Louis Lumière's very first films, the famous *Débarquement des con-*

gressistes ('Arrival of the congress participants') in Neuville sur Saône, made in May 1895, we see a crowd of photographers with still cameras slung or carried on their shoulders coming one by one over the footbridge to the station platform. Each of them either glances, looks directly or waves at their new 'colleague', who cannot be seen but who sees them looking at him. Their greetings imprint the presence of the film camera on the screen. This wonderful new power lies in the fact that it records the traces of its own presence.

Sometimes, playing on the ambiguity of the scene being filmed, the camera enters the diegesis, hiding behind the subject of the film. Thus in *Départ de Jérusalem en chemin de fer (panorama)* ('Leaving Jerusalem by train (panorama)'), scene no. 408, the camera tracks out along the railway line, leaving behind a small group of people who are waving goodbye. Who is the addressee of these friendly gestures? A traveller on the platform at the back of the train? The scene's title suggests so, yet nothing reveals this to be the case. It might equally well be the camera and, through primary identification, us the viewers. A similar situation occurs in *Arrivée de cyclistes à Turin* ('Cyclists arriving in Turin'), scene no. 1094. Are the cyclists waving to the crowd of onlookers or to the camera? The lack of a reverse shot leaves the question open. The camera both reveals and hides itself, playing on our uncertainty about the off-screen space, which is, however, explicitly referred to on screen.

However, the most frequently found manifestation, present in most of the scenes, is that of people looking at the camera. There are countless examples of all kinds of looks: discreet, embarrassed, curious, questioning, surprised, amazed, quick glances and open stares; so much so that they become almost the second subject of the film. In *Porte de France*, scene no. 211 the spectacle of the street is soon replaced by the close-up of a passer-by who, visibly intrigued by the cinematograph, stands in front of the lens and stares 'into its eyes'. In a kind of metonymic reversal, the cinema observes itself in this contemplative look.

This mechanism by which an osmotic relation is established between the object and subject of the look, quite different from the usual approach of today's cinematic fictions, seems to have been the rule in the early days of the new art. Scene no. 351 in *Repas d'Indiens* ('The Indians' meal') gives a strong indication that this was so. A small group of Indian people, pre-arranged in a semi-circle, are squatting on the ground to eat their meal; suddenly a man (the assistant cameraman?)

emerges from the background shadows, abruptly seizes the head of one of the people eating, raises it and turns it to face the camera. Leaving aside the latent racism suggested by such a total lack of respect, this might seem no more than the manifestation of a habit inherited from posing subjects for photographic portraits. While such a hypothesis cannot be ruled out entirely, it does not adequately explain the need to have the subject look at the camera or, in general terms, the virtually constant reference to the working cinematograph.

The Cinematographic

Another motivation, given by the camera operators themselves,[1] was the commercial opportunity such a look afforded. When the operators arrived in a town for the first time, the camera filming in the street would arouse a great deal of curiosity and they would often pretend to film when the camera was not loaded. Passers-by would rush to buy a seat for that evening's screening in the expectation of seeing themselves on screen. Yet, however real a practice this may have been, it hardly provides a definitive explanation.

It does, however, point to a phenomenon of far greater significance. It tells us that the newly invented cinematograph was part of social reality. It reveals the emergence into the world of this marvellous machine which not only changed the state of the world, as all inventions do, but also, and above all, provided the image of the world it was acting to transform by duplicating it. Whether consciously or not, the cinematograph's propensity to record the traces of its activity, its primary narcissism, and desire for exhibition, also manifest a form of lyricism in honour of the invention.

It is clear that what interested the Lumières was, to use the classic semiological distinction, the cinematographic rather than the filmic (Metz 1971). Of course new subjects for films, new 'events' to show had constantly to be found, but this was in order to ensure and maintain public interest in the cinematograph. It is undeniable (proof is not appropriate here) that the entire production of the Lumières (in terms of both aesthetics and commercial exploitation) follows this logic. From this perspective Méliès followed a radically different logic, that of the filmic.[2]

Thus the many traces of the camera in action constantly assert its presence in the world. The most concrete manifestation of this presence was probably the extraordinary and expanding conquests of its operators throughout the year 1896. However, and this was probably the strength of the young cinema, the camera's presence required another: that of the spectator. Due to unipunctuality,[3] optical laws and the code of perspective, the spectator's eye takes the place of the camera through primary identification during projection: I am now where the camera was yesterday. At the same time this presence of the camera in the world indicates my own presence in the world; the numerous 'panoramas' in the catalogue provide the most spectacular manifestation of this. From Moscow to Boston, via Cairo, Tokyo, Mexico and Melbourne, the cinematograph established a place in the world for both itself and the spectator. This was the miracle performed by the new invention.

From this point of view images of people looking at the camera or visibly moving to avoid it take on a new meaning. They are proof of a real situation, proof that the camera is present and also that what is filmed is real since it has been modified or disturbed by the filming process. The impression of reality that is so palpable in the famous *Entrée d'un train en gare de la Ciotat* ('Train coming into the station at La Ciotat') is reinforced by the fact that people's reactions to the camera have been caught. Thus, at the same time as the film shows us the cinematograph at work, it also demonstrates the machine's ability to capture the real. It is easy to grasp the superiority of the Lumières' invention over Edison's 'Black Maria', whose recording mechanism was very heavy and required isolation. Clearly, the Lumières' films were a way of praising their cinematograph.

Filmic All the Same

The presence of the film camera is, moreover, so strong that it is found where it is least expected, in 'staged' scenes. This happens in one of two ways, depending on whether the film is a recording of a play in the theatre or a fictional playlet.

The *Ballet de Flora*, scenes 904 to 908, the *Ballet Excelsior*, scenes 909 to 913, and *La Vie et la Passion de Jésus-Christ* ('The Life and Passion of Jesus Christ'), scenes 933 to 945, were all specially staged for the cinematograph and the camera's presence is tangible, particularly at the end of many shots, despite the fact that one might have expected it to disappear. It is not unusual for a scene to come to its close before the end of the fifty seconds of the piece of film. When this happens we see the 'actors' freeze, as though turned to stone, waiting for the end of the shot, and in this endless stillness one becomes once more strongly aware of the other scene, that of the filming process. It is of course the non-coincidence of two lengths of time, that of the scene and that of the filming, that produces this effect. In the gap between them we read the presence of the camera.

The camera manifests itself differently in many 'playlets', particularly the comic scenes such as *La nourrice et le soldat amoureux* ('The Nurse and the Soldier'), scene no. 875, *L'amoureux dans le sac* ('The Lover in a Sack'), no. 885, and many others. Spectators today almost always smile at what appears to them the actors' exaggerated, excessive, unnatural actions, unless they are regarded as an aspect of the comic genre. I am tempted to see them as a more complex phenomenon, corresponding once more to the dominant cinematographic logic. As an example I would take the scene from *Voyageur et voleurs* ('Traveller and robbers', no. 121), of 1896. Two robbers trick a traveller and steal his two suitcases. This playlet is perfectly organised in time and space and demonstrates a high degree of directorial skill. Yet one cannot fail to be struck by a disparity in the acting: while the two robbers act in a sober manner, the traveller's gestures are blatantly excessive. Should this difference be seen as 'naive' acting, corresponding to a primitive stage in the development of cinema? I would not support such a 'modernocentrist' position. Beyond the variations of cultural codes, acting which may now appear excessive and overacted in fact reflects the logic of the Lumière 'system'.

I can see two reasons for such overacting. The first is entirely deliberate and reflects the need to mark a difference: overacting tells the spectator of the Lumière scenes that they are no longer watching 'reality' but fiction. The excess acts here as a marker of genre. The second reason is, I suggest, linked to the presence of the camera. Although in producing fiction the Lumières were dealing more directly with the filmic, the camera was still present. The traveller, or more precisely the actor playing that role, is in fact addressing the camera with his acting. It is a little like the gymnasts – in a 'real' scene this time (*Sauts au cheval en longueur* ('Jumping the length of the horse'), no. 453) – who exaggerate their movements to get themselves noticed. In the Lumière system, and in the productions of a number of their later rivals, actors in a fiction film act for the camera. They have not yet learnt to think beyond it to address the imaginary spectator. They have not yet learnt to 'forget' the camera, in other words to split their performance into two actions: acting for the camera and at the same time addressing not the camera but the spectator.

This 'forgetting' of the camera in the fiction film perhaps underlies the emergence of the filmic, ensuring its separation from the cinematographic; it is thus the basis of the seventh art.

When Narcissus Hides

This separation brings about the clear delineation of two spaces: that of the filmed scene and that of the camera at work. As we know, the fictional regime of the filmic is based on a tacit convention that the work of filming remains invisible. Thus Narcissus was obliged to give up his contemplation of himself; he had to hide behind the reeds on the bank, where the image could no longer betray his presence. He had to become the voyeur in the dark.

Despite this, however, he has never stopped contemplating himself; he has just had to cheat in order to do it. Since he is no longer present on screen, he designates a substitute, or indeed a double. This process was already under way in the *Concours d'automobiles fleuries*: the operator and the camera that we see are obviously not the ones recording the film we are watching. Like the cars and spectators, they are objects in the scene being filmed. However, their status is not entirely the same since, unlike the other objects, they are very similar to the mechanism that enables them to exist on the screen. This is a form of summons: the cinematograph is summoned to appear and in order to meet this requirement it sends a representative. In the cinema any *mise en abyme* is primarily produced through metaphor. Later such a procedure was to become the most widespread practice, at least, as we have said, for the fiction film.

Let us consider for a moment Michael Powell's exemplary film *Peeping Tom* (1960), in which cinema, and more particularly the camera, is both actor and accessory in the drama, in the context of the most violent symbolism of substitution. In this film the strange and troubled relationship between narcissism (the absolute identification of the hero-film-maker with his camera) and voyeurism is taken to its extreme. Cinema and the camera-eye are thus omnipresent in the film, but of course we never see the camera that is filming what we are seeing. Instead we are shown a substitute; one, moreover, which reinforces the subject of the film itself, which is that of the camera substitute that enables the hero to satisfy his drives.

In the same way, in his emblematic film *Man with a Movie Camera* (1929) Dziga Vertov provides a metaphorical on-screen representative of his own activity as a film-maker, apart from a few moments when the film crew are glimpsed in brief reflections from windows. Despite Vertov's ideological and aesthetic choices, this film, which glorifies the cine-eye, uses the illusion of metaphor. Here too the space of the work of film-making and that of the scene being filmed are separated and rendered almost entirely distinct.

On the mirror-screen thus defined the camera can advance without showing itself, without threatening to tear the fictional fabric by which the spectator accedes to another world, that of the diegesis. In this imaginary world there is no place for cinema unless it be through metaphorical substitution.

In Conclusion

We can see thus the difference between the cinema of today and that of the Lumière brothers. As we have seen, in the Lumières' work a porosity between the space of filming and the filmed space is more or less the rule. Thus the cinematograph inscribes the traces of its activity on the image itself. It can contemplate itself on the mirror of the screen. Should this be seen as a sort of infantile stage of an art which had yet to develop? Such a biological metaphor rests on doubtful presuppositions and has little heuristic value. We shall thus abandon it in favour of another hypothesis, that of the coherence of the Lumière system, based on the primacy of the cinematographic.

For the Lumière brothers film – the positive image – has the role of attesting to the worth of the cinematograph, the machine for recording and reproducing life, and of manifesting its presence in the world. It is then only logical that it should be seen to imprint the traces of its activity and presence on the screen. Filming and what is filmed are captured in the same time and space.

In order to become the seventh art, the cinema had to follow a different logic, that of the filmic, which obliges the instrumental mechanism to disappear behind the film-product.

Paradoxically, this investigation of the Lumières' production enables us to understand better what constitutes the filmic. The filmic requires the demarcation and separation of two space-times, that of the operation of filming and that of the diegesis. In this sense the latter space-time always comes into the category of the prerecorded. Proof *a contrario* is provided every day by television: live television and 'actuality footage' (when the programme is prerecorded) are defined by the coincidence of the space-time of filming and the space-time of what is filmed. In these cases the conjunction of the two is as necessary as their disjunction is to production of the filmic.

In this light we can see that what the Lumières invented using their cinematograph was not so much the practice of documentary or fiction as of actuality, which remains fully contemporary.

Notes

1. See Rittaud-Hutinet (1985), particularly 151–9.
2. From this point of view I suggest that the outmoded historical opposition between the documentary film (the Lumières) and the fiction film (Méliès) should be relocated as one between the cinematographic and the filmic. For simplicity's sake this contrast could be formulated as follows: for the Lumières films had to serve the cinematograph, whereas with Méliès the cinema only matters insofar as it makes films possible.
3. To borrow the term used by André Gaudreault (1989) to refer to films consisting of a single shot and thus filmed from one place.

Bibliography

Gardies, A. (forthcoming) 'Les panoramas dans la production Lumière', paper given at the Congrès Lumière, 7–10 June 1995, at the Université Lumière-Lyon 2.

Gaudreault, A. (1989) *Du littéraire au filmique, système du récit* (Paris: Méridiens-Klincksieck).

Metz, C. (1971) *Langage et cinéma* (Paris: Larousse).

Rittaud-Hutinet, J. (1985) *Le Cinéma des origines* (Seyssel: Champ Vallon).

≈ CHAPTER 9 ≈

DOUBLE VISION:
NARCISSUS AND THE SILVER SCREEN

Wendy Everett

The lonely, introverted figure of Narcissus, lost in hopeless desire for his own reflection, has for centuries haunted European thought and culture. However, it is the twentieth century which has really adopted Narcissus as its own, finding in his story the basis for theories of psychology, personality, behaviour, identity, self-reflexivity and so on; indeed, the centrality of the Narcissus myth to critical thought may be seen to constitute a defining feature of the self-conscious, self-reflexive manifestations of modernism and the postmodern.

It is, unequivocally, the myth's powerful exploration of desire, its precocious recognition of the process of defining the self via the gaze, in other words its immutable conviction of the inseparability of 'I' and 'eye', that have accorded it a particular relevance to the cinema, whose silver screen may indeed mirror the ironically reflective surface of the fateful pool in which Narcissus first saw his reflection. It is therefore scarcely surprising that the Narcissus myth should have provided a powerful paradigm for film theory, particularly – though not uniquely – for the psychoanalytic writings of Lacan and Metz to which we shall be referring.

Within the broad parameters of the cinematic adoption and adaptation of the Narcissus myth, the first-person memory narratives of filmic autobiography occupy a position of particular significance. In this context, it is interesting to note that in Part 3, section 9 of *Le Signifiant imaginaire (The Imaginary Signifier)* (1977), when discussing the relationship of film and daydream, Metz comments that certain films seem, more than others, to be closely linked to Narcissus, placing in this category the autobiographical works of 'narcissistic' young filmmakers who seem particularly self-obsessed. He does go on to point out that, in a sense, all fiction films are in some way narcissistic, and that notion, particularly in relation to self-conscious narration, will emerge later in this chapter. But what is of particular significance here is that, albeit in fairly circular and uncontentious terms, Metz is overtly recognising the existence of autobiographical films (which, it must be said, other critical theorists have been more reluctant to do), and that he does so in relation to narcissism.[1]

The reasons for juxtaposing autobiography and Narcissus are, on many levels, self-evident. Autobiographical films are made when a director is attempting to restructure, to recreate, to revision the distant and fragmented world of subjective memory, *as part of a search for personal identity*. In them, the director is both narrator and narrated, both subject and object of the gaze; just as was the case with Narcissus, the eye which looks (the *voyeur*) is simultaneously the I which is looked at. Indeed, the intense self-awareness of such films suggests that the entire autobiographical endeavour may be fundamentally narcissistic; both its aims and its processes being essentially self-conscious, self-reflexive, even self-obsessed. Accordingly it is my intention to re-explore here the structure and processes of filmic autobiography through, and in relation to, the Narcissus myth, in order to provide further insight into the genre and to identify new ways in which its complex articulations may be critically addressed.

I should like to begin by recasting the now familiar myth. It concerns an adolescent, the child born of a one-night stand (which was really little more than rape), growing up in a one-parent family, with no father-figure with whom to identify. Isolated, insecure and introverted, the lonely child tries desperately to make sense of his burgeoning (and ambiguous) sexuality, and to establish or discover his own identity. Endlessly gazing at his reflection, he becomes increasingly wrapped-up in himself, indifferent both to his surroundings and to other people. Eventually he disappears, possibly pining away, more probably growing up and leaving home. However, a trace of his former self remains (for the moment, we shall call that trace a flower).

The first thing to note is that this plot provides the basic narrative structure of virtually all autobiographical films. The protagonists may be male or female, but otherwise we find in their stories only the slightest of variations; typically, we see an adolescent (for, Ovid tells us, the son of Cephisus had turned sixteen and could pass for either child or man), introverted, solitary, self-obsessed, growing up in a single-parent family (generally it is the father who is absent, uncaring or ineffectual), desperately trying to make sense of, and come to terms with, his or her growing, bewildering and often ambiguous sexuality, and to establish his or her own identity. At the time of watching this child too, of course, has vanished, faded away, and in its place we find, not a flower this time, but a film: an autobiography.

Within this application to autobiography of the Narcissus myth, what seems to me to be the key element is the process whereby Narcissus becomes flower; remembered self becomes filmic self. It is, of course, this very process which is made explicit in Dalí's painting of the *Metamorphosis of Narcissus* (1937), and I propose to allow this work to act as mediator in the move from myth to film. Dalí's well-known canvas depicts, on the left, the figure of Narcissus, his head resting on his knee as he gazes down at his reflection in the pool. To his right, and slightly more foregrounded, perfectly mirroring the youth's figure, a hand holds an egg (which constitutes the 'reflection' of Narcissus' head) from which grows a flower; a narcissus. The flower is thus both reflection and metaphor, it is the new creation, the work of art conceived by the artist's mind and created by the narcissistic hand or eye. In this case, the hand we look at provides a reference to that of Dalí himself, surely one of the most transparently self-obsessed of all artists; in the case of autobiographical films, the hand or eye is that of the adult director, creator and filter through which we see the remembered child. The flower itself appears to be growing before our eyes; it has cracked, but not as yet broken, the egg shell. The painting thus deals with the process of creation; the reflections it offers are multiple, and atemporal (both present and future are part of the same image), and must be endlessly reassessed, particularly in relation to the detailed and complex background elements. Applied to filmic autobiography, the hand which directly mirrors the figure of Narcissus through its self-conscious indication of the process of the artistic (re-) creation of the self by the self, serves to remind us of the process by which the (remembered) child becomes its filmic representation or metaphor. But it simultaneously foregrounds the essentially visual nature of this process and signals the polyphony and mobility of the autobiographical gaze.

Let us begin the attempt to understand further the nature of the autobiographical process, by applying to it the Narcissus myth which I recounted earlier. Given that, for the autobiographer, the narrative is both a rearticulation and a reappraisal of the child's search for personal identity, we might expect that the key moment in Narcissus' tale, the moment of self-discovery, will feature equally prominently in theirs; and indeed this is in fact the case. Narcissus, it must be understood, could become flower only through that moment of self-discovery, hence the warning given by Tiresias that Narcissus will live a long life only if he does not know himself, the implication being that self-knowledge inevitably destroys the status quo and engenders change. Similarly, the child we watch in an autobiographical film is able to exist as a filmic construct only via, or because of, such a moment of self-discovery. Thus, even though the autobiographical narrative, like the Narcissus myth itself, may begin well before, it is not until this moment of the gaze, this meeting across time of adult and child's I and eye, that the autobiographical process is generated. As in Dalí's painting, the rest, the complex and proliferating background details, are mere explanations, explorations, and elaborations of this central moment. Yet, while Narcissus reaches his self-awareness through contemplating his image in the clear water of the pool, the subjects of autobiographical films almost inevitably appear to reach theirs by contemplating themselves in a mirror.

The mirror, of course, is a privileged site of self-regard and, as such, has for centuries played a prominent role in Western art and literature, while its connotations of self-consciousness and self-referentiality are today paradigmatic of most of the cultural forms which may be seen to define our postmodern world, central to that process whereby: 'postmodernism rediscovers and radicalises the self-reflexive moment' (Bertens 1995).[2] The reflective surface of the mirror is perceived as fundamental to the development of a sense of the self and, by identifying the earliest formation of the I with what he calls the mirror stage, Lacan implies that, right from the outset, I and eye are entirely inseparable in the development of subjective identity, an aspect whose significance for film theory has been considerable. Indeed, much debate centres around the function and significance of the mirror as screen-within-screen and, as we shall see, particularly in relation to spectatorship and identification, the notion of screen itself as mirror (e.g., Metz

1977:89–97). Lacan sees the mirror stage as the first of the three determining phases in a child's development (along with the *fort-da* game, or development of language, and the Oedipus complex, or subjective response to social laws). It occurs between the ages of six and eighteen months when the infant, despite limited or nonexistent linguistic and motor skills, first develops the ability to recognise its own reflection in the mirror and – a key point as far as this chapter is concerned – identifies with this image: 'It is enough to understand the mirror phase *as an identification* in the full sense that analysis gives to this term, in other words the transformation brought about in the subject when that subject takes on an image...', he writes (1966:90). Since the child is in fact identifying with an image which is both self (his/her own reflection) and other (merely a reflection), the mirror stage can be seen to prefigure the whole dialectic between alienation and subjectivity which is basic to the human condition. Moreover, given that the completeness or perfection which identification with the image appears to offer can never be attained (since the image is unreal), the process is inevitably narcissistic. However, it is this reflected image, Lacan's *je-idéal* ('ideal I', Freud's ideal ego), which will provide the source of all secondary identifications, as well as making possible the child's entry into language and the formation of the ego and the Imaginary (Lacan 1966:89–97). All these aspects must be recognised as fundamental to filmic autobiography, in which we also find a close correlation between Narcissus, the search for personal identity and the mirror image.

My first textual illustration of these concerns is *Les Roseaux sauvages* (*The Wild Reeds*), an autobiographical film made by André Téchiné in 1994. Set in France during the Algerian crisis, the film provides a vivid and convincing account of adolescence in France in the early 1960s. The action takes place in and around the small town of Villeneuve-sur-Lot, in the south-west of the country, and the narrative traces the complicated and unstable relationship between François, Téchiné's alter ego, and his three friends in the year leading up to their baccalaureate examination. François is portrayed as an intelligent, introverted boy, desperately trying to make sense of the bewildering worlds of school and beyond (in particular, given the period, the relationship between France and Algeria, and the divided loyalties created by this bitter conflict), as part of his struggle to define his own identity, and to understand and come to terms with his own confused sexuality. The film thus closely mirrors the

Narcissus myth and should therefore contain, at some distance into its narrative, a representation of the key moment of self-realisation that we have posited as essential to the autobiographical process. This moment, when François confronts and accepts his homosexuality, in what we recognise as a direct reference both to Narcissus and to Lacan, occurs in a brief scene in which, late one night while the other students are asleep, he stares at his reflection in the cloakroom mirror. François and his reflection are initially depicted as separate and unreconciled, kept apart by the rigid framings and divisions of the screen: 'the child is divided from the moment it forms a self-conception' (Lapsley and Westlake 1988:69). However, a series of abrupt jump cuts, as he desperately repeats: 'I am a faggot. I am a faggot', moves us closer and closer to his reflection until, as he accepts its apparent plenitude, it fills our visual field.

In simple terms, we might represent François's moment of self-knowledge as a triangle, in which the base a-b is formed by the mirror, and the apex c is the child. The child looks in the mirror at his own reflection, which he endows with the certainty or plenitude he desires, and which he then strives to adopt as his own. However, as soon as we place this scene in its autobiographical context, we are forced to recognise that the role of the mirror and, to borrow Hutcheon's terms, the 'primary' or 'overt' narcissism which it appears to express, is in fact infinitely more complex (Hutcheon 1980:23). For we have to remember, of course, that the director himself, the adult Téchiné, in addition to representing this remembered moment of discovery, is basically setting up the screen as a mirror at which he is gazing in order to reach, through its remembered reflection, a deeper understanding of his present identity. In other words, our original line a-b must now be recognised as both mirror within screen and screen as mirror, and our original point c (the gazing child), now becomes a point on that screen which is both identical to and different from the director, whose presence is manifest only through his invisible controlling hand or eye. In this way, the very fact of the autobiographical framing inevitably complicates both the nature of the gaze and the role of the mirror.

The immediate repercussions of this framing concern the nature of the subject, the I/eye of the film: in the first case, the child is seeking his personal identity – what he means when he says 'I am' – by contemplating his reflected image (which is both self and other, first and third person). His reflection is then – as it were – projected back onto himself as his present and future identity: I am gay now; I shall continue to be gay. The creative, essentially active function of the reflected image which we observe here, recognised by Metz when he likens the mirror to a camera or film projector (1995:82–3),[3] is given added dimensions of complexity by the autobiographical context of the scene, for in fact the looking I/eye is that of the adult director; thus the basic duality of the mirror reflection is multiplied to include both adult's and child's gazes. The essentially unstable perspective of the shot is structured by constant two-way visual and temporal shifts; both the child's present and his hypothesised future belong, in reality, to the adult director's past, but they are also being recognised as fundamental to his present, and indeed future, identity. That his remembered self is projected onto the screen as if occurring in the present tense (a fundamental characteristic of the filmic image), can now equally be recognised as a basic feature of the process of remembering. In autobiographical memory, the processes of gaze and reflection are entirely mobile and open-ended. Interestingly, the fact that the movement occurs between eye and reflection, thus within an apparent stasis (child gazing motionless at his own reflection), is inevitably reflected in the camera work of filmic autobiography, characterised by its reflexive slowness and contemplative stillness.

Once we have accepted the notion that, in an autobiographical film, the screen itself functions as mirror for the director, we can recognise key moments of narcissistic identification even without the provision of overt mirror images. Thus when, for example, in *Au revoir les enfants* (1987), the face of Louis Malle's young alter ego stares out at us from within the rigid framing of a train window, as he is unwillingly and unhappily carried away from his mother at the start of term, we are aware that ultimately it is the adult Malle who is gazing at this younger reflection in search of a new understanding of his (past and present) identity. Our viewpoint, like his, switches repeatedly from first to third person as in turn we look out from, and into the train, and we need to recognise that these shifting viewpoints continually cross and confuse different times. If the child's unhappiness and helplessness are made clear to us by the way his image is trapped within the framing of the train window, it is because this is the viewpoint of the remembering, judging adult; while the hostile frozen landscape which flies past, structured by rigid ploughed furrows stretching away into the distance and the black vertical lines of bare trees, sketches the topography of Malle's personal memories. Thus we are simultaneously sharing an intimate and immediate subjective experience and a distanced evaluation or deconstruction of that experience; in this tension between gazes we sense the invisible hand of the director.

In the opening sequence of *JLG/JLG* (1994), Jean-Luc Godard poses a complex series of questions about himself as a child, about his present need to remember and to revisit that earlier self, and about the relationship of personal identity and its cultural context. Unlike the examples we have so far referred to, Godard's film does not use an actor to represent the director's alter ego, and its portrayal of the key moment of self-awareness is thus very different from theirs. The film opens with a shot of a photograph of Godard as a child, which stands on a piano in an empty flat. As we gaze at the photograph, we gradually realise that the adult Godard's shadow is falling across it, both establishing a direct link between him and the child, and providing a visible reference to the invisible hand of the director, which must inevitably recall our earlier comments about Dalí's painting. A series of jump cuts slowly moves us closer and closer to the photograph until its frame is replaced by that of the screen, which is now entirely filled by the child's face, as Godard's voice directly interrogates the image. In so doing, he jumps the time zones of the gaze, omitting the intermediate stage (child facing mirror), explicitly acknowledging that his return to an image of his younger self is a fundamental part of his current search for his own identity. The process is still narcissistic, but it is a form of narcissism which directly confronts the complexities and problems of remembering, including temporal shifts, lapses and ambiguities. Instead of artificially organising his memories into a coherent narrative structure, Godard presents us with a complex matrix of impressions in which there can be no discrete divisions between past and present, real and imaginary: distant sounds of children at play or awkward scraps of conversation, long reflective shots of Lake Geneva as the wind fragments its mirror surface or of sunlight falling across the corner of a carpet are all interwoven to suggest the child's world, and to acknowledge the fragmented and elusive nature of memory and its inevitable mediation through culture and myth. As Godard addresses the child in the photograph, in what at first appears to be a straightforward cinematic voice-over, he adopts the exaggerated tones of a horror film, thus adding a further self-reflexive layer to our reading. Meanwhile, the child's direct and unwavering stare directly implicates us within the memory process.

This sequence acknowledges that, just as the child seeks self-awareness in his/her reflected image, the adult searches the screen–mirror of memory in the same way. This is a key feature of autobiography and one which clearly distinguishes its discourse from, for example, that of the nostalgic heritage films with which it is often carelessly confused. Why this obsessive need to understand, to revisit our past selves in this way? Narcissus, it was foretold, would be fine so long as he did not know himself. And, true to the prophecy, as soon as he gained self-knowledge, he, or at least, his former self, was lost, destroyed. But the nature of being human is to desire self-knowledge, precisely in order to escape the stasis of (present) ignorance. The myth might well indicate that Narcissus has simply moved on, via his new-found sense of identity. And that seems to be the message of autobiography too, for whether we are looking at Malle or Godard, Bergman or Tarkovsky, the implications are the same: understanding an imperfectly remembered past is essential if the adult director is to break free from his present stasis and move forward. The only way this can be achieved is by transforming that remembered – but vanished – self into its own reflection or metaphor: the flower/film. In other words, the real subject of all autobiographical film is the metamorphosis of child into film (flower). And that process of metamorphosis is of course the film itself.

The metamorphosis, the transformation of child into director and thus into its filmic articulation, is initiated by the child's earliest contact with film; accordingly the narrative of autobiographical film is dominated by references to this relationship. Indeed, if I said at the beginning that these child protagonists are almost always without a parental role model, then it is equally clear that in all autobiographical films the director acknowledges, wholly or in part, the cinema as role model for his/her younger self. And, just as the film presents us with seemingly static shots of the child's face as close-up or reflection or photograph, so too it provides innumerable shots of the face of that child intently watching the screen. In other words, for the child, just like the remembering adult, the screen is performing as a mirror.

This function of film clearly fascinates the Hungarian director, Márta Mészáros and, in the first film of her autobiographical trilogy *Diary for my Children* (1982), we see how important the cinema is for Juli, her adolescent alter ego.[4] The film begins as Juli, recently orphaned, is brought back to Hungary from the Soviet Union (where her parents had been exiled before the war), through the intervention of Magda Egri, a loyal member of the Stalinist elite who is keen to act as her guardian. Juli is thus abruptly plunged into an alien world; bitterly missing her parents, she totally refuses to accept Magda as a substitute. The adolescent search for identity which the film depicts is rendered all the more poignant and confusing, suggests Mészáros, since the regime denies Juli's past, as well as that of her parents. In other words, Juli is required to renounce the very memories which would constitute her identity.

Once again we can easily situate this narrative within the parameters of the Narcissus myth, and once again we find a key scene in which the protagonist searchingly confronts her reflection in the mirror. The moment occurs when Juli is in her bedroom, sitting in front of her dressing-table. Both the lighting and the sound-track (romantic, non-diegetic piano music) are deliberately artificial, self-consciously establishing the relationship between mirror and screen that Mészáros will explore. Juli looks up from her hand-mirror and gazes at the reflection of her head and shoulders (typical filmic close-up) in the large dressing-table mirror, in the bottom right-hand corner of which is a head-and-shoulders photograph of a film star. As Juli looks at her own image, she automatically alters her stance to reflect that of the actress in the photograph. She slowly slips her straps off her shoulders, and studies her breasts, first in the mirror and then looking directly down at her body. The film then cuts to a cinema screen on which a handsome man is inviting a glamorous woman to dance. Juli is clearly viewing her own developing sexuality in terms of cinema images. The sound-track of the film she is watching (the film within the film), a sexy jazz piano, now becomes ours, as the different realities – and fictions – blend. The camera cuts to show Juli seated at the front of the cinema balcony watching the film; then to a close-up of the star; then back to Juli whose stance now perfectly mirrors that of the star. In this sequence then, Mészáros is exploring the notion of screen as mirror, as such, the function of film in the formation of identity. Just like the reflections in a mirror, screen images are shown to have the power to project themselves back onto the spectator. Throughout *Diary for my Children* Juli repeatedly turns to the cinema as role model, and it is clear that her entire view of herself is mediated through its images. Given that the stars she is modelling herself on are illusions on celluloid, shadows of shadows, we return directly to Narcissus: 'And while he drinks, struck by the image of the form he sees, he falls in love with an illusion that has no body, and thinks that to be substance which is only shadow' (*Metamorphoses* 3, 11:413–19).⁵ This close correlation between screen spectatorship and narcissism, overtly explored by Barthes when he writes about the way that fictitious characters on the screen have the power both to capture and to captivate the viewer, remains fundamental to contemporary theories of spectatorship (Barthes 1995:259).

There is, of course, one essential way in which the screen is not a mirror: it never reflects the spectator's own body. Nevertheless, as we have seen clearly illustrated in *Diary for my Children*, it is perceived as functioning as a mirror, a phenomenon Metz describes as secondary identification, possible only because the spectator has already experienced the primary mirror phase, has already been constituted as a subject (Metz 1977). For him, therefore, the images on screen enable the spectator both to lose and to discover him/herself, through a perpetual re-enactment of the first moment of identification and the establishment of personal identity. And, like the self reflected in the mirror, the screen self is perceived (or in narcissistic terminology, 'misrecognised') as whole and as perfect.

In applying these ideas to autobiographical discourse, we must again recognise the proliferating complexities which the genre creates. Perhaps the first thing to notice is the fact that the autobiographical context inevitably subverts any clear-cut distinction between spectator and actor. In *Diary for my Children*, for example, the 'spectator' we have been watching (Juli) is, of course, really an actor pretending to be a spectator; yet at the same time Juli is a reflection of Mészáros herself, so that in the child's identification with characters in the films within the film, we must recognise that of the director herself. References by film to film as creator of identity are, not surprisingly, central to autobiographical narratives, which abound with scenes set inside cinemas, clips from earlier films, and loving close-up shots of various elements of the cinema apparatus. These self-conscious references are almost inevitably extended by repeated shots of the director as child already handling a camera or film-projector and starting to make and show his/her own films. We are, of course, being shown just how the director's hand acquired the skills that would enable it to bring about the metamorphosis of Narcissus, the transition from self to film.

One film which explicitly and obsessively explores this process is *Cinema Paradiso* (Tornatore 1988), in which the entire development of the protagonist, Toto, variously depicted on screen as small boy, adolescent and – unusually – adult director, is intricately related to his developing filmic skills: his passion for the cinema, his training as projectionist, his youthful experiments with a camera, and finally his status as successful director. Not only is it clear that the cinema replaces his dead father in offering him comfort and security and in serving as role model and guide to the mysteries of sex and the universe beyond his small island, but it is also gives him an identity and a means of survival. As Toto grows up, we see the extent to which cinema shapes his vision, his language and his identity. Moreover, the film explicitly acknowledges its role in enabling him to remember, understand and come to terms with his past, and thus to move on (which we have seen to be one of the main purposes of autobiography). For the adult Toto, 'salvation' is achieved as he watches a film (made by Alfredo, the original projectionist in his local cinema) consisting of all the out-takes, the unseen moments, the passionate kisses which the local priest had censored from the original prints. The message is clear; film must be acknowledged as central to the understanding of the self and to the process whereby self can be transformed into film.

Fascinatingly, in all these examples, the transition of self into film *is* the film that we are watching, and the hand whose presence might seem to be the subject of the film, exists only by virtue of the film, which *is* the metamorphosis of the self. It is therefore inevitable that autobiographical films are totally self-reflexive: they are films about themselves, films obsessed with their own filmic identity. Thus the mirrors and reflections, the screens-within-a-screen, the tightly framed shots, the photographs and film clips and proliferating gazes are ultimately all reflections of film itself, those *mise en abyme* structures whose infinitely regressing reflections characterise all modernist discourse. Indeed, it seems to me that one of the most remarkable aspects of autobiographical film is that its entire construction can, in these terms, be seen as *mise en abyme*: film about film as reflection of the processes of film.

But of course, we cannot end our study there, for there remains one final and essential gaze to add to those we have so far seen. Outside and beyond the various layers of eyes looking at eyes, yet central to the entire process, there are our eyes: the gaze of the spectator. For surely we are being required to recognise that the processes of identification and mediation which these films explore are simultaneously at work on us; we too are using the screen as a mirror, identifying with its characters and seeing in its images our own reflections. As we are drawn into the films' subjective discourse by the immediacy of their first-person viewpoint, so too the objectivity which we have seen to be a feature of that discourse creates an ironic distance, reminding us that we too have an essentially active and creative role to play. 'What moves in film, finally, is the spectator, immobile in front of the screen', comments Stephen Heath (1981:53). In this process, in which we are watching a film in which a director is watching a film in which his or her younger self is watching a film and so on, the gaze can be neither passive nor still, since the movement of the eye towards the mirror/ screen/lake in search of self-knowledge is returned, is reflected back through all these multiple gazes to us, the spectators. And what we see obliges us, like them, to change and to look again, to make our own narratives, our own 'films'. Like mirror reflecting mirror, the autobiographical gaze is endlessly mobile and entirely open-ended.

This characteristic was instinctively recognised by Truffaut in the concluding shot of one of the earliest of all filmic autobiographies, *Les 400 coups* (1959), where Antoine's image is frozen as he gazes directly out at us from the screen, implicating us uncomfortably and irresistibly in his search for identity. Of course, he is really staring at the camera (an action entirely forbidden by classical narrative since it makes the spectator aware that he/she is watching a film), and he does so because ultimately the film as mirror must reflect itself, must reveal the process by which its identity as film was created. And that process returns us to the Narcissus myth with which we began: screen as site of the metamorphosis of child into flower.

Notes

1. For a discussion of the status and frequent misrecognition of autobiographical films, see Everett (1995).
2. See also Lyotard (1979).
3. 'Every mirror is like a camera (or a projector) since it "throws" the image a second time, since it gives it a second printing, since it has the power of *emitting*.'
4. In several sequences in which Juli is watching films, we see that she confuses their narratives with her own past, adopting their images as her remembered childhood, so that the films themselves form an integral part of her own sense of identity.
5. This very successful translation was made by Linda Hutcheon (1980:11).

Bibliography

Barthes, R. (1995) 'En sortant du cinéma' [1975], in *Oeuves Complètes* 3 (Paris: Éditions du Seuil(256–9.

Bertens, H. (1995) *The Idea of the Postmodern* (London and New York: Routledge).

Everett, W. (1995) 'The autobiographical eye in European film', in *Europa: An International Journal of Language, Art and Culture*, Spring:3–10.

Heath, S. (1981) *Questions of Cinema* (Bloomington: Indiana University Press).

Hutcheon, L. (1980) *Narcissistic Narrative: the metafictional paradox* (New York and London: Methuen).

Lacan, J. (1966) 'Le Stade du miroir comme formateur de la fonction du Je', in *Ecrits 1* (Paris: Éditions du Seuil).

Lapsley, R. and M. Westlake (1988) *Film Theory: An Introduction* (Manchester: Manchester University Press).

Lyotard, J.-F. (1979) *La Condition postmoderne* (Paris: Minuit).

Metz, C. (1977) *Le Signifiant imaginaire (Psychanalyse et cinéma)* (Paris: 10/18) 3, 9.

―――― (1995) *L'Énonciation impersonnelle ou le site du film* (Paris: Méridiens Klincksieck).

PART IV
NARCISSUS WRITTEN AND REWRITTEN

CHAPTER 10

NARCISSUS AND ECHO: FEMININE HAUNTING MASCULINE

Naomi Segal

Given that they are so genealogical, so based on alliance and consanguinity, it is not surprising perhaps that myths are often wrenched out of their contexts – but it is particularly disturbing how often Narcissus is wrested out of his essential connexion to Echo. In the book of *Favourite Greek Myths* that I had as a child, they appear in two consecutive chapters in clearly demarcated stories, Echo as 'a nymph who talked too much' and Narcissus obsessed with 'a twin sister [who] had died when she was young and very beautiful' and whom he 'missed so very much that he wished he might die too' (Stoughton Hyde 1905:54 and 56). In Ovid, however, the two figures are inextricably woven into a mesh of questions about sexual difference.

The story begins with a prologue on Olympus:

> ... it chanced that Jove,
> Well warmed with nectar, laid his weighty cares
> Aside and, Juno too in idle mood,
> The pair were gaily joking.
>
> (Ovid 1986:60)

The banter turns to the question of sexual pleasure. Jupiter maintains that women have greater pleasure than men; his wife 'disagreed'. They call in Tiresias (who once spent seven years clothed in the body of a woman) to arbitrate. He sides with Jupiter. In her anger – and a familiar refusal to 'take a joke' – Juno strikes Tiresias blind; by way of compensation, her husband grants him the gift of prophecy. The story of Narcissus is presented as proof of Tiresias' insight.

Narcissus is the offspring of a nymph, Liriope, who bore him after having been raped by the water-god Cephisus. By the time his fate comes to meet him, he is in his mid-teens and cold-heartedly proud. Of all the youths and maidens who desire him none is as interesting as

> a strange-voiced nymph, who must speak
> If any other speak and cannot speak
> Unless another speak, resounding Echo (62).

Echo has also been punished by Juno, this time for aiding and abetting Jupiter's adulterous dallying with the other nymphs; famous for her eloquence, she was posted to keep Juno talking until the girls had slipped away. For this she is condemned to be able to speak only by repeating the ends of other people's speeches. When she sees the beautiful youth, 'Echo's heart was fired'

> As when a torch is lit and from the tip
> The leaping sulphur grasps the offered flame.

The nearer she gets, the more her passion burns:

> She longed to come to him with winning words
> To urge soft pleas, but nature now opposed

she has to wait for him to speak first. Separated from his friends while hunting, Narcissus calls out: '"Anyone here?" and Echo answered "Here!"' He looks round in amazement, is unable to find the owner of the voice, and calls 'Come!' – and so does she. Still seeing no one, he cries 'Why run away?' and again Echo repeats his words.

> He stopped and, cheated by the answering voice,
> Called 'Join me here!'

Echo, 'never more glad to give her answer', echoes his phrase and comes out of the wood 'to throw her longing arms around his neck'. But he turns tail and runs away, crying:

> Be off! I'll die before I'll yield to you!
> And all she answered was 'I yield to you!' (63).

Spurned and ashamed, Echo lurks in the woods, hiding among foliage or in lonely caves.

> Yet still her love endures and grows on grief,
> And weeping vigils waste her frame away;
> Her body shrivels, all its moisture dries

but she does not die. What remains of her is an unfading voice and bones said to have turned to stone, invisible but enduring 'for all to hear, alive, but just a sound'.

About ten years ago I published a book entitled *Narcissus and Echo*. It was a comparison of ten French narratives or *récits*, ranging from the eighteenth to the twentieth century, but clustered in the nineteenth, and all with a very direct relation to Romanticism: in chronological order, Prévost's *Manon Lescaut* (1731, 1753), Chateaubriand's *René* (1805), Constant's *Adolphe* (1816), Gautier's *Mlle de Maupin* (1835–6), Musset's *La Confession d'un enfant du siècle* (1836), Mérimée's *Carmen* (1845), Nerval's *Sylvie* (1853), Fromentin's *Dominique* (1863), Gide's *L'Immoraliste* (1909) and *La Porte étroite* (1909). These texts share the following group of characteristics: they are written by, of and (by implication) to men; the protagonist recounts his confession to a paternal interlocutor and frame-narrator who serves him as double and invites him to enter the patriarchal order; his story always involves a woman, usually older and more articulate than he, and she tends to die, leaving him to tell what is now exclusively his tale. But even in the extreme cases where he has literally murdered her, his guilt is lodged in her: *femme fatale*, saint, actress or androgyne, she is to blame for his failure. In nearly all these fictions, the protagonist's mother has died giving birth to him, and as the infant who is both victim and killer in the scene of the childbed death, he must seek, desire and repeat the death of the woman who stands to him in the mother's place. And there is a further twist: as first incestuous substitute she is also (in *René* explicitly) his sister. Implicit in this sibling structure is a hint that the mother-daughter pair does not entail a childbed death – that, in one sense or another, mother and daughter can coexist without mutual murder as mother and son cannot. To see how the Ovidian narrative of Narcissus and Echo can support this set of observations, let us return to the familiar scene of Narcissus' slow death and particularly to the description of the pool in which he finds his image:

> There was a pool, limpid and silvery,
> Whither no shepherd came nor any herd,
> Nor mountain goat; and never bird nor beast
> Nor falling branch disturbed its shining peace;

> Grass grew around it, by the water fed,
> And trees to shield it from the warming sun.
> (Ovid 1986:63)

Now even ten years ago I hope I was capable of some subtlety with vulgar Freudian images, but the description of the fatal pool seems to me still to describe something so shady, immobile, foreknown and uncanny that it must recall the *heimlich/unheimlich* of the mother's genital (see Freud 1919). Here the son seeks an other and finds a double that is as indeterminately sexed, as resistant to possession as himself – or Tiresias. Four stories of women have been told immediately before this scene: Juno, who has power enough to strike but not to destroy, who is said to have pleasure but no knowledge of that pleasure; Liriope, who submitted to watery ravishment and cannot keep her child from a similar fate; the nymphs, who gather like groupies around the king of the gods, and Echo, who could talk but not enjoy (if enjoyment it is – Jupiter thinks so) and who can now do neither. The power of Juno and the desire of Echo – mother's and daughter's voices – cannot coexist, unlike the doubling of Jupiter and Tiresias, Tiresias and Narcissus or Narcissus and his beloved reflection. But, despite this diffusion and cooptation of female complexity, the text also shows how Echo's desire cannot *not* survive the death of Narcissus. If his trope is water, hers is fire: however cold a magnetism he provides, as she approaches him she 'burns with a nearer flame'. When she declines, it is into the more or less eternal mineral base while, when he slips and falls, he dissolves away like the Wicked Witch of the West. In the pool that is the stilled version of the maternal vortex he thinks he has found a true-love other, but what he unconsciously seeks is a prenatal 'I' in whom, actually, he glimpses the moment before gender in the image that must also be the female child he neither has nor is.

Mirrors are supposed to be the conventional prop of female narcissism, while the voice characterises the empowered male. But in both Ovid and (I would argue) the French *récit*, it is men who seek the mirror in which they will drown and women who survive into audibility against the odds. Virginia Woolf must have had a similar dialectic in mind when she observed in *A Room of One's Own*, 'women have served all these centuries as looking-glasses possessing the magic and delicious power of reflecting the figure of man at twice its natural size. [But] if she begins to tell the truth, the figure in the looking-glass shrinks' (Woolf 1929:35).

In *Narcissus and Echo* I was interested in 'getting the woman's voice out of the man's mirror' – that is, in intervening to read between the lines or against the grain of these apologias for young men's desire and try to piece out the female desire which can only speak through the male-voiced text. The direct appeal of a first-person narrative, couched in all the angry ambivalence of a confession, demands a reader response that neither author nor narrator can, of course, and happily, control. As brief examples, here are a few scenes in which the image of mirroring is central – three moments from 1753, 1853 and 1909.

In the second edition of *Manon Lescaut*, Prévost added a scene in which Manon plays a trick on des Grieux. They are living rather peacefully in the Parisian suburbs and he is keeping them both by judicious gambling. One day a cloud enters the idyll: he is led to suspect her of another infidelity. She has been seen talking to a new admirer, an Italian prince. His playful mistress begs des Grieux to stay at home with her for once during the day; he agrees, and she sits him down at her dressing-table to do his hair.

> As she worked, she frequently made me turn my face towards her and, leaning with both her hands on my shoulders, gazed at me with avid curiosity. Then expressing her satisfaction with a kiss or two, she made me sit back in my place and continued her handiwork. This play kept us amused until it was time for dinner. Her enjoyment had seemed so natural and her gaiety so uncalculated that – as I could not square such a loyal manner with an evil plot to betray me – I almost opened my heart to her several times, to relieve myself of a burden that was beginning to weigh heavy on me. But all the while I flattered myself that the initiative would come from her, and I looked forward to a delicious triumph. (Prévost 1753:122)

What exactly is Manon gazing at? And *is* she deceiving him? In one sense she is, though less anxiously and altogether more lovingly than he is deceiving her, as the outcome will show. What des Grieux fears and expects is the horror of a sexual betrayal, and Manon is certainly not plotting that this time – indeed we can argue that she has never plotted it, since, in her own exceptionally directly-quoted words, 'the fidelity I desire from you is that of the heart' (Prévost 1753:147).

Manon uses another mirror in the next phase of her performance. When the prince arrives, she drags des Grieux by his – presumably now undressed – hair and, thrusting a hand-mirror in the face of the prince, demands that he compare himself with 'the man I love' (123) and leave her alone. He stomps off after a few curses. But her pleasure is brief and the trick has not paid off: des Grieux rightly feels as manipulated as his rival, set up as the girlish figure of a scene redolent of both sophisticated modernity and caveman ravishment: the mirrors of Manon's wit have exceeded and feminised him in a way he will not tolerate for long. The narrative 'turns against her' from this point, so that when she sends him, to console him for a while, a young woman who resembles her rather too much, des Grieux infers all sorts of ideological thoughts about the interchangeability of women, and Manon's doom is sealed.

In Nerval's *Sylvie*, the text opens with a recollection of the time, some years before the moment of narration, when the protagonist spent every evening gazing at an actress on a stage: 'I was coming out of a theatre in which I *appeared nightly* at *the front of the house* in the full *costume* of the *suitor*' (Nerval 1853:589). In this self-reflexive sentence, again, we see a potential reversal of the gazer and the gazed-upon: the stressed terms might as easily describe an actor as a member of the audience. A similar emotional symbiosis or interchangeability is suggested in the fantasy, 'I felt myself living in her, and she lived for me alone'. But, the narrator continues a few lines later, he has never tried to meet his idol because 'I was afraid of clouding the magic mirror which cast me back her image' (590). Here the question we must ask of the mirror in the text is not what the female other might intend – she is presumably unaware of the protagonist's existence and has no intentions towards him – rather, his phrasing shows that it is in and through the image he creates of her that he is seeking what one ordinarily finds in a mirror: an image of himself. And that avoiding the apparent temptation to meet 'the real woman' is an expedient not of vanity but of *fear*. Hereafter what follows in his eventual close encounters with Aurélie the actress and his childhood friend Sylvie proves that the mirror cannot work as fantasy would wish – unless, as in the case of the aristocratic nun Adrienne, the female figure who is less an image than a frame is, icily, first incarcerated and then dead.

My third example comes from Gide's *La Porte étroite*. Jérôme is walking in the garden with Juliette, the younger sister of his cousin Alissa, with whom he is in love and to whom, already, he finds it difficult to speak *en tête-à-tête*, much easier to write to her or employ a mediator. Juliette has acted regularly as go-between to the couple; insensitive Jérôme has no idea that she is in love with him. He is holding forth to her, explaining his plans to marry Alissa – but not just yet – when suddenly he fancies that Alissa might be listening to them behind a hedge.

> 'Oh', I cried, with the somewhat pompous exaltation of my age, and too concerned with the sound of my own voice to hear behind Juliette's all the things she was not saying, 'oh, if only we could lean over the soul we love and see in it, as in a mirror, the image we have placed there! To be able to read another person as well as we can read ourselves – better even! What peace there would be in such tenderness! What purity in such love!' (Gide 1958:518)

The final result of Jérôme's vision of pure love will of course be the excess of undesire that brings Alissa to an early grave. At this point – as the narrator warns – his knowledge of the other is about as developed as his real interest in her. Alissa was indeed inadvertently listening behind the hedge. She darts off into the house pursued by her sister. It becomes clear soon after that each sister has recognised the other's desire and understands that Jérôme could make neither of them happy: that is what emerges here from the protagonist's image of the mirror. (And at the very end of the text, ten years after Alissa's anorexic decline, the narrator uses the same terms to explain to the now much-maternal Juliette why he could not love anyone but Alissa – in order to be faithful not to her memory but 'perhaps rather to the image she had of me' (597).)

These three examples show how the woman may be inferred out of, between and against the words of the man: in the first case, her dangerous strength and wit, in the second her irrelevance to a unilateral fantasy of reflection, in the third the difficulty that two women who love each other have in uniting to protect one another against a man's failure to love. And, as I have argued in a number of places (Segal 1986, 1988 and 1992), this approach sets out to lift the female character from the textual bind in which she is caught – like the object of Freud's smutty joke – in a discourse designed by a man to be consumed by a man and in which she is isolated among a veritable crowd of male doubles all down the diegetic chain of command, to unite her with the unintended female reader who can discern the echoes of her voice.

Some objections could be raised against the kind of feminist reading I have just outlined. First, that such a question as 'what does Manon really want?' or 'what might be motivating Albertine or Ellénore to stay with Marcel or Adolphe?' is as futile as the classic 'How many children had Lady Macbeth?'

since the realist projection of other possibilities hidden from view is strictly a delusion. This is true, but it is true not because characters lack 'real autonomy' but rather because as figures of fantasy they are inseparable from the implied unconscious of the author. And it is the value of such pseudo-naive questions that the readings they provoke can expose the workings of unconscious fantasy, turn the fictional game against itself, denuding the solipsistic narcissism of the romantic complaint, reading the text psychoanalytically, as Peter Brooks suggests, 'against its demand and according to its desire' (Brooks 1987:12). If the fantasy is exposed so starkly through the axiomatic Freudian riddle 'what do women want?' it is because masculinity was then and is still the dominant mode of desire in our cultural world. A second objection would query the status of a feminist reading by raising the possibility, now much arrogated, that you don't have to be a woman to 'read as/like a feminist'. I want to turn that vexed political claim against myself now and try to justify my present research which – still on Gide – is in the thriving field of queer studies.

Exactly the same objection as one might make against 'men in feminism' can be made against me as a heterosexual-identified woman doing research into the motif of pederasty and pedagogy in the writings of Gide (Segal 1998). In a political sense, it can't be answered. Issues about who speaks of whom and the claims of the authority of experience cannot be dismissed. But it is also true that to read against the demand of a male homosexual desire which by definition excludes me is a logical continuation of the feminist reading of those other texts intended to by-pass, remove and narrate the woman. And besides, the sexing of the body may no longer be the main issue for any of us. It is surely time now to investigate not the haunting of a male text by a female figure but of a masculine text by the feminine which it conjures and repudiates. The Narcissus and Echo scenario would then be the masculinity that seeks to define itself against femininity by disputing, discharging and dispelling it. This process is different from the romantic one and more complex because, while women are a group that cannot be ghettoised, the feminine is an imaginary element existing inside, outside and between bodies of both sexes. The pederastic fantasy of which Gide is a particularly acute example is a centrifugal one, striving to create precipitates of pure masculinity – shapes and systems and modes of fluid exchange from which the feminine has been drained. Gide is fascinating because in him – his writing, writing about him, the body that remains in his textual relics – everything is informed by a fundamental relation of undesire towards the feminine.

André Gide, who died in his eighties in 1951, is perhaps unique among a rich generation of French gay writers. For one thing, unlike both Proust and Wilde, he believed it right and proper to speak of homosexuality in the first person (Gide 1996:1124 and Gide 1910:46), though the ways in which he did so may seem very incomplete to readers of the 1990s. For another, his apologia for pederasty, based as it is in a Platonic tradition (or rather in the revival of that version of Greekness which was developed through an inexplicit theory of desire in nineteenth-century German classicism) seems to look both far back and uncannily forward in its strange combination of good citizenship, natural hedonism and pure masculinity. Gide is the 'straight man' of twenties gay creativity: he placed himself in more or less overt contrast to his contemporaries Wilde, Proust and Cocteau in his rejection of the inversion theory and the varieties of femininity which for him were true perversion (and hence repellent). At the same time, he lived with and lived off the feminine in a number of ways: the 'mystical orient' (Delay 1956:301) of his life was his cousin Madeleine, to whom he committed himself in early adolescence when he learned of her mother's adultery, and whom he married thirteen years later, following the death of his own mother, just a few months after he had definitively and joyously recognised his pederastic identity in North Africa. There seems little doubt that he had no sexual contact at all with Madeleine; but twenty-eight years after they married, he had a child by Élisabeth, the feminist daughter of his friend Maria Van Rysselberghe – to his sharp disappointment, it was a girl – and he lived more often in the large apartment in Paris adjoining Maria's where rooms were kept for Élisabeth and her child and his erstwhile lover Marc Allégret, than in the family estate in Normandy where Madeleine had her own extended family and waited for his visits.

And what of his desire? Gide's parents were bourgeois Huguenots, his mother from a well-to-do business family in Normandy, his father a southern-born academic. His father died when he was eleven, and the story of his upbringing is told by both himself and a string of biographers as that of an isolated boy surrounded by strictly religious women, his mother in particular, with her large square body, sideways unsmiling eyes and embarrassing dress sense, representing simultaneously all that is negative in a prescriptive and proscriptive religious education and all that terrorises Western culture as a dominating feminine. Madeleine appears to have been her desirable substitute, the mirror in which he looked for his own reflected face, the fixed point from which he continued to seek his limited distance, the pole by which he measured creative emancipation.[1] With her went the same religion, more tenderly packaged but still feminised as the wife in the house, the soul (in a more mystical than stringent guise now, or so he tried to make it) possessing the body from within – what does the body do to escape these? It dwells in closed rooms, at first, and learns of pleasure in the form of sin, battling (in a way we can only gawp at post-1960) with the tireless 'temptation' of masturbation. It later absorbs itself in friendships of an intellectually freer but still chaste kind – in his late teens and early twenties, when Madeleine was continuing to refuse his repeated proposals, Gide describes himself as 'virgin and depraved' (Gide 1996:159) – and finally defines itself in the discovery of real warmth and multiple pleasure in the wordless embrace of a brown-skinned boy in the sand outside Biskra. He is horrified by penetrative sex, seeing in it only violence and predation in the briefly evoked scene of his friend Daniel B. (Eugène Rouart) descending under a black coat vampire-like over the frail body of an Arab boy; he comments: 'as for me, who can only understand pleasure when it is face to face, reciprocal and without violence, and who often, like Whitman, get satisfaction from the most fleeting (*furtif*) contact, I was horrified both by what Daniel was doing and by seeing Mohammed accept it so obligingly' (Gide 1954:596). As an adult, he writes a solemn and frustrating journal explicitly aimed at the public for whom he begins to publish it from 1939, and a string of fascinatingly direct and indirect fictions; he travels, cruises and roosts; he plays mayor and juror in Normandy and amateur ambassador in Africa and the USSR; and he preaches a strange kind of sensual pleasure, that of *attente* ('expectancy', 'waiting') which, along with its psychological corollary of *disponibilité* ('availability') is poised midway between release and abstention. Put all this together, and we have a man who desires two things: a feminine mirror he may both fix and abjure, and a masculinity he seeks in the child who is by preference brown or bad or both. How do these equal and opposite impulses appear in his texts?

In Gide it is better to be seduced by an uncle than an aunt – or a *tante*.[2] If Gide's writing is a long apologia in which pederasty is justified in terms of pedagogy, that is, as the reproduction of masculinity down a genealogical line which avoids the mess of sexual dimorphism, the system is everywhere haunted by what it leaves out. 'Sometimes I'm afraid that what I suppressed may take its revenge' murmurs the protagonist of *L'Immoraliste* (Gide 1958:471) after he has drained his wife of those elements of her vitality – poverty and health – that in his system make blood bright in males and vampiric in females. For body fluids mark the impossibility of that clean genealogy, the survival of desire and its refusal to remain inside a closed hydraulic system. Wherever the boundaries of the body seep and sweat, what emerges from its 'proper' place is femininity.

Despite the rigidly hierarchised relation between senior lover and junior beloved in the pederastic bargain, the latter is in perpetual risk of being feminised. To receive the sperm of the *erastes* in an improper way (that is, with any signs of pleasure or immodesty) is to behave like a [female] prostitute. Anthropological theory and the history of sexuality show that the boundaries of the 'proper' depend on two things: a concept of dirt as 'matter out of place' (Douglas 1966) and the 'interconvertibility' of body fluids (Laqueur 1990), in which the difference between white and red, benign and malign is not absolute but relative, depending on where the fluid is found – inside or outside a male or female body.

Seduction by an uncle, real or honorific, is presented in both Gide's fiction and his autobiographical writings as an act of honest pedagogy.[3] In all these cases, corruption is evaded by the fact that the senior partner is always strangely innocent, even ignorant of his own desire: it is the younger partner who beckons while he hesitates or falls. By contrast, in the image of the seducing aunt Gide's terror of pollutant contamination is very clear. We can see this by comparing the fluid dynamics of two scenes in which the danger posed by feminine desire can only be wiped away by the intervention of a virgin.

In *La Porte étroite*, the aunt's attempted seduction of the nephew ends with the latter rushing to the end of the garden to wash in pure water. A page later, he glimpses her laughing with her younger children and a falsetto-voiced lover who mocks the father's name; cousin Alissa kneels weeping in her bedroom. Perceiving her utter chastity, he presses 'her head to my heart and my lips, through which my soul streamed forth, to her brow' (Gide 1958:504). The woman's bad fluids pass thus through the boy to the girl (for direct mother–daughter contamination is a yet more repressed fear) where it remains, driving the latter to a very logical anorexia that will eventually kill her.

In Gide's autobiography *Si le grain ne meurt* (1920), on the other hand, there is no seductive aunt. Instead what immediately precedes the protagonist's discovery of the angelic cousin is a description of his helpless anorexia, which 'Emmanuèle', most untypically, exploits. There is no lover, and no male is present in the house when André tiptoes past his aunt's room – it is scarcely clear what terror is produced there, except that it simultaneously excludes and seduces the male in him. When he finds his cousin weeping, the fluid exchange is the opposite of that in the earlier, fictional text: 'It was only when I felt her tears on my cheek that my eyes were suddenly opened' (Gide 1954:434). The precious fluid of her chastity flows out of her onto (into) him, once again emptying her and filling him – with what? Is it chance that after this, Gide's sexual practice will consist of a painful concentration on emptying himself, reproducing that anorexic moment before he discovered that all full bodies are potentially feminised?

The face in the glassy water may after all be the lost sister of the Romantic-Oedipal fantasy and bowdlerised classicism, surviving as the endogamic beloved whose presence ensures that one may desire what she is not. Or it may be more subtly dissolved and diffused in the fluids that lubricate all encounters between body and text. Either way it also survives as a voice broadcast as if by ventriloquism from the supposedly stony rocks and trees that frame the pool.

Notes

1. In June 1918 Gide went to England for the summer with the eighteen-year-old Marc Allégret. Madeleine revealed, the night before he left, that she knew of the relationship. He went nevertheless, returning to a seemingly calm atmosphere; but a month or so later, when he asked to consult her large collection of letters from him dating back to their childhood, she told him she had burnt them one by one: 'it was the most precious thing I had in the world' (Gide 1996:1,075). He later commented to a friend:

    I spent the whole winter suffering. For a long time, I stayed in Cuverville without going back to Paris. I did nothing else except suffer, weeping over my dead child. You can read my Journal, you'll understand what I suffered. My life was now distorted: there would be nothing left of me in the future but an incomplete, approximate, caricatural, grimacing image: my true image had been rubbed out for ever. And above all, I suffered in my love, which had remained intact, as fervent as on the first day. People don't understand what the love of a uranist is like, free from all sexual contingencies: something so strong, so perfectly preserved, embalmed, that time has no power against it. I gazed at my poor beloved, that face which for me is the very image, the radiant image of love, and told myself: 'She did that!' I thought I'd go mad. (Schlumberger 1956:193).

2. The pejorative term *tante* is common French for an effeminate gay man; for its origin in prison slang see Courouve 1985:207-9.
3. Examples from text and life are Édouard and Olivier, Georges etc., Albert Démarest and the young Gide, Gide and Marc, Maurice Schlumberger or his young cousin Paul, Corydon and Alexis, Marchant and Geneviève, the pastor and Gertrude. In other cases the avuncular–pedagogic relation is less sanctioned, for example in the case of Lafcadio's uncles, Passavant and Strouvilhou or Lafcadio's own relation to Geneviève – though again here it is the niece who makes the first move.

Bibliography

Brooks, P. (1987) 'The idea of a psychoanalytic criticism', in S. Rimmon-Kenan (ed.), *Discourse in Psychoanalysis and Literature* (London and New York: Methuen).

Courouve, C. (1985) *Vocabulaire de l'homosexualité masculine* (Paris: Payot).

Delay, J. (1956) *La Jeunesse d'André Gide* 1 (Paris: Gallimard).

Douglas, M. (1966) *Purity and Danger* (London: Routledge and Kegan Paul).

Freud, S. (1985) '*Das Unheimliche*' [1919], trans. J. Strachey, in *The Pelican Freud Library* 14 (Harmondsworth: Penguin).

Gide, A. (1910) *In Memoriam: Oscar Wilde* (Paris: Mercure de France).

—— (1954) *Journal 1939–1949. Souvenirs* (Paris: Gallimard).

—— (1958) *Romans, Récits et Soties. Œuvres lyriques*, ed. Y. Davet and J.-J. Thierry (Paris: Gallimard).

—— (1996) *Journal I: 1887–1925*, ed. E. Marty (Paris: Gallimard).

Laqueur, T. (1990) *Making Sex* (Cambridge MA: Harvard University Press).

Nerval, G. de (1966) 'Sylvie' [1853], in *Œuvres de Gérard de Nerval*, ed. H. Lemaître (Paris: Garnier).

Ovid (1986) *Metamorphoses*, trans. A.D. Melville (Oxford and New York: Oxford University Press).

Prévost d'Exiles, A.F. (1964) *Histoire du Chevalier des Grieux et de Manon Lescaut* [1753], ed. F. Deloffre and R. Picard (Paris: Garnier).

Schlumberger, J. (1956) *Madeleine et André Gide* (Paris: Gallimard).

Segal, N. (1986) *The Unintended Reader: Feminism and Manon Lescaut* (Cambridge: Cambridge University Press).

—— (1988) *Narcissus and Echo: Women in the French récit* (Manchester: Manchester University Press).

—— (1992) *The Adulteress's Child: Authorship and Desire in the Nineteenth-century Novel* (Cambridge: Polity Press).

—— (1998) *André Gide: Pederasty and Pedagogy* (Oxford: Oxford University Press).

Stoughton Hyde, L. (1953) *Favourite Greek Myths* [1905] (London, Toronto, Wellington, Sydney: Harrap).

Woolf, V. (1977) *A Room of One's Own* [1929] (London: Panther).

CHAPTER 11

GIDE'S NARCISSISM

Scott M. Sprenger

> Oh ... Freud is so bothersome! It seems to me we would have discovered his America without his help.
>
> André Gide

No doubt the most influential rewriting of the myth of Narcissus in modern times is the theory of narcissism that Sigmund Freud articulated in his 1914 article 'On Narcissism: An Introduction'. The Freudian version of Narcissus had a major impact not only on subsequent theorists such as Béla Grunberger, Jacques Lacan, and Julia Kristeva, but it has played a vital role in shaping contemporary discussions of object desire in psychoanalytic literary criticism. Freud's turn to the Narcissus myth to extend and rework his more central, Oedipal theory of desire shocked his contemporaries, such as Ernest Jones, since it appeared to undermine psychoanalysis at its foundation; but Freud insisted that certain self-absorbed configurations of desire remained inexplicable without a theory of infantile narcissism. Based on his 'observations' of egomaniacs, melancholiacs, hypochondriacs, coquettes, and other self-obsessed creatures, Freud inferred a new 'stage' of development – a narcissistic stage – that he believed must lie between the end of auto-erotic stages and the onset of Oedipal desire for the mother. His idea was that the infant first takes itself as the primary object of love, but that this self-love must later be renounced or radically modified in order for it to evolve into 'mature' object-love. In those who fail to mitigate their original self-love, excessive narcissism leads to adult object choices which do not register as a truly external reality or 'otherness', but which merely reflect back the narcissist's own self-image and self-desire.

One author often accused of self-absorption and whose semi-autobiographical novels have frequently caught the attention of psychoanalytic/psycho-biographical critics is the French writer, André Gide. This is primarily due to the cause-effect logic psychoanalytic theory establishes between narcissism and homoeroticism, coupled with the well-publicised homoerotic themes of Gide's fiction. For understandable reasons, critics have considered Gide a sort of 'testing-ground' for the psychoanalytic theory of same-sex love – a love which, according to Freud, should be interpreted as a 'pathology':

> The boy represses his love for his mother: he puts himself in her place, identifies himself with her, and takes his own person as model in whose likeness he chooses the new objects of love. In this way he has become a homosexual. ... He finds the objects of his love along the path of *narcissism*, as we say; for Narcissus, according to the Greek legend, was a youth who preferred his own reflection to everything else and who was changed into the lovely flower of that name. (Gay 1995:462–3, Freud's italics)

While the psychoanalytic/psycho-biographical approach to Gidean desire has convincingly demonstrated various parallels between Gide's fiction and his life,[1] it has also overlooked certain textual and narratological intricacies – intricacies which, ironically, seem to point to Gide's own self-conscious, fictional theorisation of the connection between narcissism and homoerotic desire.

For historical reasons and for the sake of concision, I will limit my analysis of Gidean narcissism to *La Symphonie pastorale* – a novella which has traditionally been interpreted as an allegorisation of Gide's love for Marc Allégret. According to Francis Pruner (1964), Alain Goulet (1988), Charles O'Keefe (1996) and others, the fictional pastor's love affair with the young girl, Gertrude, and his marital turmoil with Amélie correspond more or less to Gide's trip to England with Allégret in 1918 and the unravelling of Gide's marriage to Madeleine. The pastor, in this scenario, thus stands in for Gide, Gertrude for Allégret, and their illicit affair functions as a conventional (because heterosexual) screen story for Gide's far more illicit affair with Allégret. Pruner, for example, writes: 'Thus, in the major part of his narrative, Gide transposed the only great pederastic passion of his life into the forbidden love of a pastor for an adolescent girl' (Pruner 1964:18). And more recently, Charles O'Keefe has commented: 'Gide has made a transposition of sexes, so that the blind girl Gertrude is the literary counterpart of the adolescent Michel' – which we know is Gide's code name for Marc Allégret (O'Keefe 1996:194).

What such interpretations miss, however, is that Gide textually complicates the transposition of events by embedding the pastor's expression of desire for Gertrude within a subtle manipulation of the myth of Narcissus – a manipulation that in fact works to resist the psychoanalytic attribution of such a desire to an infantile or regressive 'stage'. Of course, many critics have previously observed Gide's use of Narcissus in *La Symphonie pastorale*; but the way the myth inflects the novel's textual and narrative logic, especially within a psycho-biographical context, has not been fully developed.[2] With some exceptions around the edges, critics who have studied the myth of Narcissus in *La Symphonie pastorale* have not sufficiently concerned themselves with autobiographical issues, and vice versa. Even Jean Delay, whose massive psycho-biographical study analyses the Narcissus myth in several of Gide's works, glosses over the issue in *La Symphonie pastorale*. Bringing together both lines of inquiry, I believe, may yield new insight.

To begin, it may prove more useful, according to the self-reflexive logic of Narcissus, to interpret Gertrude as a personification of the pastor/Gide's idealised, narcissistic self-image rather than strictly as a symbol of Allégret. Gertrude would then function allegorically as the vehicle through which the pastor/Gide covertly brings to life (and vicariously relives) a desire that he had repressed or compromised by choosing a life governed by religion and conventional morality. By rediscovering, resuscitating, and giving expression to this repressed self-image under the name 'Gertrude', the pastor attempts to recapture and convey a more complete picture of himself. He fictionally reunites his spiritual and erotic desires into one figure that would otherwise resist conventional narrative and morality.

Though speculative, this way of interpreting *La Symphonie pastorale* helps account for a number of details previously unaccounted for or which have traditionally troubled psycho-biographical critics. One problem that immediately comes to mind is: why would Gide have Gertrude fall so deeply in love with Jacques, the pastor's son, if the pastor is supposed to symbolise Gide, and Gertrude, Allégret? The fact that Gertrude's sympathies ultimately lie with Jacques, and not with the pastor, poses a serious stumbling block to the psycho-biographical approach. Pruner defends himself on this point by arguing that Gide uses Jacques as a vehicle to criticise his friend Henri Ghéon, who flirted with homosexuality only to renounce it through religious conversion. As Pruner shows, Jacques's love for Gertrude and his later renunciation of this love through his conversion to Catholicism parallels events in Henri Ghéon's life (Pruner 1964:21–3).

The issue, however, may be seen from another angle. If we interpret Gertrude as a resuscitation and personification of the pastor's repressed idealised desire, it would follow that the relation between Jacques and Gertrude should be interpreted as crypto-homoerotic.[3] Gide thus may be playing out his homoerotic scenario with Allégret at a deeper textual level than previously believed, and he adds an ironic twist: by scripting an interpretation whereby most conventional readers will hope for a union between Jacques and Gertrude and will be disappointed that such a union does not occur, Gide manages to trick his heterosexual reading public into an unwitting endorsement of homoerotic love. What is more, by harnessing his conventional readers' morality and heterosexual desires to his covert narrative strategy, Gide cleverly elicits (and secretly gets) the legitimisation and recognition he knew he could not get if such a love story were told more candidly in a conventional context. For example, while the relation between Gide and Allégret is often described by critics as one of father to son, it is surprising that nobody has imagined this relation reflected in the relation between the pastor and his son Jacques. Perhaps that would be too obvious? I think not. It probably has more to do with how heterosexual ideals govern our – and even Gide's – way of thinking about and constructing narratives. (Parenthetically, seeing Jacques as Marc Allégret corresponds to several critics' observation that Jacques's physical descriptions resemble Allégret.)[4]

In any case, Gide offers further textual evidence to recommend reading psycho-biography in conjunction with the myth of Narcissus. As some critics have noted in passing, just prior to discovering Gertrude, the pastor rediscovers a 'mysterious lake' that he had once known as a young man, had later forgotten, but which he had revisited in his dreams:

> I recognised ... a small, mysterious lake where I had sometimes gone to skate as a young man. I had not seen it for fifteen years, since none of my pastoral duties take me in that direction. I

could no longer have said where it was and had stopped thinking about it so completely that it seemed to me, as suddenly, in the rosy, golden enchantment of the evening, I recognised it, that I had before seen it only in a dream. (Gide 1925:12–13).

Gide's emphasis on this water image, together with the strategic contiguity of the two events – in other words, the rediscovery of the mysterious lake and the 'discovery' of Gertrude – suggests a narcissistic association between them. From this point forward, Gertrude will in fact stand in for the lake as the reflective medium for the pastor's idealised self-image or desire.

In case we miss the narrative logic of the narcissistic association that Gide creates between the pastor, the lake and Gertrude, he draws our attention to it again through a confluence of precise dates and events. Consider the following three sets of facts: (1) though the pastor had once known this mysterious lake, he had forgotten about it and had not revisited it for fifteen years ('I had not seen it for fifteen years, since none of my pastoral duties take me in that direction' (Gide 1925:12–13)); (2) the pastor had been a pastor for precisely fifteen years when he finds the lake ('for *fifteen years* I have been in the habit of holding a service twice a month' (Gide 1925:11–12, my emphasis)); and (3) Gertrude, whom he finds nearly simultaneously to refinding the lake is described as being around fifteen years old: '"How old is she?"' asks Amélie. '"*About fifteen*, I suppose!"' remarks the pastor (Gide 1925:16, my emphasis).

What is the reader supposed to conclude from this unlikely coincidence? Given Gide's strategic narrative construction, the most plausible solution is that at the precise moment the pastor became a pastor, he repressed a part of himself that had remained hidden or latent or perhaps overly ideal for fifteen years. At a moment of personal crisis over his youthful choices fifteen years prior, the pastor decides to revisit and reawaken the desires he had left behind. The fact that Gertrude is precisely as old as the pastor's becoming a pastor (which can be read as a metaphor for living a life according to conventional morality), coupled with the fact that Gertrude is metonymically associated with the mysterious lake unvisited for fifteen years, leaves little doubt that she functions as the ideal of the pastor's narcissistic desire.

As a final bit of corroborative evidence, in Gide's *Journal* we find the pool of Narcissus described as a frozen mirror used by a metaphorical skater.

Skating. Ice on which no one has yet skated looks no different from water – perfidy – you think you're sliding across water – the sun lighting up the ice, which becomes a mirror ... I ... was watching myself very closely, leaning over the reflection, like Narcissus. (Gide 1948:103)

This passage directly parallels the passage above from *La Symphonie pastorale*, in which the pastor recalls a frozen lake where he once had ice-skated as a young man ('a small, mysterious lake where I had sometimes gone to skate as a young man' (Gide 1925:12)).

A second water/Narcissus analogy comes at the moment Gertrude undergoes her 'transfiguration' or 'rebirth' under journal entry 27 February. Recall that when the pastor brought Gertrude under his tutelage, she was lifeless and inexpressive: 'an uncertain creature' (Gide 1925:15), 'an involuntary mass' (Gide 1925:18), 'a parcel of flesh without a soul' (Gide 1925:18).

The transfiguration the pastor refers to here is the sudden sign of progress that Gertrude had begun to display while under his care. As the pastor comments on Gertrude's breakthrough, he likens her metaphorically to a number of objects and events, but most significantly, he refers to a water image taken from the story of the pool of Bethesda found in John 5 in the New Testament:

Suddenly her features became animated; it was like a sudden illumination, like that crimson light in the high Alps. ... It was like a mystical coloration; I also thought of the Bethesda pool at the moment when the angel comes down to awaken the sleeping water. ... For I realised what was visiting her at that moment was not intelligence, it was love. (Gide 1925:42)

Outside the obvious water image, this biblical reference may appear to have little to do with our Narcissus reading. Closer inspection, however, points to the precision with which Gide chose it. Recall that the story of the pool of Bethesda is that of an infirm man who waits patiently to overcome his dysfunction by plunging into the pool's curative waters. As it is stated in John, what those who wait by the pool desire above all is to be 'made whole' again by the water's magical power. Let me briefly cite a few lines from the King James Bible:

5. And a certain man was there, which had an infirmity ...

6. When Jesus saw him lie, and knew that he had been now a long time in that case, he saith unto him, Wilt though be made whole?
7. The impotent man answered him, Sir, I have no man, when the water is troubled, to put me into the pool: but while I am coming, another steppeth down before me.
8. Jesus saith unto him, Rise, take up thy bed, and walk.
9. And immediately the man was made whole ... (John 5:5-9)

From a purely thematic point of view, Gide's analogy does not seem apt. Though Gertrude is, indeed, initially disabled, she is obviously not described as male, let alone 'impotent'. To be sure, impotent both in English and in French is a translation from the Greek *asthenes*, whose range of meanings includes sick, weak, morally weak, infirm and impotent (without power). The pastor thus may have simply had in mind Gertrude's infirmities of temporary blindness and dumbness; he may have been likening the curative power of his love for Gertrude to Christ's love, which is ultimately what heals the infirm man at Bethesda, not the water. The fact that the analogy in John 5 concerns a male may thus have no intended meaning or consequence.

However, when viewed in light of the Narcissus myth, the comparison between Gertrude and an infirm (or impotent) man may reflect the idea that Gide/the pastor believed that it was he who was infirm (or less than whole) for trying to live out his erotic life within the confines of religion and conventional marriage. The pastor's hope to achieve (or maintain) an idealised union with Gertrude, in this case, should be interpreted as an attempt at self-union, or self-reunion. Furthermore, the equation between Bethesda's waters and Christ's love in John 5 suggests that the logic of who cures whom in *La Symphonie pastorale* should be reversed: that is, the pastor is 'made whole' again by Gertrude's reflection of ideal love, not the other way around.

Of course, neither Gide nor the pastor is literally infirm or impotent, but in a metaphorical sense, expressions of authentic love obstructed by religious or moral stricture can be viewed as a kind of impotence. As critics have often discussed, the issue Gide is grappling with during the writing of *La Symphonie pastorale* is not simply a liberation of homoerotic desire from religious prohibition; it is the desire to resolve an internal psychological contradiction between sexual and spiritual desire, between a natural impulse and scriptural commandments that offer no divine sanction for that impulse.

A third water/Narcissus analogy appears in Gertrude's mystical vision of the lilies of the fields during one of her mountain walks with the pastor. The vision occurs soon after the pastor has learned of Gertrude and Jacques's declaration of love and their desire to marry, and just before the affair – or the 'alleged' affair – at the Grange. Gertrude's vision is significant because various details in it recall details from the two previous Narcissus scenes discussed above. In it, we find similar references to an angel and the mystically coloured Alps. But, more to the point, we find a mysterious river that recalls the original mysterious lake: 'I see a great river of milk, smoky, misty, covering a great gulf of mystery' (Gide 1925:92). Also significant are the obvious allusions to the erotic imagery from the Song of Solomon (the lilies, the milky river), which, according to the mystical tradition, would point to the pastor's continued effort, but now more obviously via Gertrude, to maintain a perfect union of erotic and divine love.

Two key issues, however, distance this scene from previous ones: (1) the mysterious lake now becomes a mysterious river, suggesting an element of temporality or a falling away from an ideal state, and (2) Jacques is now present in Gertrude's erotic ideal: 'Over there, ahead of us in the distance [are] the beautiful, dazzling Alps ... It's there that Jacques must go' (Gide 1925:92–3). In other words, as soon as the pastor's narcissistic double becomes fully animated, she no longer faithfully reflects back the pastor's image; she looks elsewhere. But again, according to the logic of Narcissus, the pastor/Gide – who appears here to be losing his grip on his ideal desire at the thematic level – may actually be getting around to expressing it at the allegorical level.

The final water/Narcissus analogy occurs with Gertrude's attempted suicide in the river after her alleged affair with the pastor and just after the operation that restores her sight. Distraught by the upheaval she believes she has caused in the pastor's family, she chooses to take her life by jumping into the river: '[The gardener] said he had seen her walk along the river, then cross the garden bridge, then lean over, then vanish' (Gide 1925:139).

I say 'alleged' affair in reference to the Grange scene because while, from a purely conventional and thematic point of view, an affair between Gertrude and the pastor is easy to imagine, it is noteworthy, especially within the context of a supposedly uncensored fictional personal diary, that the pastor never in fact describes or refers to an affair. He describes only a kiss, hinting at the rest with: 'For a long time I clasped her to me. She made no move to resist, and as she raised her face towards me, our lips met ...' (Gide 1925:131).

The narrative lacuna of the undescribed heterosexual love affair, coupled with the pastor's emphasis on the image of a face whose lips touch his own, as well as Gertrude's plunge into water, would seem to leave the door open once again to a Narcissus reading – or at least to a Gidean or French version of Narcissus. In Ovid's *Metamorphoses*, Narcissus of course dies by his inaction, withering himself away into a flower. In the French tradition, however, we find versions of Narcissus who dies by drowning, sometimes as a result of trying to kiss his reflection.

Examples of this can be found in the works of Guillaume Apollinaire, and evidently it was common enough in the early twentieth century for the Larousse dictionary of 1917 to cite Narcissus drowning as a 'commonplace': 'Narcissus, son of the river Cephisus. He fell in love with his own image while looking at himself in the waters of a spring, into which he plunged.' Parts of this version turn up in Gide's *Traité du Narcisse* as well: 'Lonely, puerile Narcissus falls for the fragile image; he leans over the river, in need of caress, to quench his thirst for love. He leans over and, suddenly, the phantasmagoria disappears; all he sees in the river are two lips in front of his own, offering themselves, two eyes, his own, looking at him. He understands that this is him – that he is alone – and that he has fallen for his own face. ... Narcissus tells himself that a kiss is impossible' (Gide 1930:25–6).

The difference in significance between the classical, Ovidian version and Gide's modernist version is that Ovid's Narcissus remains forever mystified by his ideal, whereas Gide's Narcissus ultimately breaks through the mirror and destroys the illusion. Gertrude's falling into the water thus dramatises in mythic and narrative terms what we already know from the thematic level: that the pastor's attempt to unite ideal and erotic desire is unsustainable. Or, in psycho-biographical terms, Gide/the pastor's attempt to unite Christian and homoerotic love in his relation with Jacques/Allégret would necessarily destroy the idealised Christian union Gide had maintained with Madeleine. Given the logic of Gide's own terms, something has to give here, and what gives is the purity of Gide's Christian desire. The moment he transfers what he had always reserved for Madeleine to Allégret, he must sacrifice it. Gertrude ends up then where she begins: as a reflection of his metaphysical imagination, albeit now a cracked reflection. In the end, Gertrude's life trajectory may be interpreted as Gide/the pastor's imaginary scenario of how love could have been, how he would have liked it to be, coupled with the realisation that it could never be how he wanted.

Up to this point, I have been pulling my argument from speculative interpretations of Gide's metaphors and images. Towards the end of the text, however, the characters begin to make comments that more directly support this reading. Not only do we see the pastor openly refer to his narcissistic identity with Gertrude in lines like: 'I could not tear this love from my heart except by tearing out my heart itself' (Gide 1925:133); we also witness the pastor's obsession with his self-image – in particular, he becomes obsessed with how Gertrude will see him once her operation is over: 'For the first time in my life I peered anxiously into mirrors' (Gide 1925:135). Up until the operation, the pastor sees his narcissistic ideal without being seen by it, and he controls what she (or it) sees. Now that his ideal image will see back, he knows that she will know that his love (which, in fact, she embodies) is not as pure as he claims it is. To reinforce the doubling effect, the pastor, at this point, becomes more noticeably afflicted by the blindness that once afflicted Gertrude, at the same time that Gertrude begins to see more clearly. As the pastor himself comments, it is as if their lives are running in opposite directions: 'Sometimes it seems to me that I am sinking into the shadows and that the sight that is being returned to her is being taken from me' (Gide 1925:133). Or: put more accurately, they are parts of the same divided life placed at different points in its trajectory.

Certain of Gertrude's comments and actions, when viewed in this context, take on new meaning as well. For example, when Gertrude first sees Jacques after her operation, she realises that the person she had loved – or imagined loving – all along was Jacques, not the pastor: 'When I saw Jacques, I suddenly understood that it was not you that I loved, it was him. He had exactly your face; I mean, the face I imagined you to have ... Oh why did you make me drive him away? I could have married him' (Gide 1925:147).

This apparent twist in the narrative, where Gertrude's desire swerves away from the pastor to Jacques, is obviously more satisfying to the general public since it plays into dominant heterosexual and moral narrative patterns, but such a passage can also serve as confirmation for our Narcissus reading. From the point of view of Narcissus, the return of Gertrude's sight marks the point where the pastor's desire passes from the ideal to the real, from the spiritual to the carnal. The fact that Gertrude openly declares her physical attraction to Jacques merely spells out in detail what Gide's ideal author has been communicating to the reader all along in a more covert way.

We see the same sort of thing in the section where the pastor learns that Gertrude and Jacques wish to be married. Though at the narrative's surface level, the pastor tries at all costs to prevent that union from occurring, Gertrude herself has already acknowledged that not only can she not marry Jacques, she cannot marry anybody: 'Father, you understand, don't you, that I can't marry anyone' (Gide 1925:94). But why does Gide have her say this? There is no particular reason from the surface plot why she cannot marry in general, and why she cannot marry Jacques in particular. The pastor points to her blindness as an obstacle to marriage; but for Jacques as well as for most readers, his reasoning is implausible.

Perhaps a better way to read this episode is allegorically, and to see Gertrude as the mediator of Gide's ideal author: that is, Gertrude's statement 'I can't marry anyone' merely marks at the thematic level the obstruction Gide believes exists at a deeper, structural level. This obstruction is, of course, the limits that human communities and their heterosexual ideologies place on expressions of love. The pastor:

> If there are limits in love, they do not come from You, my God, but *from men*. No matter how forbidden my love may be in the eyes of men, oh tell me that in yours it is holy! (Gide 1925:132, my emphasis)

Another plausible way to interpret this episode is psychoanalytically: the blockage of the pastor's desire thematises what Freud refers to as symbolic castration. Moral stricture and social pressure, according to Freud, work to frustrate asocial desires through an implied threat of violence (castration). Castration, in turn, links up with the theme of blindness since Sophocles's Oedipus gouges out his eyes after 'seeing' the consequences of his actions. Such a reading finds reinforcement in Gide's dialectical treatment of blindness in *La Symphonie pastorale*: at the precise moment Gide/the pastor expresses his idealised desire (via Gertrude), he learns to 'see' (again via Gertrude). But the consequence of this moral clarity of vision is a simultaneous physical blindness (the pastor plunges into obscurity) and an irremediable blockage of his desire (Gertrude kills herself).

To conclude, I would like to briefly develop Gide's use of Narcissus in *La Symphonie pastorale* by reading it in the light of his treatment of it in *Le Traité du Narcisse*, in which Gide explicitly overlaps the Narcissus myth with the myth of the Garden of Eden. This may help explain his curious overlapping of Narcissus and Adam in *La Symphonie pastorale* which, in turn, will help flesh out Gide's aesthetic response to his internal psychic and moral conflict.

That the Garden myth is simultaneously operating with Narcissus in *La Symphonie pastorale* should be obvious from a number of textual and thematic details. In a general way, Gide evokes the Garden myth by having the pastor create Gertrude, like Eve, in an ideal, pre-lapsarian space that preexists the knowledge of evil. And while the pastor lives in the world here-below and is aware of evil, the text suggests that his temporal and moral trajectory works in reverse, as if he were trying to lift himself from the fall and cross back over into the Garden.[5] From the very outset even, Gide suggests this mythic register by having the pastor attach his horse to an apple tree just before meeting Gertrude: 'I tied the horse to a nearby apple tree, then joined the child in the dark room' (Gide 1925:13); various declarations of love are made in a garden setting (Gide 1925:94); and, at the precise moment that the pastor is beginning to lose Gertrude to Jacques, he drags Jacques into the garden to discuss his intentions. The pastor: 'I had taken Jacques to the bottom of the garden; it was there that I asked him first of all, "Have you told Gertrude that you love her?"' (Gide 1925:77). In the end, Gertrude not only falls into the water like Narcissus, she falls out of the garden like Eve. Again: '[The gardener] said he had seen her walk along the river, then cross the garden bridge, then lean over, then vanish' (Gide 1925:139).

The text even insists on Gertrude's fall: 'But not having understood at first that [Gertrude] had fallen, [the gardener] did not run over to her as he should have' (Gide 1925:139). Borrowing from the Gnostic tradition, Gide's imbrication of Narcissus with Adam may have given him a way to render more conventional what is essentially a homoerotic myth. It is also a way of reinforcing, from a more familiar Judeo-Christian angle, the moral tenor of Gide's Narcissus, who becomes disillusioned and dies after desire is expressed. The price of knowledge as it is recounted in the Adam and Eve myth – in other words spiritual death – leaves little doubt that Gide wished to include a moral angle to his story. Gertrude's death, in this case, can be read as the pastor's own self-sacrifice or willed spiritual death. Put differently, *La Symphonie pastorale* functions as Gide's self-conscious recognition of having paid a high, but necessary, price for expressing homoerotic love.

Gide's narcissistic scenario transcends conventional, romantic self-aggrandisement because, instead of opting for his personal dream of uniting spiritual and (homo)erotic desire over and against moral and social convention, he holds these two views in tension. In the end, Gide/the pastor concedes that his narcissistic ideal is an illusion, that his effort to focalise spiritual/erotic desire onto a male object will probably never be recognised as legitimate from a communal/moral perspective. And yet, in spite of all that resistance, he feels compelled to give this desire its own legitimate narrative expression and textual space.

As a final point, I would reiterate that Gide's rendition of the Narcissus myth resists conventional psychoanalytic interpretation (by Delay and others), which views Gide's narcissism (and, by extension, homoerotic desire) as a regression or a primitive infantile stage of development that Gide never quite made it through.[6] It is more accurate to see Gide's strategic use of the myth producing the effect of narrative simultaneity, where unconventional desire can be expressed, but is never fixed or coopted by the dominant narrative in which it is embedded. Michael Lucey makes this point eloquently in reference to another text by Gide, but it applies to *La Symphonie pastorale* as well:

> Gide's writing seems to narrativise and to distrust the effect of narrativisation, at the same time, recognizing that whatever temporality sexuality seems to follow, no one narrative can capture it. Gide thus writes his way out from under dominant (heterosexualising) narrative patterns. (1995:141–2)

Though there are obvious benefits to be drawn from psychoanalytic readings of Gide, in the end, Gide's self-conscious representation of his narcissism is far too complex to be transposed into the master-narrative of a strict psychoanalytic schema.

Notes

1. While Pruner's article is the only full-blown psycho-biographical study of *La Symphonie pastorale*, many other critics who emphasise *La Symphonie pastorale*'s irony and textuality nevertheless operate as if the allegorical correspondences between Gide and the pastor and Gertrude and Allégret were a

given. Goulet (1988) and O'Keefe (1996), for example, come close to undermining the conventional psycho-biographical interpretation; but, in the end, they fall short.
2. Kaplan, for example, has previously argued for a narcissistic identification between the pastor and Gertrude, but her focus is on irony and landscape imagery, not on autobiography or fictional autobiography:

> This situation is encouraged by the Pastor's narcissistic identification with Gertrude, whom he substitutes for his own vision of lost youth. It is my contention that the roles of the Pastor as ironist and of Gertrude as his victim reverse themselves at the close of the text. (Kaplan 1987:24)

Pruner also comes around at the end of his article to suggest a narcissistic relation between the pastor and Gertrude. But he offers this idea only as a minor problematisation of his initial reading (in other words, that Gertrude symbolises Allégret), not as his central thesis or conclusion (Pruner 1964:26).
3. Gide openly states in his *Journal* that he often split himself in two in order to play out opposing tendencies under the cover of imaginary characters: 'I spent my entire youth pitting against each other within me two aspects of myself which perhaps were asking only to get along. Through love of combat I would invent battles and split my own nature' (Gide 1893 [pub. 1948]:42). J.C. Davies comments on this process:

> Gide, who was well aware of this phenomenon occurring within himself, likened it to Aristotle's purging of the passions. The process has been well described by him. Should one particular tendency in the author's mind become a troublesome obsession, the remedy is simple: isolate the tendency, attribute it to a character of a work of fiction, and watch it grow to alarming proportions. (Davies 1968:16)

4. Charles O'Keefe, for example, writes: 'Gertrude has been found to be the fictional/emotional substitute for Marc vis-à-vis Amélie/Madeleine in Gide's attempt at narrative self-exploration, while Jacques clearly evokes Marc physically' (O'Keefe 1996:206).
5. Cf. Lebras 1989:262-3 for further development of the pastor as Adam.
6. Even Emily Apter's otherwise brilliant book implicitly relies on this outmoded psychoanalytic causal relation between narcissism and homoeroticism:

> [Adam's] obsession with a male 'other', simultaneously alike (the same sex) yet different (the effect of alienation from one's own image) also suggests a form of autoeroticism which doubles as homoeroticism.
>
> This paradigm is implicit in the psychosexual definition of Narcissism as a complex that describes both onanism and homosexuality. Displacing his fixation on his own phallus to the phallus of other men, the Narcissist seeks to satisfy his desire for self-as-other. (Apter 1987:30)

Bibliography

Apter, E.S. (1987) *André Gide and the Codes of Homotextuality* (Saratoga, Calif: Amna Libri).
Davies, J.C. (1968) *Gide:* L'Immoraliste *and* La Porte étroite (London: Edward Arnold).
Delay, J. (1956) *La Jeunesse d'André Gide* (Paris: Gallimard).
Gay, P. (1995) *The Freud Reader* (New York: Norton).
Gide, A. (1925) *La Symphonie pastorale* (Paris: Gallimard).

—— (1930) *Le Retour de l'enfant prodigue* (Paris: NRF).
—— (1948) *Journal* (Paris: Gallimard (Pléiade)).
Goulet, A. (1988) 'L'Ironie pastorale en jeu', in *Bulletin des Amis d'André Gide*, 21:41–57.
Kaplan, C. (1987) 'Ironic Landscapes: Narcissistic Optics in Gide's *La Symphonie pastorale*', in *West Virginia University Philological Papers* 33:23–30.
Lebras, Y. (1989) 'L'Ecriture versus écriture: L'Intertextualité dans *La Symphonie pastorale*', in *Bulletin des Amis d'André Gide* 22:259–65.
Lucey, M. (1995) *Gide's Bent* (New York and Oxford: Oxford University Press).
O'Keefe, C. (1996) *Void and Voice: Questioning Narrative Conventions in André Gide's Major First-Person Narratives* (Chapel Hill: University of N. Carolina Press).
Parnell, C. (1951) 'André Gide and his *Symphonie pastorale*', in *Yale French Studies* 7:60–71.
Pruner, F. (1964) '*La Symphonie pastorale* de Gide: de la tragédie vécue à la tragédie écrite', in *Archives des Lettres Modernes* 54:1–32.

Chapter 12

Reading the Glass: Fictive Solutions to the Narcissistic Quandary in Freud and Yeats

Gregory N. Eaves

I

My context, the text that brings together the two texts that will be my focus, is an introduction written by the Yale critic Harold Bloom for a collection of essays about William Butler Yeats.[1] In it Bloom worries about an age-old question for literary scholars with an interest in psychoanalytic discourse: the implications of Freud for the analysis of the literary text. In this case, the issue is refined somewhat; Bloom, a Freudian and a Romantic scholar, considers Freud's formulation of his theory of narcissism as it is applied to Hoffmann's tale 'The Sandman' in a famous essay entitled 'The "Uncanny"'.[2] Bloom's introduction to *Yeats* identifies the uncanny with the Yeatsian experience of 'daemonic' forces within the self and with the transformative powers attributed by Romantic poets to the Imagination. But here I shall allow Bloom to voice his disquiet in his own words:

> The central formula of Coleridgean Romanticism, of which Yeats, Stevens, Hart Crane may have been the last Sublime representatives, is 'the power of the mind over the universe of death', in which the mind's power means the Imagination, and

the universe of death means all of the object-world. This formula, Freud is telling us, is only a survival, a trace retained from the repression of an earlier narcissism. (*Bloom*, 4)

In his essay Freud compares the early narcissistic stage of the self to the practice of animism in 'primitive' cultures in these terms:

> Our analysis of instances of the uncanny has led us back to the old animistic conception of the universe, which was characterised by the idea that the world was peopled with the spirits of human beings, and by the narcissistic overestimation of subjective mental processes ... [Here Freud instances the practice of magic] as well as by all those other figments of the imagination with which man, in the unrestricted narcissism of that stage of development, strove to withstand the inexorable laws of reality. (*Uncanny*, 46)

II

If I turn now to a well-known poem by Yeats and one strategic for his mature visionary poetics, 'Ego Dominus Tuus', it will be apparent just how closely Freud's account of animism/narcissism fits a poetic text in the Romantic tradition, and just how well founded Bloom's anxiety appears to be.[3] Of the two speakers in this dialogue, 'Ille' is normally taken to represent the mature Yeats, who addresses in 'Hic' a representative of a late nineteenth-century aestheticist style of poetry from which Ille is distancing himself. Ille's poetic strategy is openly magical. In their opening exchange, Hic sounds almost like Freud in his disparaging comments:

> On the grey sand beside the shallow stream
> ....
> .... you walk in the moon,
> And .... still trace,
> Enthralled by the unconquerable delusion,
> Magical shapes.
> *Ille.*   By the help of an image
> I call to my own opposite, summon all
> That I have handled least, least looked upon.
> (*VP*, 367)

The text traced in the sand is performative, intended magically to summon into presence a mysterious, hidden aspect of the self. Surely this presents an instance of the very 'overestimation of subjective mental processes' that Freud associates with narcissism; in such a text Bloom's worst fears would appear to be born out, namely, that in his essay on the uncanny Freud 'is destroying the whole enterprise of literary Romanticism' (*Bloom*, 4).

III

To defend Yeats's specular strategy against Freud's rather dismissive treatment of animism and primitive magic and, thereby, to allay the fears of a Bloom, it will be necessary to look more closely at Freud's theoretical strategies of the time. Part III of *Totem and Taboo*, published a year before 'The "Uncanny"', is entitled 'Animism, Magic and the Omnipotence of Thoughts' and clarifies and systematises several of the more ominous – ominous for Yeats and Bloom, that is – conceptual connections proposed in the essay.[4] In fact, the two texts are in this regard considered complementary. Predictably, given the genetic predisposition of psychoanalysis, Freud locates narcissism at the archaic stage in an evolutionary narrative of the self; as elsewhere in Freudian texts, there is a parallel narrative wherein phylogeny (cultural development) recapitulates ontogeny (personal development). Thus narcissism in the individual corresponds to animism and magic in human history:

> The animistic phase would correspond to narcissism both chronologically and in content; the religious phase would correspond to the stage of object-choice ... ; while the scientific phase would have an exact counterpart in the stage at which an individual has reached maturity, has renounced the pleasure principle [and] adjusted himself to reality. (*Totem*, 90)

Within the phylogenetic strand of this tripartite narrative Freud also establishes a distinction between two types of discourse; to the discourse of science, located at the mature, realistic end of the sequence, there corresponds another, originating at the archaic, animistic end. Referred to at first as 'myth' and associated with magical practices, this discourse survives, like narcissism in the personal psyche:

> In only a single field of our civilisation has the omnipotence of thoughts been retained, and that is in the field of art. Only in art does it still happen that a man who is consumed by desires performs something resembling the accomplishment of those desires and that what he does in play produces emotional

effects – thanks to artistic illusion – just as though it were something real. (*Totem*, 90)

In referring to art's illusory effects, whereby the mental or ideal is confused with the real, Freud is identifying it as fictive; his own discourse, in contrast, maintains a strict distinction between the ideal and the real, between psychic and external realities. In this binary opposition between the fictive and the analytic the latter, Freud's own discourse, is, by virtue of the narrative linking them, the privileged term. But how effectively will its senior position in the narrative series protect the analytic distinctions between ideal and real on which it depends from fiction's propensity to confuse the two?

His tripartite account of human cultural history (animistic-religious-scientific) Freud introduces out of the blue, as it were, attributing it to 'the authorities' (*Totem*, 77). It may be obvious whom he means; the idea is familiar and elsewhere he nods in the direction of Herbert Spencer, J.G. Frazer and others (*Totem*, 75 n.1). Still, when one considers not only the self-evident authoritativeness but the self-serving nature of this narrative for the authority of Freud's own investigations and pronouncements, it is tempting to take the said narrative as a necessary myth of psychoanalysis. Just as the individual psyche has matured beyond the distortions of the narcissistic stage and into a position of adjustment to the 'reality' of the 'external world'; so the scientific phase, which advocates the very renunciation of the pleasure for the reality principle so central to Freud's theories and analyses, holds pride of place over the 'archaic' animistic phase. The teleology is apparent; and this, in an argument that identifies mythopoeia with animistic consciousness (*Totem*, 77). If it seems surprising that such mythic propensities should surface in a scientific treatise, perhaps a partial explanation may be found in Freud's own words: for if 'primitive' animistic states of mind are capable of surviving alongside the 'mature' consciousness, 'latent but capable of reappearing' (*Totem*, 93), then by analogy an equivalent archaic pattern of discourse may underlie and even subvert that of science and, indeed, psychoanalysis.

Freud's model narrative allows, then, for survivals of its own archaic past; indeed, relying on his analogy with personal psychic development, one might call such survivals the unconscious of scientific discourse. So that, for all the orderliness and the exclusive categories of the critique of omnipotence of thought in *Totem and Taboo*, and despite the attempt to secure by narrative means the supersession of the narcissistic/animistic phase, there remains the threat of contamination of the superior by the inferior discourse. In Freudian analysis such a surfacing of the hidden would advertise itself as symptom – in this case, anxiety on the part of the narrator. But this would reduplicate the very experience of anxiety one is led to expect the analyst to take for his/her object in an essay on the uncanny. It would certainly fit Freud's own description of the uncanny: 'something familiar and old-established in the mind that has been estranged only in the process of repression' (*Uncanny*, 47); and again, 'as soon as something actually happens in our lives which seems to support the old, discarded beliefs, we get a feeling of the uncanny' (*ibid.*, 54).

What one might expect of Freud's essay is an objective Freudian analysis of the uncanny; what one finds instead is an essay displaying itself many of the signs of the uncanny. Here, since they are relatively familiar and well established, I allude in passing to the findings of post-structuralist readings of 'The "Uncanny"' by such as Hélène Cixous (1976), Neil Hertz (1980), Samuel Weber (1973) and Rosemary Jackson (1981).[5] Each critic addresses the implications of Freud's interweaving of his discourse with the text of Hoffman's fantasy 'The Sandman', pointing out that, on the one hand, Hoffman tends as a result to become Freud's own uncanny double and that, on the other, Freud rewrites Hoffman's fantasy in such a way as to minimise the significance of what was, according to Freud's acknowledged predecessor Jentsch, its theme of 'intellectual uncertainty'.[6] Indeed, discussion of the motif of the mechanical doll Olympia, emblem of the intersection of the real and the fictional and key instance of the broader motif of the double, is in Freud's essay relegated to footnote status – what Cixous refers to as 'a typographical metaphor of repression' (1976:537).

In the encounter between fantastic and scientific discourse the latter appears unable to distinguish itself adequately. That, at any rate, would seem to account for the repetitions, labyrinthine contortions and 'theoretical hesitations' such critics have found in Freud's essay (Cixous 1976:525, 545). It is as if Freud in his scientific coat were all too aware of the seductive appeal of fiction and fantasy and, with the backing of a supposedly secure theoretical apparatus in *Totem and Taboo*, ventured to translate literary into scientific discourse, symbol into symptom, thereby obliging the archaic to submit, belatedly, to the reality principle. After all, is this not the very claim that Bloom makes on Freud's behalf in the introduction to *Yeats*?

Yet translation turns out to be an ambivalent strategy. The closer one looks at Freud on the uncanny, on narcissism and on the omnipotence of thoughts, the more it appears that his strategy is defensive, aiming at the containment of fantasy and at its exclusion from the epistemologically safe ground of 'reality' and scientific truths. For instance, to a reader examining the introduction to Freud's essay, there seems little enough occasion to justify the scientist's foray into the alien realm of the aesthetic; in fact, the essayist disclaims any recent personal acquaintance with the uncanny and, man of reason that he is, must rely on Hoffman to 'translate' him into the appropriate frame of mind. Surely, Freud's denial is excessive and telling. His discourse in the essay, far from translating fantasy into science, proves all too vulnerable to translation by Hoffmann. As a result, the essay on 'The "Uncanny"' mediates ambiguously – or should I say uncannily – between Hoffmann's fantasy and the theory of *Totem and Taboo*, finding its textual double on either side.

IV

Something is jeopardising the ability of Freud's discourse to maintain the basic distinctions on which it depends, including the distinction between itself and fiction or fantasy. I have hinted that the evolutionary narrative that corroborates the superiority of scientific theory may be to blame; rather than keeping the threatening discourse of fiction at arm's length, it brings the latter into sequential relationship with its own, supposedly distinct, discursive position. In so doing, Freudian discourse writes its way into the interstices between science and fantasy. Surprisingly, if we now look at the discursive strategy organising Yeats's 'Ego Dominus Tuus', we will find a remarkably similar pattern emerging.

In the first place, Yeats's poem, while openly fictive, strives not to be narcissistic in the Ovidian sense. Ille, the poet's mouthpiece, announces early on his purpose of avoiding the trap of solipsism, which he associates with an outworn nineteenth-century aesthetic:

> By the help of an image
> I call to my own opposite, summon all
> That I have handled least, least looked upon.
> *Hic.* And I would find myself and not an image.
> *Ille.* That is our modern hope, and by its light

> We have lit upon the gentle, sensitive mind
> And lost the old nonchalance of the hand.
>
> (*VP*, 367–8)

Instead, using a procedure which Yeats elsewhere calls 'evocation', Ille summons 'the mysterious one' who is his 'double' and 'anti-self' by tracing 'magical shapes' in the wet sand.

For the purposes of this discussion I need not dwell on the broader significance for Yeatsian poetics of this mysterious other, except to add that he or she is 'daimonic' and represents the hidden, spiritual aspect of the self. (Bloom himself assimilates Yeats's daimon to Freudian discourse by equating the daimonic with the unconscious.)[7] Of some pertinence to the reflection/doubling theme of this colloquium is the position of 'Ego Dominus Tuus' in the Yeatsian oeuvre. It represents the earliest explicit programmatic statement of the antithetical poetics of Yeats's infamous Symbolic System, constructed around the twenty-eight phases of the lunar cycle. As such, the poem anticipates an array of textual (and often geometrical) doublings and reflections that align Yeatsian discourse with the specular strategies of the alchemical and hermetic traditions. Beyond this point I merely invite the reader to browse among the complexities of *A Vision* and the spiralling scholarship it has provoked.[8]

Of greater consequence for my discussion pairing Yeats and Freud is the strategic use of the trope of mirroring implicit in 'Ego Dominus Tuus'. In the poem the anti-self is the mirror image of Ille, or the self; it is explicitly 'an image' and an inversion, both 'alike' and 'my opposite'. Conspicuously, the mirror on which this reflection depends, instead of being invisible or neutral and taken for granted, is made active, poetic. Since the anti-self or other is not the identical self-image ('Iste ego sum') of Ovid's narrative but is instead concealed, mysterious, he, she or it will have to be summoned in a magical ritual: the tracing of what the speaker calls 'magical shapes' or 'characters' in the sand. 'By the help of an image' he calls to his own opposite, itself an image.[9] In so doing, Ille anticipates that this opposite will then, 'standing by these characters, disclose / All that I seek'. The anti-self will, in other words, interpret or translate and thus complete Ille's own text for him, providing a corresponding double for his magical script.[10] There appear to be two sets of corresponding doubles here, a personal and textual pair; or, rather, one might say that the distinction between writer and text is being erased.

Ille himself is a fictional character in a poetic text. To this extent the characters in the sand duplicate the Yeatsian poetic text, which itself serves a similar evocative purpose: to summon the poet's hidden self into creative, that is, poetic, interaction. Yeats is doubling Ille's reflexive rhetoric in announcing simultaneously his own, 'antithetical', poetic strategy. The poetic text is thus reflexive through and through and is written in such a way as to draw attention to the trope of the mirror on which its own structure depends. As before, the mirror is the text and the text mirrors: within the confines of the poem, the text inscribed in the sand acts as mirror in bringing into reflexive alignment Ille and his anti-self; and the poetic text that is 'Ego Dominus Tuus' both duplicates that mirroring activity on behalf of the poet himself and, moving onto a further level, promises to bring into alignment text (Ille's script and the poet's own) and meaning (what the anti-self will in each case disclose), occult script and translation, for all the world as if the unified Saussurian sign, signifier matched with signified, were in prospect. Such metaphysical closure is, inevitably, promised only to be deferred, a foregone inconclusion. Nevertheless, the textual strategy itself is rendered quite explicit.

Here, as elsewhere in Yeats's later works, the mirror takes up two complementary positions in the structure of the text: its overall activity shaping the discourse locates it in a *circumferential* or encompassing position (the promise of the completed sign); and its *intervention between* the two opposing selves or texts locates it in an interstitial position, at their hinge or virtual point of contact (the reflexive alignment of mirror images or opposites).[11]

Before turning back to Freud, I should like to point out that, despite the geometry of the diagram I have just drawn of Yeats's mirror, the figural strategy referred to is not complete or self-contained (narcissistic); the written text stops with the interstitial mirror, and the antithetical image remains as yet hidden, other. Unlike that of Narcissus, this mirror does not erase difference. It stands in for an absent presence and thus behaves as would any text.

V

Juxtaposed with the specular poetic strategy at work in 'Ego Dominus Tuus', Freud's perplexities in his essay will, I hope, be more readily explained. I am suggesting that his discussion succumbs to an involuntary mirror structure of a similar kind, one that occurs in the very passage quoted by Bloom in my first citation. There Freud distinguishes between the two opposed terms in his analysis: 'figments of the imagination' (associated with the 'narcissistic overestimation of subjective mental processes'), which 'strive to withstand the inexorable laws of reality', to which Freud as a scientist is loyal (*Uncanny*, 46). The binarism opposes antagonistic discourses: 'figments', on the one hand, confront 'laws' on the other, as the omnipotence of thought contends with the reality principle. An additional pair of inverse characteristics displays the unsuspected symmetry and reflexiveness built into Freud's schematism: the error to which, according to him, the omnipotence of thought is prone consists of mistaking the mental for the real or subjective for external reality; to this psychoanalysis counterposes a corrective strategy that reverses the process:

> owing to the projection outwards of internal perceptions, primitive men arrived at a picture of the external world which we ... have now to translate back into psychology. (*Totem*, 64)

Thus psychoanalysis might be said to find its own inverse image in the discourse of narcissism.

This tidy binarism assumes that Freudian discourse, such as the essay in question, may be located within the discourse of reality. Yet one struggles to locate an essay such as 'The "Uncanny"' alongside what Freud refers to as the 'laws of reality'. As I have suggested above, not only does the essay rely upon narrative and analogy, it interweaves itself with a fantastic narrative, thereby bringing into question the boundary isolating science and reality from figments of the imagination; the essay's own introduction admits as much. In addition, the essay does justice to its topic, the uncanny or the 'effacing [of] the distinction between imagination and reality', by displaying signs of the uncanny in its own textual idiosyncrasies (*Uncanny*, 50).

In fact, of course, the entire schema in *Totem and Taboo* opposing narcissism or imagination to science is a Freudian construct, so designed as to guarantee the mastery of his own discourse. But, rather than keeping the two opposed textual kinds distinct, Freud's account with its developmental narrative brings them into relation. His text can, therefore, coincide with neither but stands in an encompassing or *circumferential* relationship to both. Equally, the essay on 'The "Uncanny"' may be said to *intervene between* the two; like Yeats's poem, it enacts the role of mirror, summoning into presence the hidden, in this case all that hides behind that word 'uncanny'; and, as it happens, this hidden turns out to be the repressed narcissism of the self. Not Freud's self, mind you; after all, he had not experienced the uncanny in ages and had had to be reminded by Hoffman.

VI

Freud and Yeats are, thus and surprisingly, alike for once in their reliance on specular strategies to articulate the hidden or unconscious aspects of the self. Freud, though, in his determination to avoid 'intellectual uncertainty' – that is, by insisting on the distinction separating his discourse from the errors of magic, fiction and the imagination – conceals from himself the reflexivity built into his essay 'The "Uncanny"'.[12] Yeats, on the other hand, is deliberately fictive in his approach to poetic knowledge and has no trouble acknowledging the specular role of the written text in the articulation of the other. In any case, Harold Bloom's anxiety about the threat posed by Freud's essay to the literature of the imagination appears to have been misplaced; on the contrary, courtesy of Hoffmann's tale, the threat rebounds on Freud's own text.

Notes

1. Harold Bloom 1986:1–22. In-text citations will refer to this text as *Bloom*.
2. The edition of Freud's 'The "Uncanny"' I have used appears in Rieff 1963:19–60. In-text citations will refer to this text as *Uncanny*.
3. Allt and Alspach 1940:367–71. In-text citations will refer to this text as *VP*.
4. Freud 1955. In-text citations will refer to this text as *Totem*. This text and the essay on 'The "Uncanny"' cross-reference each other; see *Totem and Taboo*:86, n.2 and 'The "Uncanny"':46, n.19.
5. Jackson provides a useful discussion of Cixous's argument (1981:67–70).
6. E. Jentsch claims that 'intellectual uncertainty' is the characteristic source of the uncanny. Freud, however, takes pains to discredit his rival's treatment of the uncanny along such lines, dismissing his thesis as 'irrelevant' (*Uncanny*, 35; see also 20–1, 31 and 37). Freud's teleological narrative assumes an intellectual certainty that is its own *terminus ad quem* and his analysis of the essay is accordingly suspicious of any potential blurring of the distinction between fiction and reality.
7. Bloom, in the introductory essay already quoted, applies to Yeats the observations of the classical scholar E.R. Dodds on the Greek daimon (*Bloom*, 3).

8. A good place to start might be the annotated Harper and Hood (1978). To whet the appetite, it may be pointed out that Yeats's main diagram of the lunar cycle is given the mock-alchemical title of *speculum angelorum et hominorum* [sic] (*ibid.*, xix).
9. This metonymic series is typical of reflexive writing in Yeats as elsewhere: 'Mirror upon mirror mirrored is all the show' is how the poet puts it in 'The Statues' (*VP*, 610). One thinks also perhaps of the *mise en abyme* structure.
10. Further, Ille's text and his anti-self's disclosures stand in the relationship of signifier to signified and together complete the sign; whose completion is, as ever, deferred.
11. This pairing of functions, circumference and hinge, applies also to the Great Wheel (of the lunar phases) in *A Vision* and, further back, to its most obvious antecedents, such as the *specula* in the works of Jakob Boehme. (See, for instance, the 'Looking Glass of Wisdom' from Boehme's *XL Questions Concerning the Soule*, English edition, 1647.) For the concept of text as hinge I am indebted to Jacques Derrida's discussion of folds in Mallarmé (1981:209ff).
12. To the 'intellectual uncertainty' Jentsch diagnosed as the theme of 'The Sandman' corresponds the intellectual certainty Freud is aiming at. Such certainty depends (1) upon the two sides of the binarism remaining distinct and (2) upon the reality side retaining the privilege, being able to rewrite the other in its own image. But these two requirements are contradictory; for a perfect binarism would seem to depend upon narcissism's having been written as reality's exact inverse. In this case the trope of mirroring may be seen to get the better of a text that seeks to gain rhetorical advantage by incorporating its own antithesis or double, the literary text by Hoffmann.

Bibliography

Allt, P. and R.K. Alspach (eds) (1940) *The Variorum Edition of the Poems of W.B. Yeats* (New York: MacMillan).

Bloom, H. (ed.) (1986) *Yeats* (New York: Chelsea House).

Boehme, J. (1647) 'Looking Glass of Wisdom', in *XL Questions Concerning the Soule*.

Cixous, H. (1976) 'Fiction and Its Phantoms: A Reading of Freud's Das Unheimliche', in *New Literary History* 7:525–48.

Derrida, J. (1981) 'The Double Session', in *The Margins of Philosophy* (Chicago: University of Chicago Press).

Freud, S. (1955) 'Animism, Magic and the Omnipotence of Thoughts', in *Totem and Taboo*. In *The Standard Edition of the Complete Psychological Works of Sigmund Freud* 13 (London: Hogarth Press) 75–99.

Harari, J.V. (ed.) (1980) *Textual Strategies: Perspectives in Post-structuralist Criticism* (Ithaca, NY: Cornell University Press).

Harper, G.M. and W.K. Hood (1978) *A Critical Edition of Yeats's A Vision (1925)* (London: Macmillan).

Hertz, N. (1980) 'Freud and the Sandman', in Harari 1980:296–321.

Jackson, R. (1981) *Fantasy: The Literature of Subversion* (London: Routledge).

Rieff, P. (ed.) (1963) *Studies in Parapsychology* (New York: Collier).
Weber, S. (1973) 'The Sideshow, or: Remarks on a Canny Moment', in *MLN* 88:1,102–33.

≈ CHAPTER 13 ≈

'THE IDIOSYNCRATIC MODE OF REGARD': NARCISSISTIC NARRATIVE IN THE FICTION OF THOMAS HARDY

Roger Webster

Reading the story of Narcissus in Ovid's *Metamorphoses*, I was struck by its openness as a narrative: it offers a range of reading possibilities, constructed as it is around oppositions, dualisms and ambiguities, and of course, the potential for metamorphosis or transformation. Perhaps, though, the more popular associations of Narcissus with self-absorption and melancholia need a corrective. This is not to disregard the complex applications of the myth in the sphere of psychoanalytical theory from Freud onwards, which develop, in particular, issues of sexuality, gender and character both 'real' and 'literary'. Indeed, few narratives have provided such a dialogue across literary history and so many re-inscriptions. It is this dialogic dimension and palimpsest feature, combined with the potential for transformation, especially with its emphasis on visual perception, that I want to explore with reference to Thomas Hardy's fictional technique. In particular, I want to draw on the themes of imaging or imagining and representation, which seem to be strongly encoded in the myth: on the one hand a kind of mimetic duplication or verisimilitude in the repetition of Echo's responses and the mirroring or self-reflexivity of Narcissus, with its associations of stasis and closure, and yet on the other a set of quite disruptive and potentially transforming images, which go beyond the conventional associations of narcissism.

I would suggest that the forms of representation which predominate in Hardy's fictional technique, especially in his later novels, move away from the conventions of nineteenth-century realism.[1] In some of the more general formal characteristics of Hardy's fiction, several features foreground the kind of self-consciousness and self-reflexivity which, I would argue, anticipate modernism and more experimental narrative techniques. Hardy's fictional method offers a radical alternative to the conventions of realism or the ratiocinative formalism of Henry James.[2] In particular, it is his interest in visual perception and representation, allied to distorted and metamorphosing perspectives, which he termed 'the idiosyncratic mode of regard'. What Jean Ricardou (1973) terms the 'representative illusionism' of Balzac is replaced by a more experimental, poetic and subversive fiction that anticipates modernism and its *mise en abyme* techniques and which can be termed narcissistic in its self-reflexive qualities.

I would suggest that Hardy's work offers an extraordinarily rich reading when aligned with what could be termed narcissistic interpretative apparatus. For example, from a biographical perspective, his repeated infatuation with women who reminded him of his mother and his self-conscious treatment of this in his final novel, *The Well-Beloved* (1897) suggest, in Freudian terms, narcissistic injuries in youth. Hardy liked to repeat a story that he was deemed dead at birth and thrown into a basket so that the surgeon could attend to his mother, until the midwife exclaimed 'Dead! Stop a minute; he's alive enough, sure!' As a child he was sickly, his parents tended to neglect him, believing he would die young, and of course his prolonged bouts of depression and tendency to morbidity in outlook are well documented, not least by Hardy himself in his notebooks. The general tenor of these could be characterised by what might be deemed narcissistic preoccupations; the abiding image of Hardy in his later years, ensconced in his study at Max Gate, neglecting his second wife Florence and becoming increasingly obsessed with his first wife Emma, has had a profound effect on numerous readings of Hardy.

Much mainstream twentieth-century criticism has attempted to insert his work into the paradigm, or perhaps symbolic order, of realism, to organicise or apply inappropriate criteria to his writing – which indeed Hardy's narratives resist.[3] Hardy was quite self-conscious about his fiction in his critical writings and notebooks, particularly three essays which have received relatively little attention, *The Profitable Reading of Fiction* (1888), *Candour in English Fiction* (1890) and *The Science of Fiction* (1891).[4] His interest in the act of reading, combined with a shift away from the author and unitary authority to a more subjective, relativistic view of the role of the reader, bring him much closer to twentieth-century approaches, not only to more recent reader- and reception-orientated theories, but also to Proust's essay *Against St. Beuve*.[5]

The act of reading has of course been identified as a potentially narcissistic preoccupation by Bakhtin in *The Dialogic Imagination*: 'we might substitute for our own life an obsessive reading of novels, or dreams based on novelistic models'. Hardy in *The Profitable Reading of Fiction* anticipates the active participation of the reader in the interpretative process in ways which bring him closer to Roland Barthes than F.R. Leavis:

> The aim should be the exercise of a generous imaginativeness, which shall find in a tale not only all that was put there by the author ... but which shall find there what was never inserted by him, never foreseen, never contemplated. Sometimes these additions which are woven around a work of fiction by the intensive power of the reader's own imagination are the finest parts of the scenery. (Widdowson 1997:243)

Hardy's interest in the term 'palimpsest' and his view of the writing of novels, are exemplified in the following notebook entry, dated 1889: 'What has been written cannot be blotted. Each new style of novel must be the old with added ideas, not an ignoring and avoidance of the old' (F.E. Hardy 1962:218). His ideas might also be applied to the reading process, in anticipation of reception theory, and can be seen as a narcissistic, self-conscious or reflexive feature. Indeed Marcel Proust identified them as such at the point in *À la recherche du temps perdu* where Marcel explains to Albertine (1920) that a great writer or artist creates the same work over and over throughout his life:

> I returned to Thomas Hardy's stone masons. 'You remember well enough in *Jude the Obscure*, you must have seen in *The Well-Beloved*, the blocks of stone that the father quarried on the island coming by boat and piling up in the son's workshop, where they become statues; in *A Pair of Blue Eyes*, the parallelism of the tombs and also the parallel line of the boat, and

the wagons alongside, where the two lovers are, and the dead woman; the parallelism between *The Well-Beloved* where the man loves three women, *A Pair of Blue Eyes*, where the woman loves three men, etcetera, all those novels that can be superimposed on each other, like the houses piled vertically up on the stony ground of the island? (Proust 1954:376-7)

I now want to explore some scenes and narrative features in Hardy's novels which might be described as narcissistic, and how these break with the conventions of classic realism. A pronounced feature of Hardy's fictional method is that moments of heightened perception in the narrative – in particular characters' self-perceptions – tend to have a strongly visual and even painterly dimension. In some cases such scenes are represented in strongly visualised descriptions – for example in the early novel, *A Pair of Blue Eyes* (1873), the scene in which the central character Knight, having fallen over a cliff edge, clings perilously to a branch and, whilst confronting the prospect of death, finds himself looking at a fossil embedded in the cliff:

By one of those familiar conjunctions of things wherewith the inanimate world baits the mind of man when he pauses in moments of suspense, opposite Knight's eyes was an embedded fossil, standing forth in low relief from the rock. It was a creature with eyes. The eyes, dead and turned to stone, were even now regarding him. It was one of those early crustaceans called Trilobites. Separated by millions of years in their lives, Knight and this underling seemed to have met their place of death. It was the single instance within his reach of vision of anything that had ever been alive and had had a body to save, as he himself had now. (Hardy 1975:240)

What follows is a sketch of evolutionary development which rushes through Knight's mind from primitive man back to the fossil. Knight had fallen over the cliff in pursuit of the hat belonging to Elfride Swancourt, the novel's heroine, which had blown over the cliff, and he is rescued by her underwear, which with some ingenuity she turns into a rope. The significant features of the episode are its remarkable variations, shifts and modulations in language and mood, from the potentially tragic and impending death to the trivial and comic, from the instant to eternity, from the microcosmic to the macrocosmic, from high seriousness and evolutionary science to bathos and the carnivalesque. The episode also makes little pretence to surface realism or verisimilitude, verging rather on the fantastic or the imaginary; my point here is that this kind of writing refuses to conform to the conventions of the kind of unitary language associated with classic realism, but rather displays the kinds of qualities which bring it closer to Bakhtin's notions of dialogism and heteroglosssia: the layering of discourses, the contradictory shifts in tone and mood and resistance to a singular, unified reading.

Knight certainly constitutes Bakhtin's concept of the subject located in history, a subject over whom the conflictual processes of language ebb and flow and for whom there is ultimately no neat resolution. As his parodic name suggests, his moves in the novel are oblique and the kind of symmetry that Proust identifies is a kind of parodic, arbitrary organisation closer to modernism than any unifying essentialism or metaphysic which might be associated with realism. Kristeva's term 'intertextuality', which is derived from Bakhtin's category of the dialogic, indicates that language is not a self-contained autonomous system, but dynamic, with words which 'weave in and out of complex relationships' as Bakhtin puts it. Kristeva opposes what she terms 'poetic mimesis' with 'thetic unicity'. I do not want to suggest that there is a simple binarism or opposition between realism and modernism or that these can be tied to Bakhtinian or Kristevian categories, but I would suggest that Hardy's narratives slip between the more conventional surface characteristics of realism and narcissistic features which are quite subversive or radical departures from these. And, as we have seen, I would further suggest that Hardy was well aware of the limits and constraints of what he termed 'scientific realism' and sought alternatives to them. Such questions of technique cannot, of course, ultimately be separated from content or world view or whatever term we choose to use and, as Bakhtin clearly argues, a monologic or centripetal text will provide only a restricted, static, totalising order; in parallel Kristeva juxtaposes the semiotic with the symbolic, the former allowing for the intuitive, poetic and polysemous play of meaning to surface (derived from what she terms the 'chora') against the restrictions of the symbolic order that she develops from Lacanian theory.

In Hardy's later fiction moments of heightened or acute perception become increasingly pronounced. These can be termed moments of apperception and depart from realist concerns with diachronic temporal schemes, anticipating the modernist emphasis on synchronic time exemplified in, for example, Joyce's epiphany or Virginia Woolf's moments of vision. These are also often represented using a discourse which accentuates the visual or the painterly. Hardy's interest in the visual arts has been thoroughly researched over the last twenty years (see Webster 1979; Grundy 1979; Bullen 1986), but I would now argue that the innovative uses which visualising discourses are put to, their defamiliarising effects, are very much to do with Hardy's realisation that the conventions of realism were outmoded for the kind of poetic fiction or mimesis which he consciously strove to achieve. This, arguably, was why he forsook prose fiction for poetry after the publication of *Jude the Obscure* and *The Well-Beloved*, and also why he turned to painting as an alternative source of innovation.

Painting does provide a highly significant parallel to Hardy's narrative technique and experimentation. We have already seen his preference for representation which views things in 'half and quarter views' and, in a journal entry dated 1891, he stated, 'If I were a painter, I think I would paint a picture of a room as viewed by a mouse from a chink under the skirting' (F.E. Hardy 1962:235). The use of unusual, acute angles for viewing narrative events becomes more pronounced in his later fiction; for example, towards the end of *Tess of the d'Urbervilles* (1891), the landlady in the house where Alec and Tess are lodging views the scene immediately before Alec's murder through a keyhole; earlier, in *Far from the Madding Crowd* (1874), Gabriel Oak sees Bathsheba through a hole in the roof of a shed where she and her aunt are milking at night. At one level, this is a very obvious illustration of what Hardy meant by 'the idiosyncratic mode of regard', but I would like to develop this further. Hardy, in his notebooks and journals, talks at least as much about painters and painting as he does about literature; he was an inveterate visitor of the National and Dulwich Galleries whilst living in London and also visited galleries and exhibitions whilst in France and Italy. His knowledge of painting was wide and his interests quite eclectic; certainly he was able to draw on an impressive range of painters and paintings in intertextual allusions which figure in all his fictional narratives and, of course, his final novel's central character, Jocelyn Pierston in *The Well-Beloved* (1897), is a sculptor. Hardy's greatest interest was in William Turner's increasingly experimental style, and he makes some mention of the Impressionists, who were beginning to receive significant attention towards the end of the nineteenth century, when Hardy was working on his later fiction. In 1887, he states in his journal,

> After looking at the landscape ascribed to Bonnington in our drawing-room I feel that Nature is played out as Beauty, but not

as a Mystery. I don't want to see landscapes, *i.e.*, scenic paintings of them, because I don't want to see the original realities – as optical effects, that is. I want to see the deeper reality underlying the scenic, the expression of what are sometimes called abstract imaginings.

The 'simply natural' is interesting no longer. The much decried, mad, late-Turner rendering is now necessary to create my interest. The exact truth as to material fact ceases to be of importance in art – it is a student's style – the style of a period when the mind is serene and unawakened to the tragical mysteries of life; when it does not bring anything to the object that coalesces with and translates the qualities that are already there, – half-hidden, it may be – and the two united are depicted as the ALL. (F.E. Hardy 1962:185)

Two years later, on visiting an exhibition at the Royal Academy in London, he pronounces:

> Turner's water-colours: each is a landscape *plus* a man's soul ... What he paints chiefly is *light as modified by objects*. He first recognises the impossibility of really reproducing on canvas all that is in a landscape; then he gives for that which cannot be reproduced a something else which shall have upon the spectator an approximate effect to that of the real. ... Hence, one may say, Art is the secret of how to produce by a false thing the effect of the true. (F.E. Hardy 1962:216)

In 1906, Hardy also commented, 'I prefer late Wagner, as I prefer late Turner, to early ... the idiosyncrasies of each master being more strongly shown in these strains' (F.E. Hardy 1962:329). On Impressionism, he comments in 1886,

> The impressionist school is strong. It is even more suggestive in the direction of literature than in that of art ... their principle is, as I understand it, that what you carry away with you from a scene is the true feature to grasp; or in other words, *what appeals to your own individual eye and heart in particular* amid much that does not so appeal, and which you therefore omit to record. (F.E. Hardy 1962:184)

There are two other comments on art from his journal which are important in this respect. First, in 1890: 'Art consists in so depicting the common events of life as to bring out the features which illustrate the author's idiosyncratic mode of regard; making old incidents and things seem as new' (F.E. Hardy 1962:225). And later in the same year:

Reflections on Art. Art is a changing of the actual proportions and order of things, so as to bring out more forcibly than might otherwise be done that feature in them which appeals most strongly to the idiosyncrasy of the artist. The changing, or distortion, may be of two kinds: (1) The kind which increases the sense of vraisemblance: (2) That which diminishes it. (1) is high art: (2) is low art ... Art is a disproportioning – (*i.e.* distorting, throwing out of proportion) – of realities, to show more clearly the features that matter in those realities, which, if merely copied or reported inventorially, might possibly be observed, but would more probably be overlooked. Hence 'realism' is not Art. (F.E. Hardy 1962:228–9)

The point I want to make here is that I think there are very significant parallels between Hardy's fictional narrative method and Turner's increasingly experimental artistic techniques, and that Hardy consciously drew on Turner and the innovative art of the Impressionists to inform in particular the kind of moment which I discussed in relation to *A Pair of Blue Eyes*. To summarise briefly Turner's artistic development through to what Hardy called his 'mad, late-Turner rendering': in particular it is characterised by his abandonment of one-point perspective, the central feature of classical mimesis associated with Italian and Dutch painters of the Renaissance. This kind of unified, centralised or centripetal mode of perspective was usually accompanied with a concentration on material detail and exactitude, providing an apparently mirror-like reflection of what was taken to be reality. Turner's earlier works to a considerable extent conform to such classical traditions, but his later works shift towards highly unconventional treatments where a unified perspective is abandoned for a shifting, multiple representation, arguably centrifugal in nature, and little emphasis on verisimilitude, on the representation of material detail. Turner was the acknowledged precursor of the Impressionists and paved the way for forms of modernist painting such as Cubism and abstraction. I would like to extend the Turner/Hardy parallel in that they both pushed to the limits the parameters of classical realism in painting and prose fiction, anticipating the formal paradigm shift or ruptures which led to modernism. What characterises both their work, as Hardy recognises, is not mimetic duplication but divergence, variation or 'disproportioning' as Hardy puts it. Technique or form are of course not separate from content and moral or world vision, and though I cannot argue the case fully here, I would suggest that Hardy's and Turner's shifts in artistic method are linked to a much more fundamental epistemological shift, away from a symbolically unified, causally linked and unitary universe, where all is ultimately clear and palpable, whether in metaphysical or rational and scientific terms, towards a world which is increasingly represented as having no totalising, coherent, causally linked possibilities. I would argue that Hardy and Turner are at the intersection, the borderland between these opposed paradigms.

I would like to conclude by discussing briefly a scene in Hardy's penultimate novel, *Jude the Obscure*. Significantly, the scene involves a mirror; Hardy had previously used mirrors, for example in *Far from the Madding Crowd*, where Gabriel Oak's first sight of Bathsheba Everdene is of her studying herself in a mirror. Bathsheba is in several respects a narcissistic character, and Hardy would certainly have seen Jan van Eyck's painting, acquired by the National Gallery in 1842, of the betrothal of Giovanni Arnolfini and Giovanna Cenami, in which a mirror is placed in the centre background which supposedly reflects the figure of the artist. The scene in *Jude* is at the point in the novel when Jude, thinking his wife Arabella has emigrated to Australia, suddenly recognises her as the barmaid in the tavern he has gone to drown his sorrows in, ironically the same tavern in which, as an idealistic younger man and aspiring student, he had responded to a challenge from Christminster students to recite the Creed in Latin. The chapter finds Jude in a state of moral and mental fragmentation. His Aunt Drusilla, whom he has just visited, is facing a lingering death, Sue Bridehead has deserted him and he is working as a casual stonemason, ironically patching up the fabric of the very structures which have denied him access to university and the church. The scene, I want to argue, bears striking similarities to Edouard Manet's last major work, painted in 1881, *Un bar aux Folies-Bergères*. Although this source of direct influence must remain speculative for lack of conclusive evidence, it is very likely that Hardy saw the painting, as it was frequently exhibited at the Salon in Paris which Hardy visited; we know that Hardy possessed a remarkable visual memory and, although he visited the Salon in the 1880s where the painting was exhibited from 1882 to 1900, he would certainly have recollected it accurately some ten years later. There are obvious striking similarities: the physical appearance of the barmaid in Manet's painting could well pass for Arabella: both are dressed in black and white and wear flowers on their bosoms; the colours of the liqueurs are similar. Without considering Manet's painting in detail, the significant features are the complex visual relations: what is reflected in the mirror and what is not? Does the mirror reveal more indirectly than the unreflected perspective? Who is the man apparently reflected in the mirror? Manet was working from within the conventions of realist painting, but pushing them to their limits with this work; as with Turner, the unitary perspective of the viewer is dislocated and problematised and there is of course a self-reflexive dimension, which raises fundamental questions about realism and representation.

In the passage in *Jude the Obscure* the mirroring device is used to reveal Arabella's identity to Jude in ways which confirm her duplicity: Jude observes her flirting with a young man and telling him that she left her husband, in other words Jude himself, behind in Australia. The innovative use of perspective and narrative point of view reveal that Arabella's reflection is in a sense her true self, though her true self is multiple, fragmented and fractured: she is for this reason a character much better equipped to survive than Jude. This is also a culminating point in the use of visual perspective in the novel. In the first chapter Jude gazes down a well in the village where he was a child: 'The well into which he was looking was as ancient as the village itself, and from his present position appeared as a long circular perspective ending in a shining disc of quivering water at a distance of a hundred feet down'. Jude's vision becomes increasingly chimerical as the novel progresses, the lights of Christminster in particular offering an illusory vision; like Narcissus he is mesmerised by the unobtainable. Manet's painting has been described as a defining moment in Parisian culture in representing the relationship between production and consumption: the activity presented in the mirror reveals a world of the commodification and transaction of desire which parallels the scene which Jude observes in the mirror, a scene in which Jude recognises and both knows Arabella for what she is and gains some self-knowledge in the process. The mirror offers no literal mimesis, but a complex interplay of distorted perspectives which resists any attempt to unify or organicise, in much the same way that *Jude the Obscure* will not coalesce into the kind of resolution which some of Hardy's earlier fiction achieves.

The use of the mirror device foregrounds the defamiliarising techniques of Hardy's fiction, especially his later works, in which the ambivalence and binarism surrounding the myth of Narcissus provide a helpful correlative. In Lacanian and Kristevian terms, the images reflected back in *Un Bar aux Folies-*

Bergères and *Jude the Obscure* are not a narcissistic reinforcement of the subject, not a unified or unitary image, but rather a fracturing and transforming process, an idiosyncratic mode of regard, offering visual and narrative distortions or 'disproportionings' rather than reflections, all of which problematise the subject, the social and historical forces which frame the subject, and the construction of art itself.

Notes

1. Whilst not wanting to pursue the problematics of nineteenth-century 'classic realism' here, the genre needs to be addressed, given that it has been used to locate Hardy's fiction by several major critics, in particular Barbara Hardy in *The Appropriate Form* (1964) and Ian Gregor in *The Great Web* (1974). Hardy's writing has, I would argue, been misunderstood and has suffered by comparison with those writers who do exhibit more obviously the formal features of classic realism. F.R. Leavis, of course, excluded Hardy from *The Great Tradition* (orig. publ. 1948), citing Henry James's patronising comments on *Tess of the d'Urbervilles* to validate his assessment: 'The good little Thomas Hardy has scored a great success with *Tess of the d'Urbervilles*, which is chock-full of faults and falsity, and yet has a singular charm.' Comments on Hardy's work in this vein tended to emphasise the supposed crudeness of his fictional technique, for example Richard Carpenter's comment in *Thomas Hardy* (1964):

    ... he indulges in solemn, discursive speculation without transmitting his ideas imaginatively into symbol and incident. Like lumps of uncooked porridge, his concepts hang suspended in the novel or poem, indigestible and tasteless. (Carpenter 1964:22-3)

    Or Desmond Hawkins in *Thomas Hardy* (1951), who talked of Hardy's 'unmitigated solemnity', where 'the result is often lumpy, like badly cooked porridge' (Hawkins 1951:88). I think that, ironically, the unspoken presence, the implied authority informing these judgements, is Henry James: one thinks of his culinary analogies in assessing novels, for example in 'The Art of Fiction' (1884), 'a novel is a novel and a pudding is a pudding, and our only business could be to swallow it', in his caricaturing of the unrefined English critical tradition.

2. In some respects, Hardy's fiction anticipates that of Proust and has affinities with twentieth-century innovations. It is also illuminating when linked to Russian Formalism: if some of Mikhail Bakhtin's and Victor Shklovsky's theories are applied, the flaws and fractures of his novels, which resist realist organicising, can be linked readily to Bakhtin's concepts of 'centripetal' and 'centrifugal' opposition and 'heteroglossia', and to Shklovsky's notions of 'defamiliarisation': critical approaches which we associate more with Dostoevsky than George Eliot.

3. To say this is not to ignore the more recent and significant cultural-historicist work of Peter Widdowson's *Hardy in History* (1989), or the borderland and marginal readings of Hardy's fiction by Raymond Williams in *The Country and the City* (1973) and Roger Ebbatson's *Thomas Hardy: The Margin of the Unexpressed* (1993), all of which offer illuminating and alternative ways of rereading and repositioning Hardy's fiction.

4. Unlike Henry James's prefaces and essays, which were so central to the construction of early fiction criticism and have been so influential in creating an associated value system, Hardy's essays and notebooks have been quite marginalised, even in relation to much Hardy criticism.
5. This is combined with a firm rejection of what Hardy terms 'scientific realism' or 'copyism' in *The Science of Fiction*, in which he argues against the 'scientific' theory of realism:

> the impossibility of reproducing in its entirety the phantasmagoria of experience with infinite and atomic truth – the fallacy ... appears to owe its origin to the just perception that our widened knowledge of the universe and its forces, and man's position therein, narrative, to be artistically convincing, must adjust itself to the new alignment ...

Instead, Hardy advocates: 'To see in half and quarter views the whole picture, to catch from a few bars the whole tune, is the intuitive power that supplies the would-be storywriter with the scientific bases for his pursuit' (Widdowson 1997:262–4).

Bibliography

Bakhtin, M.M. (1981) *The Dialogic Imagination: Four Essays* (Austin: University of Texas Press).
Bullen, J.B. (1986) *The Expressive Eye: Fiction and Perception in the Work of Thomas Hardy* (Oxford: Clarendon).
Carpenter, R.C. (1964) *Thomas Hardy* (New York: Twayne Publishers).
Ebbatson, R. (1993) *Thomas Hardy: The Margin of the Unexpressed* (Sheffield: Sheffield Academic Press).
Gregor, I. (1974) *The Great Web; the form of Hardy's major fiction* (Totowa NJ: Rowman and Littlefield).
Grundy, J. (1979) *Hardy and the Sister Arts* (London: Macmillan).
Hardy, B.N. (1964) *The Appropriate Form; an essay on the novel* (London: Athlone Press).
Hardy, F.E. (1962) *The Life of Thomas Hardy 1840–1928* (London: Macmillan).
Hardy, T. (1975) *A Pair of Blue Eyes* (London: Macmillan).
―――― (1975) *The Well-Beloved* (London: Macmillan).
Hawkins, D. (1951) *Thomas Hardy* (London: A. Barker).
Kristeva, J. (1974) *Revolution in Poetic Language*, trans. L.S. Roudiez (New York: Columbia University Press).
Leavis, F.R. (1962) *The Great Tradition* (Harmondsworth: Penguin).
Proust, M. (1954) *A la Recherche du Temps Perdu* 3 (Paris: Pléiade).
Ricardou, J. (1973) *Le Nouveau Roman* (Paris: Seuil).
Webster, R. (1979) *Visual Imagination in the Novels of Thomas Hardy*, unpublished Ph.D. thesis.
Widdowson, P. (1989) *Hardy in History* (London: Routledge).
―――― (ed.) (1997) *Thomas Hardy: Selected Poetry and Non-Fictional Prose* (London: Macmillan).
Williams, R. (1973) *The Country and the City* (London: Chatto & Windus).

PART V

IDENTITY AND OTHERNESS

CHAPTER 14

GAUL AND WOMAN AS REFLECTED IN THE FRENCH REVOLUTIONARY'S MIRROR*

Xavier Martin

The fact that, on looking into his mirror, the French Revolutionary imagined he could see the silhouette of a Gallic warrior should be understood as an effect of the famous 'myth of origins' which had gained credence in France at the dawn of the eighteenth century. Known since as the Frankish myth, it portrayed the French aristocracy as descendants of the Franks, who had invaded Gaul long ago, while the ancestors of the commoners were said to be the Gauls, whom the Franks had defeated.[1] This story thus gave as sole justification for the preeminence of the aristocracy that it was gloriously founded on conquest, and thus on truly military virtues, which were duly passed down through the 'blood', declared pure,[2] of the so-called 'race' observed to be dominant. Paradoxically, this view based precedence in the social order on the brutality of distant ancestors, laying itself open to the objection that it was, to anyone who thought about it, rather unflattering to be descended from loutish barbarians who emerged from the forests.[3]

It is thus clear that the effect of the Revolution was not to get rid of the myth, but merely to modify its power-relations

* Translated from the French by Trista Selous.

when appropriating it. The aristocrats, who were eliminated politically, also physically disappeared in large numbers from the landscape, mainly as a result of emigration. This, in its archetypal manifestation, involved a movement towards the Rhine in a kind of long-deferred inversion of the 'migratory flow'. In a manifesto which prefigured the Revolution, Abbé Sieyès' well-known work *Qu'est-ce que le Tiers Etat?*, the author expressively proposed that the aristocracy should be invited to return to what he precisely calls 'the forests of Franconia' (Sieyès 1970:128).

The logic was fairly simple. If the so-called posterity of the Frankish people were removed from the French population, the result would be that French soil would become the sole preserve of the descendants of the ancient Gallic stock. The revolution could then be 'read' as the somewhat belated return and revenge of the Gallic people against the 'occupier'; in other words, as Benjamin Constant put it, as 'a talion law exercised by the eighteenth century against the fifth' (1960:277).[4] The myth thus survived the revolution, simply by adapting the hierarchy of its values to suit the times.

It can be seen, moreover, that events gave commoners the chance to prove that warlike qualities, for which the Gauls were renowned, had long been wrongly considered the preserve of those of aristocratic blood, who were now stripped of their rank.[5] Madame de Staël observed that 'the exploits of the republican warriors' had 'obliterated aristocratic distinctions' (1983:395). In practice, the frequent allusions during the Revolution to 'French impetuosity' clearly evoke an element of the 'Gallic' character. Thus some 'patriots' petitioned for the plan of attacking the Vendée rebels 'en masse, as the ancient Gauls did' (cited by Reinhard 1957:117).

There is other documentary evidence here and there of the French revolutionary's awareness of the possibility of rehabilitating the Gallic inheritance. The most interesting comes from Fabre d'Eglantine, a member of the Convention, who said, apropos of the famous democratic appellation the 'sansculottes' ('without knee-breeches'), 'In the most ancient times, our ancestors the Gauls were proud to bear this name' (*Archives parlementaires* 1910:503). The Romans, he alleged, called the area of Gaul around Lyon *Gallia bracata*, which can be translated as 'breeches-wearing Gaul', in other words that part of Gaul where *braies* or breeches were worn. By contrast, the rest of the country, which was freer to the extent that it was not subject to the influence of Rome, could only, and most opportunely, be 'non-breeches-wearing Gaul', to quote Fabre d'Eglantine himself, who concludes, with some pleasure, 'Our forefathers were thus ... "sans-culottes"'.

This argument, however interesting, is severely lacking in rigour. Firstly, in his haste to make a good speech, Fabre d'Eglantine confused *Gallia Lyonensis* (which it was tempting to denigrate at the very moment that the destruction of Lyon was under way) with *Gallia Narbonensis*, the area around Narbonne. Secondly, the Parisian sans-culottes had adopted the name precisely – at least so it seems – because, like the inhabitants of *Gallia bracata* with whom Eglantine's argument wrongly contrasted them, they wore trousers as opposed to the aristocratic 'culotte', which consisted of short trousers or breeches. All in all, this affair of leg-coverings was as muddled as Fabre d'Eglantine's dialectics, which we have to judge too fanciful to lend the Gallic myth any added weight, since in practice the argument twists the myth severely out of shape.

For the fact is that overall the Gallic theme appeared to remain dormant during the Revolution. Four reasons can be put forward for this, of which the last is incontrovertibly the most important, since it casts a paradoxical, but decisive light over the case.

In the first place we must mention the improbable nature of the Frankish myth, of which the Gallic myth is, as we have noted, merely the revolutionary version. That modern nobility should, over so many centuries, have monopolised the preservation of the Frankish genetic inheritance is an entirely arbitrary hypothesis, which has the effrontery calmly to assert itself as the truth, when evidence reveals it to be far more disproved than proved by established historical fact, including the royal practice of ennobling commoners. It would seem that if most people gave credence to the Frankish myth, and thus to the Gallic myth (being the same thing seen from the other side) it was more through mental laziness than actual belief.

Secondly, the desire to elaborate a Gallic myth must be seen in the wider context of the revolutionary aspiration to a return to origins. For the 'regenerators', leaping somewhat blindly backwards past about twelve centuries of French and Frankish monarchy, were not too sure where they would or should end up. The landing strip was ill-defined. Sometimes it was Gaul, sometimes Egypt; Sparta was a favourite and Rome the most frequent choice.[6] This still gave great latitude and had the disadvantage of recalling only too well that the ancient Gauls had been conquered not only by Rome, but by republican

Rome, in other words the Rome favoured by the Jacobins. So, despite its many advantages, the Gallic reference was rather lacking in glory and arguments that could really flatter the effervescent vanity of the 'patriots'.

In the third place, the Frankish inheritance of France as a whole was not so easy to dispose of, for two interconnected reasons of a lexical nature. First there was certainly, and not surprisingly, an enormous attachment to the names 'France' and 'French', which the political overthrow of the 'Frankish' myth might logically have swept before it, given the close and obvious relations between the three names. It is true that during the Revolution there were a few suggestions and proposals calling for the abandonment of the names 'France' and 'French', including that of the fairly high-ranking Jacobin Dufourny de Villiers who, on the notably 'revolutionary' date of 20 June 1792 'began a discussion on the origins of the French name and proposed changing the name of the French people to that of the free people' (Aulard 1892:26). Shortly afterwards a citizen boldly asks, 'How long will you let us bear the loathsome name French?' and ceremoniously calls for assistance and support to 'obtain from the National Convention that it gives us the name Gauls' (Allonville 1841:8, 10). These impulses deserve to be recalled, but much of their interest lies in their rarity, since clearly none of them found an echo. The terms 'France' and 'French' were too well established and people were too proud of them to cast them off lightly in the name of utopia.

Moreover – and this is the second reason of a lexical nature, directly linked to the former – the name 'Frank', from which 'France' and 'French' are derived, itself signifies 'free'. This precious coincidence was not to be ignored at a moment when the French were, as they hoped and believed, fascinating 'the universe' under their banner of Liberty. The Franks were free men right down to their name, and thus also had a vocation as liberators. According to one variant of the Frankish myth, the Franks had come not exactly to conquer Gaul but to *free* it from Roman domination (Montesquieu 1951:528; Jaucourt 1756:689; Brizard 1792:23). In other words, whether, after being conquered by the Romans, they had been liberated or conquered by the Franks, in these effervescent years when the idea of the nation was solidifying, Gaul and the Gauls did not offer a very attractive point of reference, all things considered. On the other hand, in its stormy efforts to export itself, the revolution preferred to locate itself in relation to the heritage of the great Frankish ancestors and 'genetic' liberators.

Hence, it would seem, the tangible lack of any real movement towards the establishment of the Gallic myth as a new founding myth in France at the time. All in all, explicit mentions of such a myth are comparatively rare, to the point where we can readily admit that it did not deeply mark the spirit of the age. Here we come to the fourth reason for its lack of appearance in contemporary sources, a reason which, paradoxically, entirely changes the perception of the issue we have built up so far.

This fourth and last reason why the Gallic myth was not openly woven into the fabric of the revolution was that, in a niggling, irritating way, it did not seem that implausible, as was painfully confirmed by the course of events after 1789. In other words, it seemed only too probable that this France, disencumbered of its aristocrats, had rediscovered a specifically 'Gallic' inheritance of mixed virtues which, as experience proved, did not in itself favour the disciplines which civil peace and all its benefits require. When the French people, who had made or been subjected to the Revolution in varying degrees, came to contemplate the lessons of this painful period, whose end never seemed to come any closer, a precise 'reading' of their unhappy experience sprang readily to mind. As 'Gauls together', they were manifesting the two major and interlinked failings of which Caesar himself accused the Gauls in his *Conquest of Gaul*.

The first was a constant and costly compulsion to split into rival factions at all levels: 'In Gaul not only every tribe, canton and subdivision of a canton, but almost every family, is divided into rival factions' (Caesar 1951:30), a tendency cruelly and all too clearly illustrated two thousand years later by the Revolution's turbulent unfolding, during which all the talk in the public galleries was of 'factions', while the victorious party itself was split and strife-torn.[7]

Secondly, as Caesar often observes, the ancient Gauls were what in Latin he calls *mobiles*, or *de mobilitas animi* (Caesar:II, 1; IV, 5, 13). In other words, they were impulsive, changeable, capricious, unpredictable, naively seduced by novelty, incapable of sustained thought, fond of changing masters, lacking in common sense and unable to plan for the future (Caesar:III, 8, 10, 19; IV, 5). It was hard to avoid the observation that the way that events had unfolded after the spring of 1789 seemed only to reinforce this portrait. Even before the Revolution, the French character was reputed to be thoughtless, changeable and 'mobile' (Epinay 1993:86; Grimm 1877–82, 10:47–50).[8] At the time it was possible to think that this resulted from the regime itself; however, following the events of the revolution it seemed that the unfortunate 'mobility' of which Caesar accused the Gauls was a distinguishing trait of the national temperament of a people who were 'fickle and quick to become carried away by any new matter of agitation' (*Venise...*:550).[9]

Such an observation could only be painful during years when there seemed no end to political miscalculations and, as a result, the French public began to develop what amounted to a phobia of 'mobility', whether of things, people, or the metaphorical mobility of the ground itself. Thus revolutionaries could not espouse the image of the Gaul they glimpsed in the mirror, following the reverse logic of the Frankish myth, since in reflecting them so well, as experience suggested, it augured a social destiny of endless upheavals, disputes and disorder. Thus as the years passed more and more reproachful references were made to the 'mobility', changeability and unthinking ferment of the French people, yet an eloquent silence covered the Gauls, whose failings these were.[10]

In other words, the relative nonappearance of the Gallic myth in contemporary sources stems from the paradoxical fact that it would have provided too convincing a grounding for the upheavals taking place, not only conveniently explaining them but at the same time heralding their irremediable and worrying continuation. Thus the myth did not fade because it failed to 'take'; it was consigned to silence for more subtle reasons, because it 'took' too well.[11]

This is not all. Such reticence at proclaiming themselves to be Gauls was probably all the more marked because a second archetypal image was indiscreetly superimposed on that of the Gaul in the mirror. This second image reinforced the unflattering qualities of the first and furthermore neutralised its more positive aspects. For the excessive 'mobility' whose many variations could be seen in the political context was not only a 'gallo-French' attribute. It was also reputed to be characteristic of the trans-ethnic category of the feminine. The idea that woman was 'mobile' was a commonplace around 1800,[12] it went without saying that she was thoughtless and fickle, and this belief was backed up by the 'scientists'.

To this end the medical profession used a logic which was 'materialist' or at least psychosomatic, earlier employed by Montesquieu (1951:1,278; see also 45–6). Roussel and Cabanis saw this 'peculiar mobility' of women as having organic origins (Roussel 1813:15–16; Cabanis 1980:229, 236, 312, 400). The law-makers followed them,[13] right down to Napoleon himself who, describing what he called 'the sex of inconstancy' combined in one phrase 'the weakness of women's brains, the mobility of their ideas' (1943:207).

It was, no doubt, clear what was at stake. Too close a resemblance to the great-grandchildren of the ancient Gauls would confirm or suggest that the French were themselves changeable and mobile, an observation which would have the effect of feminising the nation. The unfolding events of the revolutionary years seemed to demonstrate, to illustrate the idea that the French were and always had been capricious, improvident, unthinking and frivolous. Such characteristics were widely reputed to be Gallic faults, but they were scientifically attested to be typically feminine failings. A German feminist *avant la lettre*, the Comtesse de Bentick, even directly – and significantly – asserted to the philosopher and savant Maupertuis, an adopted 'Berliner', 'I have less French blood than you and am thus less capricious' (1997:33).

In the second phase of the Revolution, France and the French were still subject to what must be called feminising comments. Fonvielle called them a 'flighty' people, subject 'to the empire of fashion'. When, with the aim of elucidating the irrational character of the revolutionary years, he describes some of his compatriots (in other words all, or almost all of them, depending on the context) *'whose weak organs did not include the strong combinations that produce the capacity to plan for the future'* (1796:86, my emphasis), he is clearly expressing himself in exactly the same terms as those used by contemporary doctors when giving a physical justification for those handicaps of a psychological nature which were considered typical of femininity.[14]

At the same time, the Swiss pastor and philosopher Meister also clearly referred the damage caused by the Revolution to a certain femininity of the French character, due to the excessive influence of women in the highest levels of society under the monarchy (1910:173). Montesquieu had taken his expression of this idea much further; considering the excessive social dominance of women, whose 'character is not to be attached to anything fixed', he concluded unambiguously, 'There is now only one sex, and *we are all women in our minds*' (1941:84). In 1781 Raynal is also quite explicit on the page on which he states that the French 'seldom feel profound sensations' – a trait which technically distinguishes women from men according to the criteria of the medicine of sensualist persuasion. He goes so far as to say of his fellow-citizens: 'They are, in some ways, *a people of women*' (1781:105). Again in the 1840s, when the misogynist Auguste Comte had been struggling for months to prove the 'native inferiority' of women when it came to 'sustained thought' and 'abstraction' (Comte 1975:199), Stuart Mill, with some subtlety, used an argument *ad hominem* to suggest the opposite idea: 'You are French and it has always been noted that the French character contains some of the failings, as well as the qualities, of young people and women' (Comte 1975:397).

The French revolutionaries were thus unlucky. The undeniable element of virilisation that might have flattered them in the image of the Gaul suffered the disgrace of neutralisation by the unfortunate feminine connotations of the central theme of 'mobility', which became 'impetuosity' in the Gauls, while its feminine version was 'frivolity', with capriciousness, inconsistency, changeability and the rest generally applying to both. We can see the same process at work here as we noted above in relation to the Gallic image: the longer the revolution went on unfolding, and looked as though it would continue for ever, the more the French people were described in terms highly suggestive of femininity, although no one went so far as to state expressly that, strangely and depressingly, the French were both feminine and Gallic.

On the other hand, since the Gallic myth was only repudiated by the French because it was embarrassingly appropriate, it was open to exploitation from outside when the occasion arose. Emperor Napoleon, whose 'Italianness' allowed him to glimpse the reflection of Caesar rather than a Gaul, was thus more disposed both to take as self-evident the idea that 'the Revolution was ... *the reaction of the Gauls against the Franks*' (Las Cases 1968:247/2)[15] and later to note on a number of occasions certain ingredients of the French national temperament regarded as Gallic. For Napoleon, as Las Cases observed on 17 November 1815 on Saint-Helena, 'we were the Gauls of long ago: the capriciousness, the same inconsistency and above all the same vanity (1968:100/2); on 12 April 1816 Las Cases notes: 'This capriciousness, this inconsistency had come down to us from a long time ago, [Napoleon] would say, we had always remained Gauls' (1968:209/1). Napoleon the strategist also stated, more positively, 'that there is nothing one cannot obtain from the French using danger as bait; ... it is their Gallic inheritance' (Las Cases 1968:140/1).

The emperor also expressed this view in relation to his own genius for long-term calculations, which his entourage could not understand:[16] 'The Gallic fibre cannot get used to the great calculations of time' (Napoleon, 1943:32). Again, classically, the incapacity for forward planning was rhetorically imputed to women, who were thought to have missed out on their share of 'foresight of the distant future' (*Archives parlementaires* 1865:435/2). It is clear that Bonaparte was well aware of the 'femininity' of France which, as we have noted, the French revolutionaries were not keen openly to accept. The emperor makes a clear allusion when he says (and it is significant that he distances the words by using Italian): 'What predominates among the French is *la vanità, la leggerezza, l'independanza ed il capriccio*, ['vanity, changeability, independence and caprice'] (O'Meara 1993/1:315). Here again we see that typically 'Gallic' characteristics need only a slight inflection in order to become equally well, at the time, those of the 'feminine'.

Furthermore it is obvious that Bonaparte felt his relationship to France as one of masculine to feminine, at least as he saw such a relationship, a far cry from the canons and criteria of courtly love. In 1809 he confided, 'I have only one passion, one mistress, and that is France: I sleep with her. She has never failed me; she gives me her blood and her treasures' (Roederer in Massin 1969–71/8:217–18). In 1812, returning hell for leather from Russia when Malet's conspiracy had almost overthrown his regime, he says: 'With the French ... as with women, you must not be away too long' (Caulaincourt 1986:85).

In other words, the unexpected connivance between the French predisposition to national 'gallicisation' and 'feminisation', which had been vaguely understood during the revolutionary years and was enough to hold back the exploitation of the Gallic myth, had its logical place in the mental universe of Bonaparte himself. Since this was not a problem for the emperor, he used it to interpret French behaviour. This was also true, as is well-known, of nineteenth-century French historiographers, whose experience of continual political instability after 1789 contributed to their belief in the genetically 'Gallic' character of the revolutionaries.

Notes

1. See Bloch (1963:90–109); Furet and Ozouf (1979:443–4); Price (1981); Werner (1984:40).

2. As opposed to the 'impure blood' destined to water the thirsty furrows of France in the words of the 'Marseillaise'.
3. This argument was formulated notably by Voltaire. See also Mercier (1994a 1:425–6) and Chamfort (1968:160).
4. See also Constant (1986:179).
5. 'Our blood is pure Gallic', asserted a citizen named Ducalle at the time of the Convention: reported by Count D'Allonville (1841:9).
6. 'We hesitate between a great many ancestors', wrote Ozouf (1984:341).
7. In 1790 one speaker in the parliament expressed his concern that this presaged 'the most terrible misfortune: all classes of citizens are divided; there is not one village where the citizens are not split into two parties'. (*Archives Parlementaires*, 1883:640/2)
8. In a letter of 9 February 1789, the Ambassador of Venice senses the imminence of 'these sudden changes which only happen in France' (*Venise...* :269).
9. Madame de Staël observed that the great revolutionary measures were taken 'in the French way, on impulse' (1962:269). See also an allusion to 'the nation's mobile character' (Sénac de Meilhan 1987:91). Mirabeau argued that this specifically French 'mobility' justified the manipulation of minds (in Baczko 1982:97).
10. See for example Fonvielle (1796:32); Mallet du Pan (1884:50, 53, 122, 186); Mercier (1994b:12).
11. Half a century later, when Tocqueville was contemplating the changeable course of political life in France 'since the Revolution began', he never tired of noting that down the centuries this people who were 'so mobile in their thoughts ... and tastes' continued to resemble 'the portraits made of them three thousand years ago' (1986:1,078). Nevertheless, in the fairly long and suggestive passage in which he expounds this idea, he precisely does not mention the Gauls. On the contrary, in an explicit aside three years earlier, Adolphe de Circourt, one of Tocqueville's correspondents, says of the French nation, 'From the Celts, their prototypes, they take their extreme thoughtlessness about serious matters, ... their need to change masters and to have them' (Tocqueville 1983:112).
12. In 1800 Mme de Staël's first great work *De la littérature* did not escape Chateaubriand's malevolent and semi-automatic imputation that it contained 'the changeable and versatile thinking of woman' (1977:111).
13. When Cambacérès was describing women during the presentation of his third draft of the Civil Code in 1796, he attributed 'the mobility of her existence' to 'an inexhaustible source of variety in the results of her organisation', which, in the language of the time, very precisely signifies her physical constitution (*Moniteur universel* 339, 9 Fructidor Year V, 26 August 1796:1,355, 2). Portalis, who led those drafting the Napoleonic Code, considered women to be subject 'to a multitude of incessant little caprices' (in Bonaparte 1943:520).
14. See Cabanis (1980), pages already cited, notably 236: the 'sensations' of the masculine individual, 'are less sharp and quick, more lasting and deep'. See also John Stuart Mill in his letter of 30 August 1843 pointing out to Auguste Comte that 'the French have always been recognised as having, up to a certain point, the organisation [in other words the physical constitution] regarded as feminine' (Comte 1975:397).

15. See also Bonaparte, title of Chapter 3 of the 'Manuscrit de l'Ile d'Elbe': the Revolution 'has freed the Gauls from the Frankish conquest' (Las Cases 1968:469/1).
16. 'I see further into the future than others', 28.5.1817, recorded by B.E. O'Meara (1993/1:49).

Bibliography

1910: *Archives parlementaires* I, 77, Paris: Paul Dupont.
1883: *Archives parlementaires* I, 15, Paris: Paul Dupont.
1865: *Archives parlementaires* II, 5, Paris: Paul Dupont.
1997: *Venise et la Révolution française. Les 470 dépêches des ambassadeurs de Venise au Doge, 1786–1795* (Paris: Laffont).

Allonville (1841) *Mémoires secrets de 1770 à 1830* (Paris: Werdet).
Aulard, F.-A. (ed.) (1892) *La Société des Jacobins. Receuil de documents pour l'histoire du club des Jacobins de Paris* III (Paris: Jouaust, Noblet et Quantin).
Baczko, B. (1982) *Une Education pour la démocratie. Textes et projets de l'époque révolutionnaire* (Paris: Garnier).
Bentick, Comtesse de (1997) *Une Femme des Lumières. Ecrits et lettres de la Comtesse de Bentick* (Paris: C.N.R.S.).
Bloch, M. (1963) *Mélanges historiques* (Paris: S.E.V.P.E.N.).
Bonaparte, Napoleon (1943) *Correspondance ... Six cents lettres de travail (1800–1810)* (Paris: Gallimard).
Brizard, Abbé (1792) 'Eloge historique de l'Abbé de Mably' [1787], in Mably, *Oeuvres complètes* (Lyon: J.B. Delamollière).
Cabanis (1980) *Rapports du physique et du moral de l'homme* [1802] (Geneva: Slatkine Reprints).
Caesar, Julius (1951) *The Conquest of Gaul*, trans. S.A. Handford (Harmondsworth: Penguin).
Caulaincourt (1986) *Mémoires* (Paris: Perrin).
Chamfort (1968) *Maximes et Pensées* (Paris: Dagen).
Chateaubriand (1977) *Correspndance générale* 1 (Paris: Gallimard).
Comte, A. (1975) *Correspondance générale et confessions* 2 (Paris and The Hague: Mouton).
Constant, B. (1960) *De Madame de Staël et ses ouvrages* [c. 1830], in *Adolphe* (Paris: Garnier).
——— (1986) *De l'esprit de conquête et de l'usurpation dans leurs rapports avec la civilisation européenne* [1813–14] (Paris: Garnier-Flammarion).
Diderot and D'Alembert (eds) (1756) *Encyclopédie ou Dictionnaire raisonné des Sciences, des Arts et des Métiers* (Paris: Briasson, David l'aîné, Le Breton, Durand).
Epinay, Mme d' (1993) *Correspondance* 2, ed. F. Galiani and L. d'Epinay (Paris: Desjonquères).

Fonvielle, B.F.A. (1796) *Essais sur l'état actuel de la France, 1er mai 1796* (Paris: Desenne, Brigitte-Mattey, Maret).
Furet, F. and M. Ozouf, M. (1979) 'Deux légitimations historiques de la société française au xviiie siècle : Mably et Boulainvilliers', in *Annales. Economies, Sociétés, Civilisations* 3:438–50.
Grimm (1877–82) 'Notice sur le marquis de Croismare' [1772], in *Correspondance littéraire* 10 (Paris: Garnier).
Jaucourt (1756) 'Fief', in Diderot and D'Alembert (1756).
Las Cases (1968) *Mémorial de Sainte-Hélène* [1823] (Paris: Seuil).
Mallet du Pan (1884) *Correspondance inédite ... avec la Cour de Vienne (1794–1798)* (Paris: Plon).
Massin, J. (ed.) (1969–71) *Napoléon Bonaparte. L'Homme et l'oeuvre* (Paris: Club français du livre).
Meister, H. (1910) *Souvenirs de mon dernier voyage à Paris (1795)* (Paris: A. Picard).
Mercier (1994a) *Tableau de Paris* 1 & 2 (Paris: Mercure de France).
—— (1994b) *Le Nouveau Paris* (Paris: Mercure de France).
Montesquieu (1941) *Cahiers* (Paris: Grasset).
—— (1951) *Esprit des Lois...* [1748], in *Oeuvres complètes* 2 (Paris: Gallimard).
Napoleon, see Bonaparte.
O'Meara, B.E. (1993) *Journal. Napoléon dans l'exil* 1 and 2 (Paris: Fondation Napoléon).
Ozouf, M. (1984) *L'Ecole de la France. Essais sur la Révolution, l'utopie et l'enseignement* (Paris: Gallimard).
Price, R. (1981) 'Boulainvillier and the myth of the Frankish conquest of Gaul', in *Studies on Voltaire and the eighteenth century* 199:155–85.
Raynal (1781) *Histoire philosophique et politique des établissements et du commerce des Européens dans les deux Indes* 3 (Geneva: Jean-Léonard Pellet).
Reinhard, M. (1957) *L'Armée de la Revolution* (Paris: Cours C.D.U.).
Roussel (1813) *Système physique et moral de la femme* [1775] (Paris: Caille et Ravier).
Senac de Meilhan (1987) *Des principes et des causes de la Révolution en France* [1790] (Paris: Desjonquères).
Sieyès, Abbé (1970) *Qu'est-ce que le Tiers Etat?* [1789] (Geneva: Droz).
Staël, Mme de (1962) *Correspondance générale* 1, 2 (Paris: JJ Pauvert).
—— (1983) *Considérations sur la Révolution française* [1818] (Paris: Tallandier).
Tocqueville, (1983) *Oeuvres complètes* 18 (Paris: Gallimard).
—— (1986) *L'Ancien régime et la Révolution* 3 (Paris: Laffont).
Werner, K.F. (1984) *Histoire de France. Les Origines* (Paris: Fayard).

≈ CHAPTER 15 ≈

THE POLITICS OF EXTREME NARCISSISM IN THE DISCOURSE OF THE *FRONT NATIONAL*

François Nectoux

Notwithstanding its split into two factions in December 1998, the success of the *Front National* (FN), the far-right French political party, has been remarkable since it erupted on the political scene in the early 1980s. Its leader, Jean-Marie Le Pen, obtained 14.4 per cent and 15 per cent of votes in the 1988 and 1995 presidential elections. In 1995 the FN gained control of five medium-sized town councils, including Toulon, where it started to implement elements of his 'national preference' programme. It has several MEPs in the European Parliament and, in 1998, forced traditional right-wing groups into an unholy alliance for control of some regional councils. In two decades, the FN has gone from being a pariah, to becoming an accepted part of the French political landscape. It has done this without altering much in its populist politics, maintaining its nationalistic, xenophobic, racist and intensely authoritarian ideology, largely based on an organic, if not biological, vision of society, national identity and history.

The way in which the FN has 'broken the mould' of French politics has inspired numerous analyses. Two explanations have often been put forward. First, with the deep social crisis, so-called 'social fracture' and mass unemployment, a number of social groups, feeling threatened in their identity and economic existence, are ready to seek reassurance and salvation in the FN fold. Second, the whole body politic is also in a serious crisis. 'Traditional' parties have been unable to articulate convincing policies in response to the social crisis. Perceived as remote from ordinary citizens, they have not been helped by a series of corruption scandals. Furthermore, traditional political forces have sometimes used the new popularity of the FN for their own tactical calculations (for instance, the introduction of proportional representation by President Mitterrand in 1986 is widely seen as such a ploy), but it has usually resulted in the FN becoming an even more 'acceptable' party. In contrast, the themes and perspectives developed by the FN may appear to provide an antidote to this political deliquescence for specific categories of the population. Furthermore, in many areas (especially in Provence, Alsace and parts of the Paris suburbs) the FN has built up a network of supporters and activists, providing a framework for electoral success.

The nature of the FN's political discourse has also been identified as an important contributing factor to the party's advance. It can be argued that the effectiveness of this discourse has been significantly enhanced by the use of rhetorical tools (such as semantic displacement) and themes whose narcissistic features are intended to convey a specific sociopsychological charge for the target audience.

My aim here is to assess the validity of this hypothesis. This will be done in a number of stages: first, some of the most relevant rhetorical effects will be presented, then the constant emphasis on 'naming' and 'hidden identity', a striking element of FN discourse, will be discussed. This will open the way to a discussion of narcissism in the context of the FN politics.

Discourse is taken here in its wider sense, to include all forms of organised, referential-symbolic relations; however, my analysis will focus on a corpus of recent texts, both written documents and public speeches. Most come from Jean-Marie Le Pen, the boisterous, historic leader of the FN, with a few from other leaders such as Bruno Mégret, Bruno Gollnich or Samuel Maréchal. It should be emphasised that the FN leadership is not a homogeneous group. Deep ideological and political differences run between factions of varying origins. Even before the 1998 split between the Le Pen-led 'historic' Front National and the Mégret-led 'FN-Mouvement national', dissenting views had appeared on many issues, from the Croatian/Serbian conflict, to support for the Iraqi regime or the relationship with the traditional conservative parties.

However, this does not prevent the collective discourse from remaining fairly homogeneous. There was no problem finding similar effects in speeches or writings by different authors. Even Le Pen's bombastic and snide discourse is very similar to those of other leaders, and is carefully controlled (Magoudi and Jouve, 1990). This is not really surprising, since the core ideological and political concept – used by all the leaders and which forms the backbone of FN ideology – is that of national identity. Identity is also the focus of narcissistic conceptualisation, as will be argued later when discussing the function of 'naming' and 'identification' in Front discourse.

TheRelevance of Discourse Analysis in the Case of the FN

The importance of discourse analysis in the political sphere no longer needs to be demonstrated. It has been made especially apparent in the context of totalitarian political discourses such as Stalinism and Nazism, and in France the work of Jean-Pierre Faye (Faye 1972; Faye 1996) represents a major reference for the study of the Nazi language and discourse. Faye has shown that language was deeply integrated into the very essence of Nazi ideology, providing an instrument that enabled the Nazis to force their political ideology and practice upon the German people. The primary concept used by Faye is that of 'acceptability'. Through his analysis of Nazi narrative (using a methodology he called 'critical analysis of the narrative economy'), Faye sought to understand how language could act to make extremist, abhorrent policies and practices (such as totalitarian social control, ultra-nationalism and, ultimately, genocide) acceptable, normalised and trivialised. At the same time, a number of studies have focused on the role and forms of political discourse in the progress of the FN. Those by Pierre Taggueiff (Tagguieff 1991; 1996) are particularly well known. More recently a French team conducted a computer-based semantic analysis of FN discourse, using Faye's conceptual framework (Souchard et al. 1997). The results of this study will be used later.

The FN leadership has always indicated that language is a fundamental issue in their political strategy. Since the late 1970s the ideological and political discourse of the Front has indeed become a carefully constructed device. Any modern political party seeks to maximise the efficiency of its political communication, but few have set out to control and reinvent the semantic structure of their discourse as the FN has done. Le Pen himself declared in 1984: 'Semantics are not neutral'; the political struggle is 'a fight in which words sometimes kill more than bullets' (Le Pen 1984). Other FN leaders have similarly emphasised the role of language in politics. Bruno Gollnish, the FN General Secretary, claimed that: 'Political struggles are semantic struggles. ... He who can force his vocabulary on another imposes his own values, his own dialectic, and draws the other into an unequal fight on his own ground' (*Le Figaro* 21/6/96). These views have led the FN to set the parameters of its political discourse carefully. An internal document of the *Institut de Formation Nationale* ('National Training Institute', training FN activists) insists that:

> No word is innocent. ... It can indeed be said that words are weapons, because an ideological and political background is hidden behind every one. ... One of the successes of the Marxists was to make their adversaries use elements of their vocabulary. Any politician who did so unwittingly became a Marxist activist. (*Le Monde* 10/5/90; *Le Nouvel Observateur* 20/6/96)

In this context, analysis of the rhetorical tools used in FN discourse provides a number of clues as to its intended purpose.

Some Semantic and Thematic Effects in FN Discourse

The FN uses well-known rhetorical techniques, such as 'substitution and reversal devices', 'renaming' techniques, strategies of 'retaliation and amalgam' and 'the use of stereotypes' (Fiala 1997). Following Maryse Souchard and her colleagues (Souchard et al. 1997), two sets of tools can be identified. First, some semantic effects are particularly relevant, especially the 'evidence effect', the 'ambiguity effect' and, most importantly, 'semantic displacement'. Secondly, in many discourses similar themes reappear, such as violence, victimisation, plot and organic society. These themes, which do not at first seem connected, form a coherent thematic landscape which informs the whole FN ideological framework.

The first rhetorical effect is that of 'evidence', produced by presenting opinions, ambiguous or wrong statements as incontrovertible facts. This may be obtained by taking the audience into the confidence of the speaker or writer: 'As you know, or as you instinctively feel' (Le Pen 1998); or by asking questions whose answer is self-evident. However, this effect only works fully in the context of the second, that of semantic 'ambiguity'. This consists in appearing to be as clear as possible, but using an inappropriate context or thematic register in discussing a particular issue. An example would be Le Pen's well-known interview on RTL radio (13/9/87): 'I do not say that the gas chambers did not exist. I could not myself see any of them. I have not especially studied the matter. But I believe it to be a point of detail of the Second World War.'

Another well-known example is his declaration on the same radio station (14/4/85): 'The Papal encyclicals fully endorse the basic tenet of the Front National's political approach, in other words national preference, and the hierarchy according to which men prefer their daughters to their nieces, their nieces to their cousins, and so on.'

We can see that this utterance mixes three different referential domains – the public, private and religious spheres. This ambiguity allows the speaker to claim rhetorically that the FN policy of 'national preference' (in other words of denying social benefits and public services to immigrants under the pretext of giving 'rightful' French people their due in a new kind of apartheid society) is only a question of common sense, accepted by the Catholic church. In a word, proper contextualisation becomes impossible.

However, the most important effect in FN discourse is that of 'semantic displacement'. Quite a few authors have observed this technique. For instance, Balibar and Wittenstein noted the way words change their meanings in racist vocabulary (Balibar and Wittenstein 1991). Semantic displacement involves replacing one word or expression by another, or creating a new association between words in relation to a given referent, in order to change, veil or modify the connotative environment. A typical example is Le Pen's expression 'the 1914–1918 holocaust' (*Le Figaro* 23/2/83).

Le Pen favours semantic displacement through the creation of neologisms, wordplay and associations generating racist, medical, sexual or scatological innuendo. One of the best examples is the adjective *sidaïque*, meaning 'Aids sufferer', instead of the normal French *sidéen*. This is coined from SIDA (AIDS), with the added suffix *aïque*, clearly modeled on *judaïque*, an old adjective meaning 'Jewish' which is often used by anti-Semitic groups (contrary to Simmons's interpretation, it has nothing to do with *mosaïque* (Simmons 1996)). Other examples are 'Eurofederast' (a play on the words 'Eurofederalist', and 'pederast'), or the extraordinary sentence: 'Verily I say unto you, Monsieur Chirac-Juppé is an *acculé*' (Le Pen 1996). This sentence is remarkable because of a striking difference in idiomatic register between the classic biblical, respectable expression of the beginning and the scatological innuendo that follows. The unusual use of the past participle *acculé* (meaning 'cornered') as a noun creates an effect of semantic displacement. Any French-speaking listener would immediately make the connection with another, similar-sounding past participle, which is often used as a noun: an *enculé* ('arsehole').

Alongside these rhetorical devices, one linguistic trait and some particular themes are especially relevant to our consideration of narcissism. Personal pronouns of the first person singular or plural (I, we, us, me ...) are unusually frequent in Le Pen discourse, comprising 69.5 per cent of all personal pronouns, according to one study (Souchard et al. 1997). This linguistic trait may indicate a self-referential relationship between the enunciator and his audience – in other words, I/we exist more than others.

A frequent theme in FN discourse is that of the organic society and nation. This is commonly found in other far-right ideologies, such as Maurras's Action Française early in the twentieth century, which assigns a role to each group, profession or class, as if an immutable destiny had given them an organic function in society, generation after generation. The FN view is not as developed, and probably not as conservative. In essence, it is a pathological view of the nation-as-body (Hastings 1996). With France perceived as a physical person, Mégret speaks of national identity as 'an almost carnal awareness of our national reality' (1996). For Le Pen, 'France is flesh' (1998), and he speaks of 'France's biological substance' (*Libération* 14/10/96). Samuel Maréchal, leader of the FN Youth Movement, declares that: 'Nations are fleshly beings, just like men and women, and are just as different from each other' (Maréchal 1996). In this context the FN's opponents, and any threat or danger to the nation, become physiological threats, like viruses or illnesses. Thus Maréchal accuses the judges of the Constitutional Court of suffering from 'an especially insidious form of mental AIDS' (1997). Le Pen creates a neologism from wordplay: 'The fight against the pretend "racist" threat in our country has the function of "AIDS-dumbing" [*sidération*] public opinion' (1997a).

Alongside the commonly found 'mental AIDS' (Simmons 1996), many other infection metaphors are coined, using expressions such as 'gangrenous', 'cancerous cells', 'France infected by the virus of ...' These are not 'slips of the tongue' (Magoudi and Jouve 1990).

Another theme is that of the victim, who may be the FN or the French people: 'the insidious enslavement of French people' (Mégret 1996); 'we are hated because we are the last defence of the nation' (Le Pen 1998). Souchard notes that Le Pen's discourse is reactive; linguistically, it contains more verbs of position (indicating constraints) and fewer verbs of action than other political discourses. Le Pen's discourse 'has a dual structure: on the one hand it shows his interlocutors that they are victims of a system that is too much for them; on the other, he suggests they escape this situation by giving him the power of action' (Souchard et al. 1997).

An accompanying theme is that of violence. In fact, this is the most commonly found: in Souchard's computer analysis, violence appears in 64 per cent of thematic effects, more frequently than politics, economics or foreigners (Souchard et al. 1997). The violence is mostly social in nature and is presented within a moralistic discourse. It is also violence exercised against the FN itself, as defender of the nation: 'Politicians urge violence against the National Front'. 'Newspapers and the extreme-left free radios urge violence against the National Front' (Le Pen 1997a).

Following these last two themes, the figure of the 'conspiracy' is also a constant fixture in FN discourse. Internationalism in particular is a conspiracy on the part of

> an anonymous and all-conquering minority ... This conspiracy aims to destroy nations and the framework of natural order through the promotion of supranational structures, the elimination of borders, the subjection of nations, anti-birth policies and policies of massive immigration and naturalisation. (Le Pen 1997b)

The theme of conspiracy is used as an answer to any dislike of the FN. For instance: 'The immense political and media hype around the launch of the "European Year against Xenophobia" reveals in reality a carefully orchestrated campaign against the defence of French identity and national feeling' (FN press release 20/3/97).

The ideological construct emerging from this discussion is that of a nation and its defenders (the FN), organically bound to France, violently infected by sick and anonymous plotters and 'viruses'. A return to the theme of identity will deepen our understanding of this picture.

From Naming to the Idealisation of Identity in FN Discourse

An intriguing comment can be found in the speech that Le Pen gave at the end of the 1997 FN National Conference in Strasbourg. This Congress provoked a nationwide reaction. As it fell on 1 May, there were concerns that Le Pen would use it to celebrate Joan of Arc as a nationalist heroine. Fearing public disorder, the leader of the Strasbourg city council, Catherine Trautman, decided temporarily to remove the sculpture of Joan of Arc. This provoked the ire of the FN leader: 'Strasbourg is in a state of siege, not because of the FN Conference, as dishonestly stated by Madame Argence, now Mrs Trautman, but because of her friends' (Le Pen 1997a).

Madame Argence, now Mrs Trautman: why should Le Pen suddenly remind his audience of the council leader's maiden name? This was part of a series of attacks against Madame Trautman, and was clearly intended to provoke a negative reaction against her on the part of the audience. The key lies in the connotations attached to the two names. The maiden name sounds archetypally 'French', untainted by external influence. The second, married name has a sound that could seem Germanic, brutal, in a word, foreign: this woman dared to marry outside her pure French identity.

This 'naming', a kind of 'outing' of which other examples can be found, follows an old practice of the extreme-right in France, whose presence can be traced from Drumont's anti-Semitic tracts onwards. The importance of 'naming' people's 'roots' reflects the organic view of society. The other is a virus that has to be expelled from the perfect body of the nation. The naming process helps the FN's supporters to identify both their enemies and each other, who bask in the glory of their 'true' French identity.

These remarks lead us to the well-trodden path of the psychological analysis of extreme ideological and political movements, in which, since Freud, the role of narcissistic disturbance has been an oft-used analytical tool.

The Narcissistic Psychology of Extreme Ideology and Politics

Narcissism is self-love, the identification of one's own existence as a unique individual and an important stage in the development of personality. It was in his 1914 work on narcissism that Freud first signalled the link between the development of narcissism and adult personality and socialisation, through the ego ideal: 'In addition to its individual side, [the ego ideal] has a social side; it is also the common ideal of a family, a class or a nation' (Freud 1914).

The maturation of narcissistic tendencies is a positive development, helping socialisation. Later, however, analysing love/hate relationships, Freud noted that:

> Closely related races keep one another at arm's length; the South German cannot endure the North German, the Englishman casts every kind of aspersion upon the Scot, the Spaniard despises the Portuguese. We are no longer astonished that greater differences should lead to an almost insuperable repugnance, such as the Gallic people feel for the German, the Aryan for the Semite, and the white races for the coloured. (Freud 1921)

And Freud comments:

> In the undisguised antipathies and aversions which people feel towards strangers with whom they have to do we may recognise the expression of self-love – of narcissism. This self-love works for the preservation of the individual, and behaves as though the occurrence of any divergence from its own particular lines of development involved a criticism of them and a demand for their alteration. (Freud 1921)

Freud adds that we do not know the source for this 'readiness for hatred ... to which one is tempted to ascribe an elementary character' (ibid.). We are left with the idea that there is a basic insecurity in relation to the other, expressing itself in racism and xenophobia for 'self-protection'. Later on, as the tragic developments of the twentieth century unfolded, others furthered the analysis. For instance, the concepts of 'narcissistic rage' and the 'grandiose self' were developed by Kohut (1971) and applied by Miller to Hitler (Miller 1980). Again, from a Jungian perspective, Jacoby discussed Kohut's work and briefly notes its application to nationalism (Jacoby 1995).

In balanced social interchange, discourse is the recognition of each other's identity/discourse (Todorov 1989; 1995). The self acts as the mirror absorbing the other's discourse and reflecting back to the other, who does the same. The self's own 'otherness', the fact that we are ourselves strangers, both to others and in and to ourselves, the strangeness that lies within us is thus revealed to us. As Rimbaud put it, 'I is an other'.

Julia Kristeva links this to Freud's concept of the unheimliche, which is translated as 'uncanny' in English (Freud 1991b). In German, however, as Freud notes, it is close to 'un-homely', or 'un-familiar'. The French translation is quite interesting: étrange étrangeté ('strange strangeness'), which makes us 'strangers to ourselves' (Kristeva 1988). This traumatic process is often rejected violently with the other, especially when people feel their own identity to be threatened by a crisis. At such times people tend to reject and oppose others, who are held responsible for the crisis simply because they are others or, even more simply, because they are not perceived to be as much threatened by the crisis (Levinas 1991; Sibony 1997).

This approach, which signals the link between narcissism and a refusal of social mirroring (in other words the reflection of the other, the stranger, in the mirror of the self) can be applied to FN discourse. As noted earlier, organic ideology means that the nation is the body identical, in which nationalists (Le Pen, his followers: 'us') recognise and lose themselves, keeping themselves clean on the mirror of the Nation, in a process of idealisation and identification. In practical terms, this indicates a refusal to acknowledge the other's place in the same living space and, to a greater extent, as part of the self:

> One of the foundations of Jean-Marie Le Pen's discourse and ideology is that the other, the one who is different, is instantly identified as a potential or actual threat. Speeches on the dangers threatening society and the enemies who are the source of these dangers are an expression of the rejection of the other. (Souchard et al. 1997)

This leads us to an analysis of the internal organisation of the narcissistic features of FN discourse.

Narcissism and its Impact in FN Discourse

The purpose of this last part of the discussion is briefly to explore the ways in which narcissism operates within FN discourse, through the organisation of themes and use of rhetorical effects. An easily constructed case relates to racist themes. The way that these themes are organised and work together is presented in table form below, where chains of rhetorical effects are illustrated by quotations. Selection was made difficult by the considerable number of very similar quotes – FN discourse is quite repetitive in its core ideological themes, such as racism.

The first level of FN discourse on racism is built upon simple primary distancing – the denial of any racism, anti-Semitism or xenophobia. This starts at the top, with the leader, Jean-Marie Le Pen, then extends to the whole of the FN, before progressing to the whole French nation: racism becomes a non-concept that cannot be related to the French identity. The second rhetorical level is based on semantic displacements, whose aim is to justify the political principles of 'national preference' and 'separate development', rhetorically distancing them from the racism in which they are grounded. This starts with an affirmation of the existence of races, and moves to the insistence that, obviously, this implies differences and thus relative inequalities. In 1996, when speaking about a previous interview, Le Pen stated that, 'asked by a journalist: "Do you believe in inequality between races?" I answered "yes", because this seemed obvious to me, as it is to the overwhelming majority of French people' (Le Pen 1996).

Yet, in the same speech, Le Pen later spoke of 'relative' inequalities between races (insisting, as an example, on the 'fact that races are not equal in all sports, blacks being better on the track, and whites in the swimming pool'). A preference by people for others of the same race/nation (another ambiguous mix up between race and nation) is then claimed as being normal, as people prefer closer relations – hence the normality of 'national preference'. Those who oppose 'national preference' are opposing patriotism, since patriotism is simply expressing preference for one's nation.

The third expression of racism in FN discourse is a 'counter-mirroring' device, consisting of turning criticism back on the other. The first and easiest counter-attack is to use any documented instance of racism by FN opponents. Hence references to historical icons of the left who were supporters of colonisation and racists, such as Jules Ferry, or to the shabby treatment by the French state of war veterans from the ex-colonies. This helps to prepare the ground for the main thrust of this approach, which is rhetorically to demonstrate that anti-racist pressure groups and the establishment are obviously racist themselves, the victims of this racism being idealised 'French citizens', in a role reversal typical of narcissistic attitudes. This process is summarised in the following statement:

> This international propaganda must not make us forget that our fellow citizens are frequently the first victims of a concealed racism, scandalously unpunished anti-French racism, and that

Table 1 The organisation of rhetorical effects in the FN discourse on racism

Primary distancing	Semantic displacement and other rhetorical effects	Counter-attack: the 'counter-mirroring effect'
I/We do not claim the absolute superiority of a race: 'I have never, myself, claimed the absolute superiority of one race over another'. (Le Pen 1996)	*Races exist*: 'Races exist. Races exist in real life'. (Le Pen 1996)	*Historical figures of the left were racists*: '... Léon Blum or Jules Ferry speaking of "superior races"...'. (Le Pen 1996)
The FN is not racist: 'The Front National is not racist and speaks to French people of all religions. It is not xenophobic'. (speech by Le Pen, 11/11/96, quoted in Maréchal 1997)	*Races are different, and there are relative inequalities*: 'But it is not to be racist to admit, as the Constitution does [sic], that races are different, unequal, according to periods and activities'. (Le Pen 1996)	*The political establishment does not respect people from the ex-colonies who have fought for France*: 'It is you who treat veterans of the French army, who became foreigners in 1962, Algerians, ... Malians, as dogs, by giving them insulting pensions'. (Le Pen 1996)
Racism does not exist in France/racism is not a problem: 'Everybody can see for themselves that, according to [the dictionary definition], racism is nearly non-existent in our country and that, in any case, nobody is laying any claim to it'. (Mégret 1996)	*The FN prefers French people; this is not racism*: the FN is '... not xenophobic, but Francophile: it prefers French people, and that does not mean that it does not like foreigners. It is not anti-Semitic. ... We prefer French Jews to foreign Jews, and we prefer those who love us'. (speech by Le Pen, 11/11/96, quoted in Maréchal 1997)	*Anti-racist organisations are racist*: 'Anti-racism ... is a reversed racism, an anti-French, anti-white, anti-Christian racism'. (Le Pen 1998) *The anti-racist establishment is part of an international plot against the nation and the FN*: 'While pretending to fight against racism, in reality the establishment targets all those opposed to its cosmopolitan project to make the French nation disappear'. (Le Pen 1997a)
	Love of the nation is assimilated to racism by FN: '... patriotism, which is nothing other than the love of one's country, implies a definite preference for one's country, a preference that the followers of human rights interpret as an exclusion of other nations, in other words as a manifestation of racism. One can see how, little by little, patriotism can be assimilated to an opinion that can be condemned in a court of law'. (Mégret 1996)	

they are too often treated as pariahs or second-class citizens in their own country. (FN press release 20/3/97)

This completes the set of expressions of racism, in a circular ideology that starts with the claim that the FN is not racist and ends with the affirmation that French citizens, as the real victims of racism, must defend their identity and what is rightfully theirs.

We could have selected a theme other than racism, such as immigration or human rights, for which similar articulations and appeals to narcissistic tendencies could have been found. Typically, the same rhetorical tools are used: '... how the rights of citizens are permanently violated here under the cover of an hypocritical defence of Human Rights' (Le Pen 1998). 'How can we fail to see that this new ideology [of human rights] is gaining a totalitarian-like hold on our country? With its priestly cast and its gurus, it deals out anathema and excommunications' (Mégret 1996).

Conclusions

At this stage, two tentative conclusions can be drawn. The first is that FN discourse displays many of the characteristics of a narcissistic approach to political argument and language. The FN leadership appears to have undertaken to convince people that they should exclude socially any different, threatening forms of identity and that the FN is the mirror in which they should reflect their recovered selves.

The second tentative conclusion is that, in this narcissistic environment, the circularity of rhetorical arguments on, say, racism makes it very difficult to respond effectively. This is partly due to the devices being used, which subtly shift concepts and meanings. However, the main difficulty is that this discourse fits the psychological profile of many of those at whom it is targeted. These are people who perceive their identity to be threatened by the evolution of society or who are really suffering from social upheavals beyond their control, and seek solace in a discourse that reaffirms their individual existence within a social identity.

The effectiveness of these narcissistic approaches and countermirroring effects in upholding the beliefs of the FN's activists and electorate reduces the opportunity for transparent, reflective dialogue in the political arena, since FN followers perceive themselves to be victims of a lack of opportunity and transparency.

No rational or humanistic anti-racist response to FN discourse would convince its electorate, or even be listened to, as long as this response does not take into account the need to make secure uncertain identities that tend to become more dispersed in different directions by an uncertain world (Dortier 1998). The task of providing such a response remains considerable.

Bibliography

Balibar, E. and I. Wittenstein (1991) *Race, Nation, Class – Ambiguous Identities* (London/New York: Verso).

Dortier, J.-F. (1998) 'L'Individu dispersé et ses identités multiples', in J.C. Ruano-Borbalan (ed.) *L'Identité – L'individu, le groupe, la société* (Auxerre: Sciences Humaines).

Faye, J.-P. (1972) *Languages totalitaires – Critique de la raison, l'économie narrative* (Paris: Hermann).

—— (1996) *Le Language meurtrier* (Paris: Hermann).

Fiala, P. (1997) 'Le language de Le Pen', in *Politique, la revue* 4, April–June 1997.

Freud, S. (1991a) 'On Group Psychology' [1921], in Penguin Freud Library 12: *Civilization, Society and Religion* (London: Penguin).

—— (1991b) The Uncanny [1919], in Penguin Freud Library 14: *Art and Literature* (London: Penguin).

—— (1991c) 'On Narcissism: An Introduction' [1914], in Penguin Freud Library 11: *On Metapsychology* (London: Penguin).

Hastings, M. (1996) 'Front national: des mots pour faire mal', in *Le Monde*, 24/25 November 1996:12.

Jacoby, M. (1995) *Individuation and Narcissism – The Psychology of Self in Jung & Kohut* (London: Routledge).

Kohut, H. (1971) *The Analysis of the Self* (New York: International Universities Press).

Kristeva, J. (1988) *Etrangers à nous-mêmes* (Paris: Fayard).

Le Pen, J.-M. (1984) *Les Français d'abord* (Paris: Carrère).

—— (1996) Speech at the Blue-White-Red celebrations, 29 September 1996, http://www.front-nat.fr/bbr963.html (downloaded 01/03/97).

—— (1997a) Closing speech, 10th Congress of the Front National, Strasbourg, 31 March 1997, http://www.front-nat.fr/strasb.html (downloaded 25/04/97).

—— (1997b) Speech celebrating Joan of Arc, Paris, 1 May 1997, http://www.front-nat.fr/jeanne.html (downloaded 12/05/97).

—— (1998) Closing speech, Front National Summer University, Toulon, http://www.front-nat.fr/discours/udt98.htm (downloaded 15/09/98).

Levinas, E. (1991) *Entre nous – Essais sur le penser de l'autre* (Paris: Grasset).

Magoudi, A. and P. Jouve (1990) *Les Dits et les non-dits de Jean-Marie Le Pen* (Paris: La Découverte).
Maréchal, S. (1997) *Ni droite, ni gauche... Français!*, http://www.front-nat.fr/livre/livre9.html (downloaded 26/5/97).
Mégret, B. (1990) *La Flamme* (Paris: Robert Laffont).
—— (1996) *L'Alternative nationale – Les priorités du Front national* (Paris: Editions Nationales); http://www.front-nat.fr/livremegret (downloaded 24/2/97).
Miller, A. (1980) *For Your Own Good* (New York: Farrar, Straus, Giroux).
Sibony, D. (1997) *Le Racisme ou la haine identitaire* (Paris: Christian Bourgeois).
Simmons, H. (1996) *The French National Front – The Extremist Challenge to Democracy* (Boulder, Co. and Oxford: Westview Press).
Souchard, M., S. Wahnich, I. Cuminal and V. Wathier (1997) *Le Pen les mots – Analyse d'un discours d'extrême-droite* (Paris: Le Monde-Editions).
Soudais, M. (1996) *Le Front National en face* (Paris: Flammarion).
Tagguieff, P. (1991) *Face au racisme* (Paris: La Découverte).
—— (1996) 'La Rhétorique du national populisme – Les règles élémentaires de la propagande xénophobe', in M. Mayer and P. Perrineau (eds) *Le Front national à découvert* (Paris: Presses de la FNSP).
Todorov, T. (1989) *Nous et les autres* (Paris: Editions du Seuil).
—— (1995) *Essai d'anthropologie générale* (Paris: Editions du Seuil).

Chapter 16

Self-Reflection through Language*

Magda Stroinska

'But was Narcissus beautiful?' said the pool.
'Who should know that better than you?' answered the Oreads. 'Us did he ever pass by, but you he sought for, and would lie on your banks and look down at you, and in the mirror of your waters he would mirror his own beauty.'
And the pool answered, 'But I loved Narcissus because, as he lay on my banks and looked down at me, in the mirror of his eyes I saw ever my own beauty mirrored.'

Oscar Wilde, The Disciple

Introduction

Myths are products of cultures to which they both belong and contribute. The story of Narcissus has been one of the most popular themes in Western literature and in art, giving inspiration to numerous literary works, poems and paintings, depicting various scenes from and various aspects of the myth. Greek myths provide a handy behaviourist framework and readers have always felt tempted to fill the skeleton of the

---

* I would like to thank Yasuko Obana (Chinese and Japanese Studies, University of Queensland) for her insights in the area of cultural anthropology and for her patience in discussing with me many ideas presented in this chapter. Any errors in interpretation are entirely mine.

story with various psychological interpretations. More recently, the name of Narcissus has become famous 'as the psychoanalyst's word for self-adoration and self-absorption which makes a man or woman dead to the whole external world' (Grant 1995:336).[1]

I would like to focus here on yet another aspect of narcissism. I am concerned with the role of language in some basic cognitive processes involved in self-recognition, self-reflection, reflexivity and identity assertion. I argue that those issues receive culturally determined answers: narcissistic in the West but not necessarily so elsewhere. Indo-European languages reflect and perpetuate this narcissistic tendency, as if they were purposefully designed to allow the speaker to create his or her own linguistic reflection.

Language has often been viewed as a mirror of the internal world of the speaker/author and thus a means of their self-reflection. I shall argue that, within Western culture (of which Greek mythology is an important part), the self-centred perspective is the most *seemingly* natural one. It is the perspective immanent in an individualising social structure, the one assumed therefore as the *default* in semantic interpretation and, in fact, one that is condition *sine qua non* for making sense out of what the others say. I would like to present an argument in defence of Narcissus, based on the claim that it is the general structure of Indo-European languages, which, as I argue, is anthropocentric, speaker-focused and egocentric. In short: narcissistic.

Any example from spoken or written discourse could show how the speaker's viewpoint comes across on the basis of the assumption that every text is, to a certain degree, a self-reflection of the author, although self-reflection may not be the primary objective. We also know ourselves through a process of self-reflection: our identity, what we know about ourselves, is the combination of our public self (in Erving Goffmann's terminology, see Goffman 1959), in other words the image that the others form on the basis of our behaviour, both verbal and nonverbal, and our private self, established in part by linguistic introspection. Language is therefore instrumental in the process of self-reflection.

Finally, I shall argue that the individualistic approach typical for Western culture is not universal. Our narcissistic tendency for self-reflection is part of our membership in Western civilisation. Other cultures may attach different value to the concept of self and to the question of individual identity.

The Concept of *Self*

Self-consciousness has long been considered one of the uniquely human abilities and traits. It has been argued (e.g., Humphrey 1982) that some level of self-awareness was a necessary condition for our ancestors to be able to predict the behaviour of others, which, at times, could have been a question of survival. This kind of 'getting into the other person's skin' allowed them to realise how they would have felt and behaved in similar situations. However, there are studies suggesting that, in fact, self-consciousness may not be a uniquely human feature (see Gallup's 1977 study on chimps' reactions to their reflection in the mirror, as described in Mayes 1990:246). The 'bottom line' of research in this area is the assumption that, as Gallup put it, without an identity of your own, it would be impossible to recognise yourself. Gallup attributed the inability to recognise oneself, as is the case with monkeys, as opposed to primates, to the absence of a sufficiently well-integrated concept of self.[2]

I shall focus here on the human concept of self and I shall use the notion of *self* to mean 'the core of identity', as perceived by an individual.[3] It is the 'Mind's I' (see Hofstadter and Dennett 1981), the centre of our consciousness, with consciousness being 'both the most obvious and the most mysterious feature of our minds' (ibid.:7). It is the *I* that is the subject of all our experiences, such as joy and happiness or pain, fear and suffering (thus the phenomenon of the so-called first-person sentences, as discussed by Evans 1982). Glover defines a person as 'someone who can think I-thoughts' (1988:62). We can talk about various features of that *I*, such as distinctiveness ('I am not you') and continuity ('I am the same person I was yesterday'). We have an insider's view of ourselves but others see us from outside. The maintenance and adjustments of a concept of the 'presentation of self' in our daily life (see Goffman 1959) and in the course of social interactions of various kinds, is one of the focal points in the study of any social encounters (see Watts et al. 1992:1 for a discussion).

Development of Self-Consciousness

A widely discussed topic in contemporary philosophy is the assertion that human beings are 'self-interpreting animals' (see Taylor 1985:45). It is an accepted view that the sense of self depends on having a highly developed capacity for symbolic thought which allows us to reflect on our own internal states and actions, as well as on the reality around us. Such reflexive awareness is 'the human capacity to be aware of one's self as being a particular person distinct from all others, and to reflect on the experience of being that person and who that person is' (Stevens 1985). Symbolisation is thus the necessary condition for representation (see Stevens 1991:76), and the ability to recognise objects and persons in our environment is the necessary condition for self-recognition.

Some sixty years ago, George Herbert Mead (1934), American social philosopher and psychologist, investigated the question of how people develop into social beings. He claimed that the most interesting case of symbolisation is the possibility of representing yourself to yourself. We create an image of ourselves in our minds, which stands for what we think we are. We can then manipulate that image. However, as Hewitt (1984:55) argues:

> Individuals do not learn about themselves or experience themselves directly ... The person does not define himself as an object 'from the inside out'. Rather we see ourselves as others see us: In the simplest sense, we learn to use the name given to us by others; more subtly, all the terms of value, respect, hatred, liking, hope, social location and definition that people apply to themselves, they learn from members of their families and the other groups to which they belong.

We may gain some insight into the development of the awareness of self in children by the observation of the development of linguistic means used by the child to refer to itself and to refer to other people in its environment. While infants begin to react to objects and faces at a very early age, they are able to name those objects and persons much later, starting at approximately one year. They learn names of other people before they are able to refer to themselves. It is not surprising that the ability to name more distant and thus distinctive people precedes the ability to name those who are particularly close (such as the mother or primary carer) and so more difficult for the child to separate from itself. When shown pictures of themselves, children may react by saying 'baby', without necessarily linking the picture to themselves. Mayes (1990:247) points out that children learn their own names at about two years of age and begin to use personal pronouns for self-reference some six months later. 'The ability to name oneself and talk about oneself comes rather late in relation to other names, presumably because it requires the child to be able to take a different perspective; i.e. figuratively, it requires the ability to see ourselves as others see us' (ibid.). It has to be noted here that the observation of linguistic behaviour alone cannot be treated as satisfactory evidence of self-awareness, as children may be aware of themselves without being able to demonstrate it through their language use. Nevertheless, it is interesting that both linguistic evidence and results of experiments involving mirror-confrontation suggest that self-awareness seems to emerge at approximately two years of age and that it appears to be linked, in some way, to the ability to identify oneself linguistically. How is this self-awareness constructed?

We grow up surrounded by other people's attitudes towards us, and our social self is acquired by internalising those attitudes. Cooley (1902) stated that 'our selves are always looking-glass selves'. He gave this process an interesting metaphorical description. 'We look to society for an image of ourselves and the image society reflects back becomes our self' (Wetherall 1991:79). Once our identity has been formed, we are capable of creating new self-reflections, 'rejecting some possible selves in favour of some other selves' (ibid.). This ability to be aware of oneself as a kind of object gives us control over ourselves because we may now see ourselves as having the power of changing that object.

Language and Identity

My own interests focus on the representation of the speaker's self-reference and address forms used in communication between different cultures (see Cecchetto and Stroinska 1996; 1997). The system of pronouns used by speakers to refer to themselves, as well as the forms of address used when speaking to others, are one of the most basic parts of linguistic competence. As such, they are often transparent enough to escape our attention. Pronouns are, nevertheless, important tools of self-presentation, able to influence our perception of each other and our mutual attitudes. Therefore, they play an active role in the formation of social images of other people. The erroneous (from the point of view of a given culture) use of forms of reference and address may thus give rise to stereotyping about other people. One standard example is the assumption made by some native speakers of English that the second person singular pronoun is an appropriate form of address in other languages.[4] These native speakers of English may then be labelled arrogant or overly self-confident if, when speaking languages other than their own, they use the informal form of address where it is seen as inappropriate.

But the question of means of reference available to the language may shed light on questions much more intricate than those of culture-specific politeness strategies. Language may be seen as a way of discovering the theory of identity of the people who speak it. It is 'the vehicle of ... reflective awareness' of its users (Taylor 1985:229), an awareness inseparable from language. 'Language realises man's humanity' (ibid.:233).

Indo-European languages use a set of pronouns to distinguish between the speakers (*I*, *we*), persons spoken to (inclusive *we* and *you*) and those spoken about (*he*, *she*, *it*, *they*). Wetherall (1991:71ff), reporting the works of Harré (1983), notes that these distinctions indicate that:

> our sense of strong personal identity, distinct from others and of the self (the 'I') as a substance which acts on the word. [Harré] points out that the Eskimo or Inuit Indian language, in contrast, doesn't emphasise personal identity so strongly and talks about qualities or states of mind which incidentally happen to find expression in individuals. Thus to feel indignation is not 'I feel angry' but 'there is annoyance', 'I hear him' becomes 'his making of a sound with reference to me', and in answering the question 'Who is preparing dinner?' we might say 'I am', the Inuit Indians would say 'the being here mine'. (ibid.)

In Indo-European languages, expressions used to refer to *human agents* typically coincide with the grammatical subjects of action verbs. With the subject–verb–object word order being the unmarked and neutral choice, the subject may further coincide with the topic (defined as the first element of the sentence, often corresponding to the 'given' information). This gives Indo-European syntax a particularly anthropocentric perspective and enforces an agent-relative interpretation.[5] Harré also discusses the impact of this point of view on the perception of creative actions: while we stress the role of the active self, other languages may present the same event as 'bringing forward or releasing the possibilities which are already present in the material itself' (Wetherall 1991).[6] It may be the case that people in such holistic[7] cultures would have difficulty understanding the story of Narcissus, if individual identity and self-reflection are not so much of an issue for them, although reflection may take place in other ways in these societies.

The link between language and identity is a very complex one. Both linguists and sociologists consider language as one of the markers of group identity; however, much less is known about the link between language and individual identity. Although not all languages are equally self-reflexive, one thing seems certain: whenever we talk, we always bring into the act of communicating our culturally conditioned set of beliefs and speech habits. Being somewhat conditioned by the time and place where we grew up, those norms and habits are not universal but culture-specific. What we accept as the only logical and natural norms of verbal (and nonverbal) behaviour, is normal and natural within our own culture and by no means can be assumed to be equally natural in other cultures. What we see as a natural behaviour is a result of our culture.

Whenever we speak or write, we are putting together pictures of ourselves. As Roland Barthes (1967) put it, it is impossible to write (or for that matter to say) anything without labelling ourselves. What we say and how we say it, when we speak and when we decide to keep silent, contribute to the social image of ourselves, as constructed by the others.

Language reveals more than we want it to reveal. It may also reveal what we would very much want to conceal. Victor Klemperer, the German philologist best known for his diaries from the Nazi years and his insightful study of the language of the Third Reich,[8] comments on Talleyrand's saying that language serves to conceal the thoughts of a diplomat. Klemperer suggests that, in fact, the opposite is true. Whatever we try to hide, be it from others, be it from ourselves, the language we use and the way we use it will reveal it *'Le style c'est l'homme'* (Klemperer 1982:16). What people say may be full of lies but the style of their language and the choice of linguistic means mercilessly bring their true nature to light.

Identity and Culture: Egocentric Particulars

Language is thus a vehicle for our self-representation and self-presentation. We reflect upon ourselves in a language and we use language to let others know our innermost thoughts. Both these activities are parts of the process of constructing a picture of our public self. In order to achieve this goal, we use various linguistic means, and most obviously deictic expressions. These are personal pronouns and adverbs of time and place: *I, me, you, here, there, now* and *then*, the so-called 'egocentric particulars', as Russell called them, as their meaning depends on the speaker's identity and location in space and time. Apart from such obvious means of self-representation, the language we use is saturated with various direct and nondirect ways of self-reflection. The type of society we live in determines the level of such saturation.

After Narcissus was born, 'the prophet Tiresias was asked if the baby would live to a ripe old age. He replied: "if he never knows himself"'(Grant 1995:334). We know how this prophecy was fulfilled and we continue to search for the answer to why the knowledge of oneself should become a death sentence for Narcissus.

Heelas (1981:3) argues that 'it is not possible to live as a human being without having an idea of what it is to be human. People have always considered their nature. Their speculations have run along well-worn and reliable paths – those provided by religion, culture and society.'

Knowledge of oneself is the assertion of one's identity. But is this identity only the matter of our self-perception? Or is it, like almost everything else about us, a product of the social environment in general, and the culture in particular? If it were, then we would be asserting that identities are formed differently in different cultures.

Identity in Western societies is built of social categories (position, education, social class, gender, sexual orientation etc.), as well as some more personal categories (such as a sense of being a unique individual with a private 'inner life', with a distinctive personality and individual experience, and a sense of agency). This sense of agency allows us to see ourselves as potential actors, able to cause or shape events, performing actions, that is 'doing things'. Although it may appear obvious that all human beings share those personal feelings of uniqueness and distinctiveness, studies in cultural anthropology clearly show the perception of self as culture-dependent and therefore not universal across cultures and societies. The individualism of Western societies may be contrasted with the collectivism of some more communal social structures.

These differences may easily be seen if one compares, for example, decision-making processes in different cultures. In Western societies (or in individualistic social structures, of which American society is a prime example – see Stewart 1972), the individual sees himself as having the power and right/responsibility to make decisions. Others, for example, experts, counsellors, doctors and friends can only help one to reach the best decision or make an informed choice. In other cultures, where the membership in a social structure is more important than self-assertion, the responsibility for decision-making may be shifted to the group or to the elders. While we tend to believe that personal expression is both valuable and important, the Javanese, for instance, believe that it is vulgar and uncivilised. Geertz (1984:128) described their ideal as follows:

> Through meditation, the civilised man thins out his emotional life to a kind of constant hum; through etiquette, he both shields that life from external disruptions and regularises his outer behaviour in such a way that it appears to others as a predictable, undisturbing elegant and rather vacant set of choreographed motions and settled forms of speech.

Some researchers argue that the belief in agency, individualism and will-power, which is so typical for Western societies, may only apply to the powerful in our society. If it was so, then those who are less powerful, for example, women, might have a different, more communal and less individualistic theory of self (Lykes 1985, after Wetherall 1991:73).

On the other hand, group membership itself, in other words the identification with an in-group set of characteristics, as distinctive from those of the out-group members, may be an equally important factor in the construction of self, no matter how powerful or marginal the group may be. Group membership, however, usually fosters group solidarity, which itself plays down the individualism of group members.

Edinger, in his discussion of the changing relationship between the *Self* and the *ego*, two elements of the human psyche distinguished by Jung, introduces the notion of the 'inflation' of ego. This is the state when ego (the subjective identity) 'has arrogated to itself the qualities of something larger (the Self – i.e. the objective identity) and hence is blown up beyond the limits of its proper size' (1992:7). It may be the case, that Indo-European anthropocentric and *egocentric* perspective in syntax is simply revealing the inflated ego of Western civilisation.

The Indo-European Egocentric Perspective

Various languages offer various means for the speaker's self-reflection. Indo-European languages in general are both anthropocentric and speaker focused, that is, they provide special grammatical constructions that either favour human subjects, or they have special vehicles for expressing the speaker's viewpoints and attitudes. Let me return to the example of the so-called impersonal constructions, in other words structures from which the acting participant has been removed. In Indo-European languages these are permissible only for verbs that take prototypical agents as subjects in the active mode (see note 6). The reference to the acting participant can then be deleted but it is still possible to retrieve the prototypical agent even if there is no mention of it in the surface structure of the sentence (see Chomsky 1965, who argued that only recoverable deletions are permitted in language). This property of Indo-European languages has been pointed out by E. Benveniste (1948), who said that impersonal constructions are allowed only for verbs that have inherently human agents, therefore reference to some kind of human agency is always implied by the semantics of the predicate itself. Prototypical agents are obviously human, exercising their volition in a conscious way, with a purpose in mind (see Taylor 1985).

Many languages give a special status to the speaker and often also to the person spoken to, by allowing the omission of the first (and second) person pronouns, as was the case in Latin, and as is the case in modern Italian or Polish, for example. It appears natural that the speaker and the person spoken to have a different status than those spoken about, as they are those who originally had to be physically present in the act of communicating. There was therefore no need to specify the gender of pronouns referring to the speaker and to the addressee. Similarly, there was no need to encode the gender information in the present tense of verbs in languages that do that in the past tense forms (cf. some Slavic languages, e.g. Polish).

In many languages, not only Indo-European, sentences with no expressed 'subject' are interpreted as referring to the speaker. The so-called first-person sentences are also known to have a special ontological status – they may express assertions that only the speaker is able to make. Expressions like 'I am in pain' are meaningful only as self-ascription, as we are unable to truly assert such inner states to anyone but ourselves. One could say that Indo-European languages are narcissistic in their core grammar, giving the speaker a powerful tool to create his or her own reflection.

While we take it for granted that we may refer to ourselves using the first person singular pronoun 'I',[9] speakers of Japanese have to choose one of four different pronouns, depending on the level of formality and the relative status of the conversation partner. Some languages encode kinship relations in their system of pronouns. In Adnyamadhanha, an Aboriginal language in Australia, there are some ten pronouns corresponding to the English inclusive 'we' (meaning 'you and I'). The choice depends on family membership, kin relation and generation distance. In Chinese, the forms corresponding to the English 'I' look more like titles or self-descriptions, for example 'less worthy one' or 'young brother', while the forms used to address the conversation partner may mean 'wise one' or 'big brother' (examples taken from Romaine 1994:28). Thus, in some languages, speakers are not able to refer to themselves without 'taking into account how they fit into society' (ibid.). Concepts and choices that are perceived as fundamental to a culture are incorporated in the grammar of its languages. The anthropocentric and speaker-focused way of presenting actions and events that is characteristic for Indo-European languages is a linguistic reflection of the individualism of Western societies.

Despite the fact that, in other cultures, self-reflection through language may take different forms, most languages use the focus on the speaker as a default interpretation. The story of Narcissus may 'sound Greek' to many Japanese because Japanese culture has less understanding for self-admiration and self-centred representation of reality. The Japanese language, however, is also speaker-centred in much of its semantics. Any departures from this self-centred way of speaking, unless licensed by literary or other specific purposes,[10] may create confusion or will simply make no sense. We may therefore assert that, at a linguistic level, narcissism is the default strategy of grammatical encoding and decoding, a natural one, with no value judgements attached. The Western egocentric perspective in language reveals an additional emphasis put on the individual psyche of the speaker and the inflation of the subjective element of human identity, thus creating the most suitable background for the interpretation of the Narcissus story. Narcissism is namely just an exaggerated form of the self-centred identity that is one of the foundations of our individualistic society.

Notes

1. The term narcissism, describing this attitude, originated with Havelock Ellis (1898). It was later defined more narrowly as a person's treatment of his/her body as the sexual object. For further discussion of the history of the term narcissism see Grant (1995:333ff).

2. An interesting study done on pigeons has shown that, with appropriate training, it is possible to make pigeons peck at marks on their own bodies reflected in a mirror. The authors (Epstein et al. 1981) do not suggest that we should attribute self-awareness to birds but rather that mirror behaviour in primates and human babies may need to be reinterpreted.
3. The Jungian distinction between the *Self* (the ordering and unifying centre of human psyche, both conscious and unconscious) and the *ego* (the centre of the conscious personality of an individual) will not be discussed here in any detail, as it does not seem to have direct relevance for the topic of this chapter. For an interesting discussion of the relationship between these two notions see, for example, Edinger (1992).
4. Such use of the informal address may be, and often will be, seen as inappropriate in other languages, where there is a distinction between an informal address (second person singular) and a formal address (be it second person plural in French, special pronoun *Sie* used with the third person plural of the verb in German or a special form Pan/Pani/Panstwo – equivalent roughly to Sir/Madame/Plural – used with the third person singular form of the verb in Polish).
5. It is interesting to note that the so-called impersonal constructions (such as passive or reflexive structures, with descriptions of weather phenomena forming an exception) in most Indo-European languages, are possible only for verbs (actions) that assume a human agent. Thus, they are not truly impersonal but rather indefinite. The proper impersonal expressions, on the other hand, often have a similar syntactic form (i.e. a dummy subject, as the English 'it' in 'it rains' and an agreeing verb) to sentences with a subject referring to human actors (for example 'the baby cries'). For a more detailed discussion see Stroinska (1993).
6. This may open some interesting possibilities for analysing religious discourse of different cultures. Does the language in which the religious texts have been written influence their interpretation? The Bible has been translated into hundreds of languages, as it is believed that the message it contains is universal. The same is not the case with the Koran, which, as it is sometimes maintained, cannot be properly understood from outside the culture and language of Islam.
7. Term used by Shweder and Bourne (1984) for cultures that do not make a clear distinction between the individual and society.
8. The 1995 German edition of Klemperer's diaries of 1933–45 (Aufbau-Verlag) became an instant bestseller. The English translation was published in 1998. Until the full version of his diaries appeared, Klemperer was best known for his book on the language of the Nazi propaganda, *Lingua Tertii Imperii*, first published in 1946.
9. There are, of course, exceptions to this rule even in English, for example, the 'royal we' used by monarchs or the indirectly referential expressions used in scientific texts, where the author uses hedges to present the words as a result of a scientific inquiry.
10. The present situation is different from earlier stages of narrative techniques within our civilisation. See Scholes and Kellog (1966) on the development of narrative strategies since antiquity. They indicate, for example, that first-person narration was rare in pre-Roman times and even eye-witness accounts were given in the third person, as 'a document aspiring to achieve truth of fact had a better chance of being appreciated as factual if it did not seem too personal' (243).

Bibliography

Barthes, R. (1967) *Writing Degree Zero*, trans. A. Lavers (London: Jonathan Cape).
Benveniste, E. (1948) *Noms d'Agent et Noms d'Action en Indo-Européen* (Paris: Adrien-Maisonneuve).
Benviniste. E. (1966) *Problèmes de linguistiqie générale* (Paris: Gallimard).
Cecchetto, V. and M. Stroinska (1996) 'Systems of self-reference and address forms in intellectual discourse', in *Language Sciences* 18, 3–4:777–90.
——— (1997) 'Systems of reference in intellectual discourse: a potential source of intercultural stereotypes', in A. Duszak, (ed.) *Culture and Styles of Academic Discourse* (Berlin and New York: Mouton de Gruyter) 141–54.
Chomsky, N. (1965) *Aspects of the Theory of Syntax* (Cambridge, MA: MIT Press).
Cooley, C. (1902) *Human Nature and the Social Order* (New York: Schocken).
Edinger, E.F. (1992) *Ego and Archetype* (Boston and London: Shambhala).
Edwards, J. (1985) *Language, Society and Identity* (Oxford: Blackwell).
Ellis, H. (c.1936) *Studies in the Psychology of Sex* (New York: Random House).
Epstein, R., R.P. Lanza and B.F. Skinner (1981) 'Self-awareness in the pigeon', in *Science* 212:695–6.
Evans, G. (1982) *The Varieties of Reference* (Oxford: Oxford University Press).
Gallup, G.G. (1977) 'Self-recognition in primates', in *American Psychologist* 32:329–38.
Geertz, C. (1984) 'From the native's point of view: On the nature of anthropological understanding', in Shweder and LeVine, 1984.
Glover, J. (1988) *I: The Philosophy and Psychology of Personal Identity* (Harmondsworth: Penguin).
Goffman, E. (1959) *The Presentation of Self in Everyday Life* (New York: Anchor Books, Doubleday).
Grant, M. (1995) *Myths of the Greeks and Romans* (New York, London, Victoria, Toronto and Auckland: Meridian).
Harré, R. (1983) *Personal Being: A Theory of Individual Psychology* (Oxford: Blackwell).
Heelas, P. (1981) 'Introduction: indigenous psychologies', in P. Heelas and A. Lock (eds) *Indigenous Psychologies* (London: Academic Press).
Hewitt, H. (1984) *Self and Society: A Symbolic Interactionist Social Psychology* (London: Allyn and Bacon).
Hofstadter, D.R. and D.C. Dennett (1981) *The Mind's I: Fantasies and Reflections on Self and Soul* (Toronto, New York and London: Bantam).

Humphrey, N. (1982) 'Consciousness: a just-so story', in *New Scientist* 95:474–77.

Klemperer, V. (1982) *LTI – Notizbuch eines Philologen* (Leipzig: Verlag Philipp Reclam jun.) Translated 1998 as *I will Bear Witness* by M. Chalmers (London: Random House).

Luce, L.F. and E.C. Smith (eds) (1986) *Toward Internationalism, Readings in Cross-Cultural Communication* (Boston: Heinele and Heinele).

Lykes, M.B. (1985) 'Gender and individualistic vs collectivist bases for notions about the self', in *Journal of Personality* 53:356–83.

Mayes, P.L.A. (1990) *Introduction to Psychology: An Integrated Approach* (London: Fontana).

Mead, G.H. (1934) *Mind, Self and Society* (Chicago: Chicago University Press).

Romaine, S. (1994) *Language in Society* (Oxford: Oxford University Press).

Schneider, D.J., A.H. Hastorf and P.C. Ellsworth (1979) *Person Perception* (Reading, MA: Addison-Wesley).

Scholes, R. and R. Kellog (1966) *The Nature of the Narrative* (Oxford: Oxford University Press).

Shweder, R. and E.J. Bourne (1984) 'Does the concept of the person vary cross-culturally?', in Shweder and LeVine 1984.

—— and R.A. LeVine (eds) (1984) *Culture Theory: Essays on Mind, Self, Emotion* (Cambridge: Cambridge University Press).

Stevens, R. (1985) 'Personal Worlds', Block 4 of D307, Social Psychology: Development, Experience and Behaviour in a Social World, (Milton Keynes: The Open University).

—— (1991) 'Personal Identity', D103 Social Science Foundation Course, Unit 1, in *Block 5: Identities and Interaction*, The Open University.

Stewart, E.C. (1972) 'American assumptions and values: Orientation to action', in Luce and Smith 1986:51–72.

Stroinska, M. (1993) 'Interpretation of reference for syntactic null arguments', in Darski, J. and Z. Vetulani (eds), *Sprache – Kommunikation – Informatik* 1 (Tübingen: Max Niemeyer Verlag) 201–8.

Taylor, C. (1985) *Human Agency and Language: Philosophical Papers* 1 (Cambridge: Cambridge University Press).

Watts, R.J. et al. (eds) (1992) *Politeness in Language* (Berlin and New York: Mouton de Gruyter).

Wetherall, M. (1991) 'Social Identity', D103 Social Science Foundation Course, Unit 20, in *Block 5: Identities and Interaction*, The Open University.

Wilde, O. (1994) *Complete Short Stories*, ed. I. Small (Harmondsworth: Penguin).

CHAPTER 17

BLACK NARCISSUS: REFLECTIONS ON IDENTITY IN AFRICAN NARRATIVE

Patrick Corcoran

In 1948, in the form of a preface to L.-S. Senghor's *Anthologie de la nouvelle poésie nègre et malgache*, Jean-Paul Sartre wrote an important essay which, in both tone and content, could be read as an official stamp of approval for francophone African and Caribbean literature. He called the essay 'Orphée noir' (Sartre 1948). Apart from the rather emblematic connection between poets in general and Orpheus, there is little within the essay to justify the appeal to Greek mythology in the context of African/Caribbean writing. It does include a rather oblique reference to Aimé Césaire as an Orpheus who walks backwards out of Hades, but little more. More recently, Peter Hawkins and Annette Lavers published the collected papers of the first ASCALF conference on African and Caribbean literature in French under the title *Protée noir* (Hawkins and Lavers 1992).[1] The reference to Proteus in the title is not picked up in any specific way inside the covers of the book. It would seem to have been chosen because in some very general sense the disparate collection of papers had a coherent core, just as the works from the black diaspora under scrutiny in the papers could be seen as in some way homogeneous, and the figure of Proteus – a god capable of changing his physical attributes but nevertheless remaining the same – adequately expressed the notion of durability and coherence in a world of multiple forms.

In a postcolonial context such appeals to Greek mythology, however unfocused they may be, are not unproblematic since they posit a connection with the Western cultural tradition that ultimately engendered the colonial movements, which in turn effectively denied any value to the indigenous cultural systems of the colonised. Between 1948 and 1961, when he wrote the preface to Frantz Fanon's *Les Damnés de la terre*, Sartre seems to have become more acutely aware of some of the difficulties that can arise from positing such connections. On the subject of recent French colonial policy he wrote:

> The European elite undertook to manufacture a native elite; young men were selected, the principles of Western culture were branded onto their foreheads with red-hot irons, behind the gags that had been stuffed into their mouths were grand slogans that stuck to their teeth; after a short stay in France they were sent back home, broken things. They had become living lies that no longer had anything to say to their brothers; they were mere echoes; from Paris, London, Amsterdam we would call out 'Parthenon! Equality! Brotherhood!' and, somewhere in Africa or in Asia lips would mouth : 'thenon ... ality... erhood!' This was the golden age. (Sartre 1961:37)

It is worth reflecting in a little more detail on why the positing of connections between classical antiquity and African cultural tradition is problematic. It is self-evident that establishing such connections could serve many different purposes and could even be viewed as a strategic choice. There are, for example, very serious works of scholarship which, in Western eyes, might be interpreted, rather unkindly, as attempts to legitimise an undervalued African cultural system by illustrating its historical, generic or structural links with (again in Western eyes) the decidedly unproblematic, indeed highly prestigious, cultural legacy of classical civilisation. Probably the best example of such a work is by the Senegalese scholar and philologist, Cheikh Anta Diop, whose *Nations, Nègres et Culture* (1979) demonstrates that strong historical links existed between the Egypt of the Pharaohs and sub-Saharan Africa. A second, much more recent example would be *Myth, Literature and the African World* (1976) by the Nobel-prize winning Nigerian, Wole Soyinka. This offers an analysis of African drama and narrative which, on the one hand, makes many links with archetypes from classical antiquity and, on the other hand, provides a critique of the two contrasting world visions which underpin Western and African cultural production.

To interpret such detailed references to Western cultural traditions as attempts to legitimise or give greater prestige to African cultural activity is ultimately a way of perpetuating the colonialist (not to say racist) cast of mind that created the problem in the first place. What really concerns Soyinka is the possibility of apprehending a culture by the use of reference points which are taken from within the culture itself. This is an ambition worth pondering in some depth and to which I shall return later. For the time being, it is worth simply recognising the fact that both Cheikh Anta Diop and Wole Soyinka are not merely engaged in producing works of academic scholarship. They are also inevitably engaged in a form of activity that not only involves culture but questions of power relations as they are manifested in and through cultural activity.

A second purpose in making connections between the two traditions might be in order to determine whether classical antiquity provides archetypes which can be seen as relevant to aspects of the African tradition as a whole or indeed to particular narratives. If this is so, then the case for arguing the existence of some form of universalist theory of culture, whether evolutionist or functionalist, is strengthened. Who might find solace in such theories is, of course, another matter. Given that the archetypes in question are drawn from the Western tradition, it is perhaps a way of legitimising that tradition as the universal tradition. In two recent studies on the problematic of fatherhood, I examined father–son relationships as they are presented in a number of African narratives (Corcoran 1997:83–96 and 1998:147–58). In these cases as now, the question would seem to involve considering whether the very different forms of social organisation and corresponding cultural activity in sub-Saharan Africa make it meaningful to talk of the Oedipus complex or narcissism in such a different cultural context. In other words, are such concepts themselves universally meaningful and applicable to all men or are they culturally determined and constrained?

So what of Narcissus? In the first instance, the way I would formulate the question is this: to what extent can the myth of Narcissus be considered to offer insights into the overall context of African cultural production? If the myth itself can be read as an allegory, how should the various elements of the myth be allocated meanings in the specifically African context? The key feature that I would like to place at the heart of any rereading of the myth is the act of looking. The fate of Narcissus is determined by this act. Once he has viewed his own reflection in the water of the pool, his fate is sealed. He will continue to look into the pool until death overtakes him. He is captured by the gaze which locks him into a relationship from which he cannot escape. What is striking about Ovid's text at this point, is the time it takes for Narcissus to recognise himself. Recognition dawns, but it is not to be taken for granted. And in this gap it is possible, and perhaps necessary, to raise the question of identity and otherness. It is also worth remembering that Narcissus, gazing into the water, is at no point looking at himself, he is looking at his own reflection: an objectified reality that exists outside himself and which may be seen as a symbol of identity, but which is nevertheless of another order of reality to the organic body of Narcissus, and is essentially other. A subtle interplay is set up when we begin to try to decide whether the reflection in the water is readable as otherness or identity. But such considerations should not deflect us from recognising that what is essential in the Narcissus story is not how we interpret the significance of the act of looking so much as the fact that the act of looking is itself paramount. It is this act which consumes Narcissus and it could be argued that it is this act which informs the whole of colonial and postcolonial relationships.

The colonial relationship is at best a toned-down version of the master–slave relationship as it is embodied and institutionalised, for example, in *Le Code Noir* of the late seventeenth century,[2] and which, even after the abolition of slavery in 1848, continued to be synonymous with fundamentally unequal and nonreciprocal relations. In this type of relationship the African is objectified in such a way that his individual character, not to speak of the African personality and such abstract corollaries as African culture, are systematically denied or travestied because they are invisible. Within a colonial relationship the eyes of the Western master cannot see reality and substance here, because he does not possess a conceptual framework by which the act of looking might be transformed into an act of seeing. His understanding of what he sees is permanently coloured by a feeling that the African is somehow a less-developed, less-perfected version of the humanity he alone fully represents, both as an individual and through his culture. From the Middle Ages onwards, from the literature of exploration and eventually conquest through to the exoticism of the 'Roman colonial', the Western view of Africa and Africans attests to this inability to see the African object other than as a series of stereotypes (see *Notre Librairie* 1987 and 1988). Moreover, the remedy to these shortcomings was implicit in the colonial policy of assimilation, that French version of the white man's burden, which can be summarised as the mission to turn the black African into a black Frenchman or, in other words, to transform alterity into identity by making this 'unsatisfactory' other just like me.

When Africans themselves begin to write their own narratives focusing on the colonial relationship, this motif of poor or defective vision on the part of the whites is omnipresent. The vast majority of novels and stories dealing with the conflicts of the pre-independence period (Mongo Beti, Sembène Ousmane, Henri Lopes, Hampaté Bâ and Ferdinand Oyono), when portraying the type of relationships that existed between coloniser and colonised, often present the perspective of the white Westerner as one that proves incapable of differentiation. Here is an example from Oyono's *Une Vie de Boy*:

> M. Janopoulos doesn't like natives. He has a habit of setting his huge wolfhound on to them ... The ladies enjoy that. Today they had a field day. ... At the first sign of trouble I was jostled, knocked to the ground, trampled on. I sensed the Greek's dog at my heels. I don't know how I managed to get to my feet and climb to the top of the giant mango tree to safety. The Whitemen were laughing ... My own Commandant was laughing with them. He didn't recognise me. How could he have recognised me? To the Whites all blacks look alike. (Oyono 1956a:43–4)

In this novel, the black Africans are perceived as an undifferentiated mass or, on the occasions when a degree of differentiation is achieved by a white, it struggles to go beyond identifying an isolated function: servant, washman, cook and so on, and never manages to recognise the possibility that the individual is endowed with a whole personality.

> 'Toundi, you'll never get the hang of what it means to be a houseboy ... When will you understand that as far as the Whiteman is concerned you only exist through the services you provide for him and that is all! I'm a cook. The Whiteman only sees me through his stomach ...' (Oyono 1956a:131–2)

The same absence of differentiation and the tendency to fragment the personality into single functions is central to another novel by Oyono, *Le Vieux Nègre et la Médaille* (1956b). In this instance the protagonist, Meka, is awarded a medal for services to France. During the official ceremony he is the centre of attention, all eyes converge upon him. Once the ceremony is over he once more blends into the mass and can no longer be distinguished as an individual, much less an important personage. Lost in the town, he is picked up by the police and unceremoniously thrown into prison. Like Toundi, who naively believes that his position as houseboy has given him a head start on the road to acculturation and assimilation, only to find that this is an empty promise, so Meka learns that the temporary VIP status he has been accorded is a mere sham and there will never be any recognition of the true personality locatable behind the façade. Colonial relationships are not based on the recognition of realities but on the fostering of illusions.[3]

The very fragmentation of this Western view of the African is not without its consequences and these African narratives show that the black African's sense of his own identity does not come unscathed through the experience of being subjected to the gaze of the West. The postcolonial context would seem to confirm this point. If the typical colonial situation is one in which the object of the act of looking is not really seen or is seen badly, the postcolonial situation is typified by the primacy of a different type of act of looking. The gaze of the West is demoted to a secondary position and it is the gaze of the African that takes its place in the order of importance.[4] Struggles for independence from colonial powers have often been referred to as attempts by the colonised to find a voice and to win the right to tell their own story or to write their own versions of their history. This process could, however, equally well be expressed in terms of the act of looking. Independence also means the freedom to look at oneself through one's own eyes and not to be imprisoned under the uncomprehending gaze of the other.

When André Gardies came to write the first comprehensive book of criticism on the cinema of black francophone Africa, the departure point for his analysis was precisely this notion that independence meant reconquering not only a space but a sense of identity. One of the first functions of the new cinema was the act of showing Africans to Africans and it was to be accomplished by Africans:

> What is completely taken for granted in the West – talking about oneself – was a right that had to be won here, since colonisation involved, at one and the same time, an act of spatial dispossession and a loss of identity.
>
> In black francophone Africa, it was first and foremost a question of being able to show oneself to oneself: this was the first thing to be accomplished, the foundation stone, without which nothing could be built. (Gardies 1989:14)

The passage from the first act of looking to the second (in other words, from a situation in which the African is an object of the Western gaze to a situation where he is both subject and object – where he is finally able to look at himself) although it may appeal to our sense of justice is none the less problematic. If the sense of identity and the self-image are at least partly functions of how we perceive others seeing us, if we firstly see ourselves by trying to understand how others see us, then it is easy to imagine how the problems of vision detected in colonial relationships must breed problems.

In what ways it is problematic is probably best illustrated by considering the following question: what makes a postcolonial narrative a postcolonial narrative? Is it somehow related to the situation of the writer who produces the narrative or something to do with the particular way readers receive the narrative? Is it related to the narrative's explicit subject-matter: a particular set of social, political and cultural issues and relationships that are typically dealt with? Probably, it is related to all of these, but they cannot be considered as defining postcolonial narrative. The nation states of Europe are living in the same time frame as the ex-colonies and they too are living in a postcolonial era, but who would think to categorise the mainstream English or French literature of the 1990s as postcolonial? To answer my own question, then, I would suggest that what defines the term 'postcolonial' in a cultural context is the inescapable necessity of mediation through and by reference to another culture or other cultures. In order to understand the all-pervasive nature of the mediation process one only has to reflect on the linguistic choices that face African writers, and indeed writers from the black diaspora in general. More often than not they are faced with a choice between expressing themselves through the medium of a language which will give them access to only the most restricted public or using the language of the former colonial power. This problem was articulated by Sembène Ousmane as long ago as 1963, when he wrote: 'If I tried to write in Wolof, who would publish me, who would read me?' (Ousmane 1963:49). His words have been echoed by numerous writers since. An example from the anglophone setting can be found in Ngùgì wa Thiong'o's *Decolonising the Mind* (1986), but this problem also continues to preoccupy creolophone writers from the Caribbean, such as Patrick Chamoiseau, or from Réunion, such as Axel Gauvin.

Once the notion of mediation through another culture has been posited as the defining feature of the 'postcolonial', it is interesting to try to imagine what type of African narratives could be considered as escaping the label 'postcolonial'. The sort of texts that spring to mind are those which seek to escape the clutches of Western influence by a retreat towards a sense of authenticity that can only be located in a precolonial past. *Les Contes d'Amadou Koumba* by Birago Diop (1961), *Le Maître de la Parole* by Camara Laye (1978) or certain of the stories by Amadou Hampaté Bâ, such as *Kaydara* (1978), would fall into this category. But clearly such hankerings after the past are not examples of living culture so much as attempts to breathe life into a culture under threat. A different sort of mediation is going on here.

One of the effects of contact between sub-Saharan Africa and the West has been to supplant an essentially oral tradition with a written literature. For many years, certain writers and scholars have been engaged in a race against time to attempt to collect the stories that compose the oral heritage of the region from the lips of the story-tellers (the griots) before they are lost for ever. The situation is probably best summed up in the phrase attributed to Hampaté Bâ: 'With each old man that dies, a whole library goes up in flames' (in Chevrier 1984:5). There is, however, a paradox at the heart of these efforts to preserve the oral tradition and consign it to print so that it will not be lost for future generations. The very act of preservation can be seen as speeding up the process itself, which is the passage from oralcy to literature.

What these examples show is that African culture in a postcolonial setting involves a constant struggle to assert independence in a variety of forms, but each act of assertion is simultaneously subject to various forms of mediation which bring it back within the orbit of the ex-colonial power.

So the attempt to reread the Narcissus myth as an allegory applicable to the African context, while it may illuminate some of the general problems of postcolonial cultures, is ultimately doomed to failure. In the colonial setting, the African was the object of the act of looking rather than the subject, but when the African achieved the notional freedom to gaze upon himself (a freedom to be located in the postcolonial period) he is as dissatisfied with what he sees as the white man was, albeit for different reasons. When the white claims to see only otherness, this allows some sort of justification for the project of transforming otherness into identity and thus provides an ideological framework for colonialism. When the African, the Black Narcissus perhaps, gazes at the reflection looking back at him from the pools of the white man's eyes, he cannot fall in love with the image. Nor is he, like Ovid's Narcissus, able to feel that the other he perceives can become recognisable as himself. Indeed the very myth in which I have been seeking to insert him can be seen as another form of the cultural mediation which has already obliged him to use the voice of others, the languages of others and the art forms of others.

Notes

(All translations are my own)
1. ASCALF is the Association for the Study of African and Caribbean Literature in French.
2. *Le Code Noir* of 1685 . The text of the code can be accessed on the following website: http://julienas.ipt.univ-paris8.fr/~aceme/
3. It is perhaps true to say that the African view of the white colonialist is no less imperfect and lacking in comprehension, but there is nevertheless a key difference. When the African looks at the European and his customs it is not in a context of cultural conquest. The African is not involved in a proselytising mission to systematically devalue any manifestation of white culture and proclaim its inferiority to his own. The technological and military superiority of the colonisers was somehow seen as a proof of their moral and ethical superiority and was used to justify the worst abuses.
4. This volte-face which leads to the seer suddenly being seen is also referred to by Sartre in 'Orphée noir', where he writes of 'the shock of being seen' (1948:ix).

Bibliography

1987: *Notre Librairie 90: Images du Noir dans la Littérature Occidentale* (Paris: CLEF).

1988: *Notre Librairie 91: Images du Noir dans la Littérature Occidentale* (Paris: CLEF).

Chevrier, J. (1984) *Littérature Nègre* (Paris: Armand Colin).

Corcoran, P. (1997) 'Fathers and sons in African fiction', in J.P. Little and R. Little (eds), *Black Accents* (London: Grant and Cutler).

―――― (1998) 'Politics and Fatherhood in the African novel: *Le Chercheur d'Afriques* by Henri Lopes', in L. Spaas (ed.), *Paternity and Fatherhood* (London: Macmillan).

Diop, B. (1961) *Les Contes d'Amadou Koumba* (Paris: Présence Africaine).

Diop, C.A. (1979) *Nations, Nègres et Culture* (Paris: Présence Africaine).

Gardies, A. (1989) *Cinéma d'Afrique Noire Francophone* (Paris: L'Harmattan).

Hampaté Bâ, A. (1978) *Kaydara* (Dakar: Les Nouvelles Editions Africaines).

Hawkins, P. and A. Lavers (1992) *Protée noir* (Paris: L'Harmattan/ ACCT).
Laye, C. (1978) *Le Maître de la Parole* (Paris: Presses Pocket).
Ngùgì wa Thiong'o (1986) *Decolonising the Mind: The Politics of Language in African Literature* (London: James Currey).
Ousmane, S. (1963) *Afrique 25*.
Oyono, F. (1956a) *Une Vie de Boy* (Paris: Presses Pocket).
——— (1956b) *Le Vieux Nègre et la Médaille* (Paris: U.G.E. 10/18).
Sartre, J.-P. (1948) 'Orphée noir', in L.-S. Senghor, *Anthologie de la nouvelle poésie nègre et malgache* (Paris: Quadrige/PUF).
——— (1961) 'Preface', in F. Fanon, *Les Damnés de la terre* (Paris: Gallimard).
Soyinka, W. (1976) *Myth, Literature and the African World* (Cambridge: Cambridge University Press).

PART VI
THE FATE OF NARCISSUS

≈ CHAPTER 18 ≈

JOUY'S *CÉCILE* AND THE NARCISSISTIC ROMANTIC HERO

Allan H. Pasco

> He who is estranged seeks pretexts
> to break out against all sound judgment.
> Proverbs 18:1

Romantic heroes, those wonderfully vain, deeply melancholic characters that punctuate French literature at the end of the eighteenth and beginning of the nineteenth centuries, have a number of traits and features in common. Self-absorbed, profoundly narcissistic, they commit themselves as their primary activity to self-analysis, without ever gaining understanding; they see themselves as above the common herd, though they seldom gain positions of authority, and they remain both morally isolated and deeply dissatisfied with surrounding reality (Holmes 1977:59).[1] Manifestations of the generic Romantic hero form a continuum extending from one extreme that Emile Durkheim termed anomic to the other that I would call anaclitic. Though the basic narcissism of the Romantic hero can be seen in either variety, the two differing ways that they live out their lives are also evident. Anomic characters lack direction or purpose. Primarily inwardly orientated, because they feel so little connection with the outside world, they are indecisive and unempowered and tend to wallow in isolated anguish.

The other variety of Romantic, literary creations, while no less self-centred, extends their self-definition to include the goal or the object of affection into the image and definition they have of themselves. Such goal-defined and orientated, anaclitic characters tend to be fairly confident and empowered, while being no less narcissistic or self-absorbed. Whether they succeed or fail, they choose to commit themselves absolutely to incorporating the object of their affections or obsessions into their personal lives. Vigny's Chatterton of 1835, for example, sees Kitty Bell as a part of himself.

Erich Fromm believed that human narcissism is always a pathological development of love towards self and others (Bacciagaluppi 1993:104). While that seems true as well of literary manifestations, the pathology may be either muted or explosively obvious. Consequently, Fromm's distinction between narcissists that are benign, on the one hand, or malignant, on the other (ibid.:98), is very useful. Benign narcissists are passive and harmless to themselves and to others; malignant characters are both aggressive and dangerous. Because characters are not necessarily fixed in either of the extreme varieties I suggest, they may swing from one excess to the other: from anomic to anaclitic and, in both categories, from benign to malignant. Most often changes occur when anomic characters that have no clearly defined goals awaken to the desire for something or someone outside themselves and, thus, become anaclitic. Whether anomic or anaclitic, benign characters may become malignant if they feel empowered. They become dangerous if anything blocks satisfaction in their attempt to dominate some aspect of themselves, if internally directed, or, if externally orientated, to subordinate and control another in the outside world. Malignancy usually comes from the frustration that is part and parcel of all Romantic heroes who have trouble distinguishing themselves clearly from the object of their love. When that object resists, or when other forces try to separate self and 'other', Romantic heroes tend to react violently and destructively. Even when malignant, of course, anomic characters are seldom harmful to others, but they may turn on themselves and commit suicide. Malignant, anaclitic personages may also harm themselves, though their impulses are more commonly, and more generally, outward and outwardly destructive.

Anomic Romantic heroes often claim to have 'read all the books' and 'experienced' everything, though we soon learn that they have never left the home parish. As their most important trait, these obsessively inward-looking characters have no fixed goals. They whine piteously, because they are outside normal societal structures and thus without power. Unappreciated and unwilling or unable to make appropriate compromises and choices, they remain disengaged, if not explicitly rejected. Although anomic characters are, like all Romantic heroes, narcissistic and thus egoistic, they are unable to understand anything outside themselves. So it is with René in 1802, with Obermann in 1804, with Adolphe in 1816, and with legions of others. Such characters may have once successfully formulated a desire for something or someone beyond themselves, but they were never able to integrate the external object into their self-image. They are either permanently frustrated, as when René's sister Amélie dies, or forced to recognise that the goal is insufficient to bring contentment, as when Adolphe finds himself chained to Ellénore. In either case, they resemble flotsam helplessly and miserably caught in the wash of daily life. Empathy with or even consciousness of others is fleeting and shallow.

Anomic characters may vary in detail from one another, but their overall description remains relatively consistent. Stendhal's Fabrice del Dongo diverges in a minor way from many of his brothers and sisters, for example, in that he merely floats without the normal accompaniment of continuing despair (Pasco 1991:361–78). Most are, however, supremely conscious that they do not know what they want. Were they to have clearer understanding and consequently be able to formulate a goal, they would still be mired in the expectation that they will be victimised by a pernicious society, a cruel father or a selfish husband. They cannot work for the fulfilment of desire, because they have little idea of what would bring satisfaction. Their only certainty is that they are bitterly unhappy, and they suspect that their dismal fate will never end. When benign anomic characters turn malignant, because they are so self-centred, the damage they wreak is to themselves. There are exceptions. I think of Raphaël in Balzac's *La Peau de chagrin* (1831), who kills the young man in a duel almost by accident, through inattention. George Sand's *Indiana* of 1832 is more typical. After being betrayed by Raymon, she drifts, 'sunk in a stupid daydream, in meditation without ideas ... Unawares she stood by the water' (Sand 1962:119–20), where Sir Ralph rescues her from self-destruction.

Anaclitic characters are also capable of suicide, but with them self-murder becomes a public performance, meant to communicate with someone else. They all say, in essence, 'You'll be sorry if I die!' For these Romantic heroes, self-destruction is designed like Werther's to make an impression on others and thus enmesh the other, whether God or the beloved, or both, into the act itself. Indiana's second attempt at killing herself is particularly interesting, because her lack of success indicates a change in her character. Although the reader is not privy to the details of the conversion process, she has extended her ego-centred self-definition beyond herself to include Sir Ralph. She has then become goal-defined; Ralph has become a part of her self and the new self-image, what psychology would call an extension, includes both parts of the new entity. Consequently, because she and Ralph are now one, she successfully avoids despair and suicide.

Anaclitic or object-seeking and defined heroes who pursue an impossible goal and are unwilling or unable to consider an alternative are perhaps the most common variety found in the novels, plays and poems that exemplify Romanticism in the classroom. These characters are so fixated on their desire for some object or person outside themselves that they are rigidly incapable of changing goals. Their self-definition extends to include the other and they cannot see themselves in isolation from the extension of their desire. If the other refuses to take part in this relationship, the Romantic hero's frustration becomes permanent, for he is usually incapable of accepting a substitute. Psychiatrists consider this obsessive fixation on a particular goal or object an inability to 'form a transference'. Anaclitic Romantic heroes and heroines are almost always prevented from attaining and tasting success because the goal is impossible. That impossibility is often represented in literature by the class structure. Because Romantic heroes are generally born in a class somewhat below what they consider their just deserts or below that of the object of their love, the higher class and, as well, the idealised object they configure is closed to them. They have, in short, unacceptable heredity.

Anaclitic narcissists define themselves extensively in relation to the subjectified image of their desire, and their self-definition incorporates their goal. The object (or extension) of their affection becomes part and parcel of their self-image. Unlike anomic characters, who are incapable of making attachments to anyone but themselves, who indeed seem incapable of focusing on external goals for more than a few passing moments, anaclitic Romantic heroes are so extensively focused on whatever it is they want that they are unable to shift their affection from one object to another. To do so would be to change their very entity. Unable to make such transference, they tend to struggle ceaselessly and vainly to gain success. An important and widely recognised characteristic of the Romantic hero is his or her insistence on becoming desperately enamoured of someone whom society or family forbids. The young Saint-Mégrin of Dumas père's *Henri III et sa cour* (1829) falls in love with the Duchesse de Guize, wife of one of the most powerful men of the day. The title character of Ducray-Duminil's *Victor* (1821) is the son of an outlaw who loves the daughter of the powerful Baron de Fritzierne. Children of outlaws like Hernani (1830), foundlings like Dumas's Antony (1831), orphans of another race like Duras's Ourika (1824), are for example denied the fulfilment of love in a marriage that would have moved them into the upper reaches of society. Just as Romantic love must *post hoc, ergo propter hoc* be frustrated, so social success is likewise impossible. Even when the principal characters of Romantic literature adopt a new name, like Lucien de Rubempré or Julien Sorel de La Vernaye, they will be found out, exposed, and expelled or crushed. Very commonly, they choose as the object of their wondrously total love the wives of powerful men. Often the female object of affection fulfils her romantic destiny as well, by defying her husband and falling in love herself, before suffering a lifetime of remorse – most often a short lifetime (I think, for example, of Madame Cottin's Claire d'Albe of 1799). Those heroes, like Julien Sorel and Chatterton, that repeatedly throw themselves against goals they know to be impossible are the most common manifestation. While they may occasionally succeed, as in the case of Julien, they will continue to raise the ante until they fail, crushed by what they loudly proclaim to be a brutish, unfeeling society. Many Romantic characters fit this sad pattern.

Malignant, anaclitic heroes are particularly interesting, whether they are born in the category or shift over during the narration. These are usually the freebooters, the larger-than-life adventurers. While such heroes have chosen impossible goals, they may, by one means or another, successfully impose their will on whomever or whatever is involved. Because only their own, personal desire has significance for them, other people and the laws of society are important to the degree that they help or impede the realisation of the goal. Whether the means of attainment is moral or immoral matters little, as long as it moves the heroes appropriately towards stabilising the object of their affection or desire as a part of their self-definition. They are indifferent to possible offence against man or God as they attempt to gain success. Only victory or defeat is significant. Such heroes may, like Stendhal's Gina, sink to prostitution and murder. No crime is too abhorrent, no sin too base. Whatever stands in the way, for example, of the Count de Monte Cristo's vengeance will be swept aside. When Alphonse Karr's Edward steals Magdeleine from his friend Stephen and marries her, for another example, Stephen then exacts revenge by killing Edward in a duel before seducing his widow (*Sous les tilleuls* 1832). Without regard for standards, rules, conventions or laws, such characters confront life and struggle at any cost to impose their own personal will on the world.

It does happen that such characters occasionally exhibit a streak of inherent decency that makes them anxious to avoid committing a truly revolting crime that hurts others. As a result readers find them sympathetic. Hugo's Jean Valjean (*Les Misérables*, 1862), or Suë's Rodolphe (*Les Mystères de Paris*, 1842–3), or even Balzac's Victor, Hélène d'Aiglemont's corsair lover in *La Femme de trente ans* (1830–42), come to mind. Most often, however, they have few scruples, and like Balzac's Vautrin, Ducray-Duminil's Roger, in his *Victor ou l'enfant de la forêt* (1798), or Alphone Karr's Stephen in *Sous les tilleuls*, only success matters. If they eventually meet destruction, as does Balzac's Victor, or are overcome by repentance, like Karr's Stephen, the change occurs almost as an afterthought, with little textual preparation. Etienne Jouy's Anatole is cut from this mould. Because his incestuous love, which he consummates by riding roughshod over church, family and society, so clearly reveals his narcissism, he emphasises certain traits that mark all Romantic heroes, whether anomic or anaclitic. One might even suggest that he serves as a sort of *summum genus* of the Romantic hero.

Anatole's adventure is recounted in Etienne Jouy's *Cécile, ou les passions* (1827),[2] an obvious pot-boiler that uses what was at the time the outmoded form of an epistolary novel, with little stylistic discrimination between the various letter-writers, shallow characterisation and poorly integrated digressions of considerable length. The slipshod quality is a problem, since by the time of its publication, Jouy, known primarily as Monsieur de Jouy, was a thoroughgoing professional of both experience and success. He was the author of the well-known 'Hermite' series, descriptive essays about Paris and the provinces that had enormous popularity (for example, *L'Hermite de la Chaussée d'Antin* (1813–15), *Guillaume Le Franc Parleur* (1815), *L'Hermite de la Guiane* (1816–17)). Claude Pichois wonders whether the collaboration of Philarète Chasles might not be responsible for the stylistic flaws and structural imbalances of the final result (1965:176) but, for whatever reason, from an aesthetic point of view, little recommends the novel. From a perspective of sociology and literary history, however, it sheds important light on Romanticism. As Pierre Larousse puts it, *Cécile* is a novel 'which in itself is sufficient to characterise the literature of the period in which it appeared. Convoluted ideas ... endless dissertations on suicide, the barbarism of French law, prejudice, infanticide, Seneca, manichaeism, and so on, and so on' (1867:663). Larousse does not mention either incest or personal violence, which are among the novel's most important themes and also its most important narrative functions or motivations.

Leaving aside quality and concentrating on devices, themes, character, and story, *Cécile* seems a typical Romantic novel. The heroine has just been released from the Laguich convent. On returning to her family, she learns that the socially prominent, wealthy Comte de Montford wishes to marry her. She, however, finds him repugnant and cannot understand why her insensitive father would force him on her. She dreams of her mother's brother, Anatole, who is soon to return from exotic adventures in Ceylon and India. Among his other feats, Uncle Anatole saved his best friend, Charles d'Epival, from a life of slavery by a combination of self-sacrifice and military prowess. Not all of Anatole's adventures were so successful. When his Sinhalese mistress's family accepts a local man's offer of marriage, for example, the new fiancé tries to keep the girl from Anatole by hiding her in a temple to which foreigners are forbidden entrance. Anatole explodes with activity to save his mistress for himself: he breaks into the holy place, assaults a priest, joins with friends to combat local troops, and ends up in a Dutch jail. In the course of the tumultuous events, the girl is knifed and dies. Charles manages to break his friend out of jail, though at the cost of considerable violence against the Dutch. This seeming digression sets the pattern for the future. Anatole's personal desires are more important than social conventions and laws, more important than the welfare of others.

Clearly, Jouy had a particular character type in mind. In fact, Anatole exhibits the characteristics considered typical of a narcissistic personality disorder: (a) a longstanding pattern of grandiose self-importance; (b) fantasies of unlimited sex, power, brilliance or beauty; (c) an exhibitionistic need for attention and admiration; (d) either cool indifference or feelings of rage, humiliation or emptiness in response to criticism, indifference or defeat; (e) various interpersonal disturbances, such as feeling entitled to special favours, taking advantage of others and an inability to empathise with the feelings of others (American Psychiatric Association 1980 in Schimel 1993:67).

These traits and features appear in Anatole to varying degrees, but each is a part of his psychological make-up. His extreme egoism is undeniable. On returning home, Anatole tells of his many adventures to an admiring audience. Since he is gifted at explaining difficult concepts, he agrees to tutor his niece and godchild, Cécile, whose education has been neglected. Mme de Clénord, Cécile's unsuspecting mother and Anatole's sister, is pleased to note that he 'seems ... to have retained the tender affection he had for her in her childhood' (23.55). Cécile was five when he left and is now a very pretty girl of fifteen. Their mutual attraction soon blossoms into love and his friend Charles warns him to flee: 'Stop deluding yourself about the nature of your feelings for your niece' (23.171). As with any narcissist, Anatole's own wishes are paramount, however, and he remains. Finally, finding themselves alone in an isolated wing of the family chateau, 'I took Cécile in my arms, I dared to put my sacrilegious hand on her chaste breast ... My frenzy reawoke her reason ... she pulled away' (23.293). Both characters fill page after page with evidence of their passion and of the recognition that it is an impossible love. Not only are they too closely related to avoid ecclesiastical strictures, but her father would also oppose their union. Anatole thinks of suicide in the family crypt, but instead seduces the teenager on the tomb of his and, consequently, her maternal ancestors (23.314). 'This love', he tells her, 'is a crime on earth, but here [in the catacombs of my maternal ancestors' tombs] we are no longer in the world of men' (23.314). 'Cécile', Anatole later explains to Charles, 'lost, prostrated on the maternal tomb [in other words 'my mother's tomb'], clutching, in one hand, the urn of ashes, was no sacred object to me ... incest and sacrilege were consummated' (23.314) Finally, Cécile writes her friend Pauline, 'I am lost, defiled, guilty in the eyes of religion, nature and society, I shall bear the mark of opprobrium on my forehead forever' (23.306). She has succumbed to Anatole. As is common in incestuous Romantics (Pasco 1997:109–32), when Anatole thinks of Cécile, 'all the feelings of a father, brother, lover and friend came together within me' (24.19). His sister, Mme de Clénord, agonises, however, over 'the idea of witnessing a union that nature, religion and law all condemn' (24.58).

As a result of their meeting among the dead in the family sepulchre, Cécile is pregnant. Although Anatole wishes to marry her, there is little chance of swaying the girl's 'unnatural father' (24.123). After Cécile gives birth secretly, M. de Clénord offers her the choice of marrying M. de Montford or taking religious orders. She chooses the latter. Anatole, who hears of her decision only on the day she is to take her vows, acts precisely as before when he was frustrated in Ceylon. He rushes in a fit of anger to the convent, assaults a religious and tries to carry off Cécile, before being clubbed unconscious and taken away. Modern psychiatrists would recognise his rage as one of the 'intense rage attacks (narcissistic rage), which narcissistic patients commonly experience when frustrated in their narcissistic needs' (Kernberg 1984:291). Certainly, to Cécile and his friend Charles, Anatole gives every evidence of insanity, leaving Cécile little choice but to proceed with her commitment to the church. Later, after Anatole regains his reason, he breaks into the convent and steals her away. Eventually they end up in the New World, find a complacent priest who blesses their union, and establish an idyllic community. They remain until they hear of the Revolution in France, at which point they return home, ready to take part in a new world where such marriages as theirs will be allowed.

Although the publication date of 1827 means that Etienne Jouy was very early in choosing to deal openly with consummated incest, as one would expect from an ardent social conservative and literary classicist (however Romantic the subject matter), he fills *Cécile, ou les passions* to overflowing with guilt. The title character bears a name that means 'blind' – it is also the name of Cleveland's daughter in *Le Philosophe anglais ou les mémoires de Cleveland* (1732–39), whom the Abbé Prévost saved from incest with a last-minute revelation. Unfortunately, Jouy's Cécile is not blind. Both Anatole and Cécile are aware of their close, blood relationship and, as uncle and niece, they understand that what they are involved in is incest, thus taboo, thus a vile crime and mortal sin. Their friends Charles and Pauline point out that it is occasionally possible to gain ecclesiastical permission for the marriage of even such closely related relatives, given sufficient money (a common ancestor up to and including a great-grandparent requires ecclesiastical dispensation), but this case would be particularly difficult, given Cécile's father's vigorous opposition. Nonetheless, Cécile writes to Anatole, 'I love you' (24.56), and he responds similarly (24.81).

I have argued elsewhere that from the late eighteenth to the mid-nineteenth centuries incest may well have been a significant social problem (1997a and 1997b). We cannot be certain, for arrest records are unclear and untrustworthy. All we know is that incest was one of the most common themes in the literature of the day. It was not simply that Oedipus served as the subject of a number of works (such as Guillard and Sacchini's opera *Oedipe à Colone* (1787) and both *Oedipe chez Admète* (1778) and *Oedipe à Colone* (1797) by Ducis); the theme of incest itself became a commonplace.

Although the mention of incest may bring Rousseau's Mme de Warens to mind, since Jean-Jacques insistently refers to her as *maman* (*Confessions* 1782, 1789), Rousseau and Mme de Warens were not related by marriage or blood. Consequently, using recent definitions of incest as 'any sexual activity – intimate physical contact that is sexually arousing – between non-married members of a family' (Justice and Justice 1979:25), in this case there was in fact no incest.[3] Still, for incest as a literary topos, it is not so much the actual reality of incest that has importance as the suggestion, the suspicion, the odour of incest. Variations on this hint that the age-old taboo had long been significant; it did not begin with Rousseau. Crébillon père's *Rhadamiste et Zénobie* (1711) and *Sémiramis* (1717) turn on it, as does Voltaire's version of *Sémiramis* (1748) and his never-performed *Les Guèbres* (1769), as do many others. Rousseau's *Les Confessions* and *La Nouvelle Héloïse* (1761) are, however, worth noting as a separate category, since their enormous popularity doubtless had much to do with taking incest as an occasional literary theme and establishing it as a topos.

Likewise, before Saint-Preux was adopted into the family, his and Julie's affair was unethical because he was her tutor, but they were not related and thus there was no incest. After he was adopted into the family, however, only Julie's death preserved them from breaking the taboo. One of the interesting aspects of *La Nouvelle Héloïse* consists in the way Rousseau suggests, but avoids, incest. In doing so he configures a variation on the literary topos 'the avoidance of incest' that was an important narrational function from early in the eighteenth century. I have already mentioned, for example, how the title character of the Abbé Prévost's *Cleveland* falls in love with Cécile, whom he later discovers to be his own daughter. Because of the discovery, they are saved from incest. There is also reason to believe that the main reason Virginie had to die in *Paul et Virginie* (1788) was so the author could avoid marrying them to each other and the ensuing consummation of unacceptable affinitative incest. One might also wonder whether Zilia and Aza might have had more success getting together in Françoise de Graffigny's *Lettres d'une Péruvienne* (1747) if they had been less closely related. Whatever the case, by the end of the century and well into the next, the hint of incest wafts across multitudes of French works. By the 1820s it was almost a cliché.

Eighteenth-century writers and thinkers were fascinated by the fact that the Bible apparently permitted incest in at least the two instances of Adam's and Noah's families. In Sade's *La Philosophie dans le boudoir* (1795), Dolmancé reminds his student, Eugénie, that the families of Adam and Noah were incestuous, and far from being repulsed he claims that incest is very natural. 'If love, in a word, is born of similarity, where is this more perfect than between brother and sister, father and daughter?' (Sade 1966:420). Diderot's chaplain puts the matter somewhat differently in his discussion with the Tahitian: 'Well, I grant you that *incest* may not hurt nature in any way' (1956:496). The issue arises repeatedly. In Guillaume Grivel's *L'Isle inconnue* (1784–7), the Chevalier des Gastines and Eléonore are shipwrecked on a deserted island. 'Aren't we in the same position as our first parents?' asks Gastines (Grivel 1784–7:1.236). Later he will allow his many children to marry among themselves. 'We were convinced that we should deviate from the rules observed in policed nations only when it was not possible to observe them' (4.4–5). He might have found a justification in Charles Fourier's much later analysis of biblical incest: Fourier concludes that God must have approved of the incestuous relations of Cain, Abel and Seth, since He could have avoided the need by creating a second 'first' couple. While recognising that incest is no longer permitted, Fourier opens the possibility that at some future time, God may reintroduce the old statutes (1841–8:4.81–4).

Literary incest is almost never consummated. The father's return prevents what Freud called 'the horror of incest' between Dorval and Rosalie in Diderot's *Le Fils naturel* (1757).[4] In Beaumarchais's *Le Mariage de Figaro* (1784), when Count Almaviva and the complicitous Judge Bridoison intend to force Figaro into marriage with Marceline, at the last moment they discover her to be his mother. With the unveiling of the true, blood relationships, Figaro is saved for his much-loved Suzanne and simultaneously preserved both from his horrendously unattractive mother and from incest. The danger of incest is likewise overcome in Beaumarchais's *La Mère coupable* (1792) only by the revelation of the parents' respective adulteries. René's sister Amélie resists incest in Chateaubriand's famous story (1802). Atala (1801) is preserved by poison from her adopted brother Chactas. Similarly, when Eugène Sue's Fleur-de-Marie learns in *Les Mystères de Paris* (1842–3) that Rodolphe is her father, she understands the feelings that draw her to him. If late eighteenth- and nineteenth-century characters are allowed to marry, we can be almost sure that they are not related, despite the pet names they have for each other: whether the *maman* of Rousseau's *Les Confessions*, the *petite maman* of Faublas (1787), the *ma soeur* of George Sand's *Indiana*, the *mon enfant* of *François le champi* (1848), or the *ma fille* of *La Mare au diable* (1846). Only in pornography or melodrama and the closely related *roman noir*, which feed on the violation of taboos, do authors permit the consummation of incest. There are exceptions, like Jouy's *Cécile*, but when they occur the result is for the most part exemplary, as in Balzac's *La Femme de trente ans* (1830–42), where Julie dies from shock on learning that her daughter is having an affair with her half-brother. Dumas goes further when the thrill value of the theme had abated and allows the half-brother and sister of *Ingénue* (1853–5) to marry, but only in a Polish netherland far from France. Mosca is quite within the expectations of his society in Stendhal's *La Chartreuse de Parme* (1839) when he comforts himself with the thought that his mistress Gina 'loves [Fabrice] like a son … In this lies all my hope: *like a son*' (1952:2.154).

The 'avoidance of incest' narrative function must have served as a means for Romantic readers to indulge in the titillation of the 'horror' without sharing the guilt. That they were indeed drawn to incest is revealed by the very numbers of works published, and reprinted, where incest played an important role. Furthermore, as the amazing frequency of incest in the literature of the day reveals, there can be little doubt that the perversion held sway in the fantasy life of many who bought Romantic novels and admission to Romantic plays. I wondered in my *Sick Heroes* whether the obvious attraction that Romantics felt for incest might come from their egregious narcissism. Restif de La Bretonne's quasi-fictional Monsieur Nicolas mused, 'Is it true then that in love, it is not the object that we love, but the immediate charm it gives our existence, and that the love we feel for a mistress is nothing other than the romantic, fairytale love of ourselves?… I think so.' And he goes on to explain that he believes so because he had loved a number of his own daughters. 'Ah! We are all Narcissuses!' (1989:2.213). And as Jouy's Anatole remarks to Cécile, 'We were (as you said as you clasped me to your breast), "two halves united in one person"' (24.26). The incest emphasises the narcissism of Cécile and Anatole but, in truth, whether the temptation of incest that is so prevalent in Romantic works is consummated or not, the mere suggestion of incestuous attraction emphasises the narcissism that is essential to the Romantic hero. The enthymeme is very simple: all Romantic heroes are narcissistic.

With *Cécile*, the incest topos, which had been reserved for those Romantic heroes who were destined for eternal frustration, since they were unable to transfer their goals to a more possible object, is freed for other purposes. Incest committed reminds us that all Romantic heroes, whether anomic or anaclitic, are in the process of making love with themselves. The malignant, anaclitic character like Anatole who actually completes the union merely takes the narcissistic desires of all Romantic heroes to the extreme. He successfully gains victory over the impossible. In doing so, the other that he loves is so completely integrated into himself that it is as though there is no other, no objectified desire. Whether anaclitic or anomic, the Romantic hero looks only to himself; he lives only in the mirror. As Eric Fromm puts it,

> The selfish [narcissistic] person is interested only in himself, wants everything for himself, feels no pleasure in giving, but only in taking. The world outside is looked at only from the standpoint of what he can get out of it: he lacks interest in the needs of others, and respect for their dignity and integrity. He can see nothing but himself; he judges everyone and everything from its usefulness to him; he is basically unable to love. (Cited in Schimel 1993:201)

René is so occupied with contemplating his own unhappiness that he is unaware of his sister's love. Chatterton commits himself to his desire without regard for the outcome, and Anatole breaks one of the strongest taboos of civilisation in order to satisfy his desire. But whether the Romantic hero is unable to break out of his subjective ego or whether he succeeds in integrating an external, objectified 'other' into himself, Narcissus reigns.

Notes

1. See also: Ridge (1961); Garber (1969:213–27); Furst (1979) and many others.
2. Both the edition I shall use – volumes 23 and 24 of Jouy's *Oeuvres complètes* (Paris: Jules Didot aîné) – and the five-volume separately published version

by Tastu came out in 1827, although the *Oeuvres complètes* carries an erroneous publication date of 1823. Claude Pichois considers the novel's publication and authorship in detail (1965:1.166, especially nn.128-9). Although the title page gives only Jouy's name, Pichois notes that Quérard's *Les Ecrivains pseudonymes* and L. Louvet credit Chasles with the authorship, as do Talvart and Place (1930:2.383). Pichois finds hard evidence only that Chasles helped with proofreading, but the – for Jouy – uncharacteristically Rousseauistic flavour of many passages leads Pichois to suspect that Chasles did indeed collaborate on the work (1965:166-76).
3. For a brief discussion of other possible definitions, see Mary de Young (1982). The relationship between the young Jean-Jacques and his *maman* would, however, doubtless fall under the shadow of 'spiritual incest' – see Aristénète [François-Félix Nogearet] (1787).
4. Suzanne R. Pucci (1997) argues that Diderot's incest in *Le Fils naturel* is a function of the reproduction and representation of family intimacy.

Bibliography

American Psychiatric Association (1980) *Diagnostic and Statistical Manual of Mental Disorders* (Washington, DC: American Psychiatric Association).
Aristénète (pseudonym) [F.-F. Nogearet] 1240 [1787]: *Manuel des boudoirs ou essais érotiques sur les Demoiselles d'Athènes. Ouvrage plus moral qu'on ne pense, tiré en partie du porte-feuille secret du secrétaire grec du Scythe Anacharsis Cythère, avec license des Amours, l'an du plaisir & de la liberté*, trans. A.-R. Lesage, A.-G. Meusnier de Querlon and authors unknown, ed. C.-F.-X. Mercier de Compiègne. 4 vols. (Cythère [Paris]).
Bacciagaluppi, M. (1993) 'Fromm's Views on Narcissism and the Self', in J. Fiscalini and A.L. Gray (eds) *Narcissism and the Interpersonal Self* (New York: Columbia University Press).
Diderot, D. (1956) *Supplément au Voyage de Bougainville*, in P. Vernière (ed.), *Oeuvres philosophiques* (Paris: Garnier).
Fourier, C. (1841-8) *Théorie de l'unité universelle* [1822], in *Oeuvres complètes* (Paris: Société pour la Propagation et pour la Réalisation de la Théorie de Fourier).
Furst, L.R. (1979) *The Contours of European Romanticism* (London: Macmillan).
Garber, F. (1969) 'Self, Society, Value, and the Romantic Hero', in V. Brombert (ed.) *The Hero in Literature* (New York: Fawcett).
Grivel, G. (1784-7) *L'Isle inconnue ou mémoires du chevalier des Gastines, recueillis & publiés par M. Grivel*. 6 vols. (Paris: Moutard).
Holmes, G. (1977) *The 'Adolphe Type' in French Fiction in the First Half of the Nineteenth Century* (Sherbrooke, Québec: Editions Naaman).
Jouy, E. (1827) *Oeuvres complètes* 23 and 24 (Paris: Jules Didot aîné).
Justice, B. and R. Justice (1979) *The Broken Taboo: Sex in the Family* (New York: Human Sciences Press).

Kernberg, O. (1984) *Severe Personality Disorders: Psychotherapeutic Strategies* (New Haven: Yale University Press).

Larousse, P. (1867) *Grand Dictionnaire universel du XIXe siècle* 3 (Paris: Administration du Grand Dictionnaire Universel).

Nogearet, F.-F. (see Aristénète).

Pasco, A.P. (1991) 'The Unheroic Mode: Stendhal's *La Chartreuse de Parme*', in *Philological Quarterly* 70:361–78.

—— (1997a) *Sick Heroes: French Society and Literature in the Romantic Age, 1750–1850* (Exeter: University of Exeter Press).

—— (1997b) 'Incest in the Mirror: Bernardin and the Romantic Tradition', paper given at *Narcissistic Reflections* colloquium, London, UK, 31 May.

Pichois, C. (1965) *Philarète Chasles et la vie littéraire au temps du romantisme*. 2 vols. (Paris: José Corti).

Pucci, S.R. (1997) 'The Nature of Domestic Intimacy and Sibling Incest in Diderot's *Fils Naturel*', in *Eighteenth-Century Studies* 30, 3:271–87.

Restif de La Bretonne, N.-E. (1989) *Monsieur Nicolas ou le coeur humain dévoilé* [1790–7], ed. Pierre Testud. 4 vols. (Paris: Gallimard).

Ridge, G.R. (1961) *The Hero in French Decadent Literature* (Athens: University of Georgia Press).

Sade, D.-A.-F. (1966): *La Philosophie dans le boudoir* [1795], in *Oeuvres complètes du marquis de Sade* 3 (Paris: Cercle du Livre Précieux).

Sand, G. (1962) *Indiana* [1832] ed. Pierre Salomon (Paris: Garnier).

Schimel, J.L. (1993) 'Love and Sexuality in Narcissistic Personalities: A Clinical Report', in J. Fiscalini and A.L. Gray (eds), *Narcissism and the Interpersonal Self* (New York: Columbia University Press).

Stendhal (1952) *La Chartreuse de Parme* [1839], in *Romans et nouvelles*, ed. H. Martineau (Paris: Gallimard).

Talvart, H. and J. Place (1930) *Bibliographie des auteurs modernes de language française (1801–1927)* (Paris: La Chronique des Lettres Françaises).

Young, M. de (1982) *The Sexual Victimization of Children* (Jefferson, NC: McFarland).

CHAPTER 19

NARCISSUS' ATTITUDE TO DEATH*

Tivadar Gorilovics

Death is an integral part of the story of Narcissus, being its necessary denouement. Without death the myth would not be what it is. Any other version is thus of no interest to us, including that given by Pausanias in his *Description of Greece* (31:6-9), in which Narcissus falls in love not with his own image but with his twin sister. When she dies he finds some consolation by looking at himself in the water and imagining he sees her face. However, the myth requires it to be Narcissus himself, and not some double, who dies.

As the myth has been retold and reworked countless times, one must obviously choose which versions to consider. For reasons of method as much as simplicity, I shall apply my approach to only two texts which are, however, from my point of view, both consistent and representative. These are Ovid's classic original story in *Metamorphoses* and, as my example of a modern reworking, Oscar Wilde's *The Picture of Dorian Grey*, which will make it possible to examine the way in which the myth can be updated to suit the needs of modern realities and requirements.[1]

Narcissus' death is usually interpreted as the final consequence of a punishment inflicted upon him at the request of one of his many victims by Nemesis, in other words 'divine vengeance', responsible for preventing 'excess', in this case the

---

* Translated from the French by Trista Selous.

young man's pride and unforgivable coldness. Narcissus is punished for seeking to escape the common law of shared love.[2] We should note, however, that in Ovid's work neither Echo nor any of the other victims of his coldness ask for such a punishment; on the contrary, Ovid's Echo is an opinionated and indeed obstinate lover, who intends to stay with Narcissus to his last moments.

My intention here is not to comment on this moralising aspect of the myth, but to look at how Narcissus sees death, investigating his attitude as he reaches the last stage in his destiny. How does he face up to it? Does he see himself as guilty? Does he repent? Is he in despair or has he become hardened?

We cannot imagine Narcissus as anything but young and beautiful. Death thus cuts him off in his youth, as he says himself (l. 470). Yet Tiresias the seer originally told his mother, the nymph Liriope, that he would live to 'the lengthy days of a ripe old age' (347) on the well-known condition that 'he does not get to know himself' (348). Thus Narcissus is capable of ageing like anyone else and dying of old age: his story, unlike that of Dorian Grey, has no place for a dream of eternal youth. Narcissus is young and extraordinarily beautiful, which is enough to explain why 'many men, many girls desired him' (353), led by the nymph Echo. This is as it should be. What is not as it should be, however, is his inflexible disdain for his flock of male and female lovers: 'but (there was in his delicate beauty so stiff a pride) / no men, no girls affected him' (354–5).

Was Narcissus as cold as marble? Let us not jump to hasty conclusions. People who 'hate all that' are anything but frigid. His disdain might be nothing but a show, a deceptive appearance hiding not a simple aversion, but fear and panic at the mere idea of a lovers' embrace. When Echo approaches him Narcissus cries out in alarm: 'He fled and, as he fled, "Hands off, do not embrace me, / I would die", he said, "before I would offer myself to you"' (390–1).

'I would die ...'? Did Narcissus suffer some serious sexual trauma in early infancy? Whatever the case, his reaction is that of any individual confronted with the radical difference that the sexual represents, the eruption of the Other within oneself,[3] except that his reaction is extreme in its violence.

Yet Narcissus' cry, his visceral fear and mortal anguish contrast with what happens following the consummation of the 'crime', which Narcissus moreover commits in all innocence. What happens exactly? He understands that he is burning with love for himself in the paradoxical situation of a lover who wants to be separated from the object of his love, saying 'Oh would that I were able to withdraw from my body; / and, a strange wish in a lover, I should like what I love to be apart' (467–8). However, far from feeling the slightest guilt, he gives himself over to his suffering (469–70) and undergoes a radical transformation to become the paragon of the perfect lover in some story by Marguerite de Navarre, whose passion ultimately consumes him. Thus, in place of a violent death or suicidal despair,[4] we find a model of the 'fine death', a slow pining away, similar to that of Echo, whose unhappiness in love causes her to grow visibly thinner until finally, as Ovid tells us, 'her body's moisture went off into the air' (397–8). Things happen similarly for Narcissus:

> he could not bear it any longer but, just as yellow wax
> will melt before a low fire, or the morning frost
> in warm sunshine, so was he wasted and dissolved
> by love and slowly consumed by its hidden fire.
>
> (487–90)

Finally we learn that 'that body was no more, which Echo had once loved' (493).

Ovid gives a full depiction of Narcissus' last moments:

His last words were these, as he gazed into the familiar spring,
'Alas, oh boy adored in vain', and the place returned
those very words, and when he had said farewell, 'Farewell',
   said Echo too.
He lowered his weary head onto the green grass,
death[5] closed the eyes still admiring the beauty of their lord .

(499–503)

In fact Narcissus' 'stoic' resignation relates to what is called in psychoanalysis the narcissism of death. We shall return to this later. However, here death may also be a victory over destiny and, in particular, over Nemesis, at least if we are to believe Pliny the Elder,[6] who said that the power to leave life is an advantage that men have over God himself.

Death is no burden for me, for in death I shall lay aside this
   pain:
but I would wish that he that I have adored might live longer.
As it is, the two of us will die in a single breath.

(471–3)

This ending reveals the character's self-destructive logic, to borrow an expression from Michel Picard (1995:57), since

Narcissus is condemned to love without hope and to die of this love, as if to prove that his mortal anguish when confronted with Echo's desire was justified. Faced with the impossibility of satisfying a desire of which he is himself both the consenting and the unattainable object, he is taken over by a 'desire for non-desire'. This seems to me to illustrate what André Green says about the narcissism of death:

> The search for satisfaction is continued beyond all satisfaction – as though this had in fact taken place – as though it had reached its aim in the abandonment of any search for satisfaction. – It is here that death takes the form of the absolute being. Life becomes equivalent to death, since it is deliverance from all desire. (1983:22–3)

Referring to Freud's *Beyond the Pleasure Principle*, Green continues: 'It is not unpleasure that is substituted for pleasure, it is Neutrality. We should not think of depression here, but of aphanisis, asceticism, an anorexia of living.'

Although in Oscar Wilde's novel the myth retains some of its constituent elements, it nevertheless undergoes important changes. Like Narcissus, Dorian Grey is young and beautiful, but he discovers his admirable beauty not in the waters of a spring but through a portrait carried out with all an artist's skill by a painter friend who admires and is clearly attracted to him. The portrait shows him as he is seen through the admiring eyes of others. For Dorian sight of this painting marks the decisive moment in his narcissistic awareness of himself, which here takes the classic infantile form and which the narrator describes explicitly by relating Dorian's reactions:

> When he saw it he drew back, and his cheeks flushed for a moment with pleasure. A look of joy came into his eyes, as if he had recognised himself for the first time. ... The sense of his own beauty came on him like a revelation. He had never felt it before. (33)

But Dorian is incapable of mentally grasping his own image by himself, hence his constant need to know what others think of him – a preoccupation which is, and with good reason, completely foreign to Ovid's Narcissus. Dorian's portrait is explained and commented upon by the character who takes the role of his teacher (another new development in the treatment of the myth), a mentor characterised by Wilde as a superior intelligence towards whom Dorian acknowledges his debt: 'You have explained me to myself, Harry', he tells him, not without adding a compliment whose pointedness is evident, since Harry has exonerated Dorian of the death of his first victim, Sybil Vane: 'No one has ever understood me as you have' (121).

It is Lord Henry who makes him aware of the value of youth and, more seriously, of the fragility of youth:

> you have the most marvellous youth, and youth is the one thing worth having. ... Some day, when you are old and wrinkled and ugly, when thought has seared your forehead with its lines, and passion branded your lips with its hideous fires, you will feel it, you will feel it terribly. Now, wherever you go, you charm the world. Will it always be so? ... You smile? Ah! when you have lost it you won't smile. ... Yes, Mr Gray, the gods have been good to you. But what the gods give they quickly take away. You have only a few years in which to live really, perfectly, and fully. When your youth goes, your beauty will go with it. ... You will become sallow, and hollow-cheeked, and dull-eyed. You will suffer horribly ... (29–30)

It is this terrible picture of old age painted by Lord Henry that gives rise to the dream which will bring about Dorian's ruin, the dream of eternal youth. It begins with the bitter thought: 'How sad it is! I shall grow old, and horrible, and dreadful. But this picture will remain always young' (34). We know what comes next: Dorian's desire to remain forever young, while the picture ages. He thinks, with a superficiality of which he is not aware at the time:

> This portrait would be to him the most magical of mirrors. As it had revealed to him his own body, so it would reveal to him his own soul. ... When the blood crept from its face, and left behind a pallid mask of chalk with leaden eyes, he would keep the glamour of boyhood. ... Like the gods of the Greeks, he would be strong, and fleet, and joyous. (124)

The portrait changes as Dorian loses his innocence and gives himself up to indulging his worst instincts and vices. All these things that ravage the man and his youth leave their marks not on his body or, particularly, his face, but on the portrait instead. It is here, of course, with this doubling of the narcissistic image that Wilde makes his most radical departure from Ovid's model, in which Narcissus' beauty apparently remains intact, even through his physical decline and death, since Narcissus can still contemplate himself in the waters of the Styx.

Dorian, this rich and adored young aristocrat of late nineteenth-century British high society in London, is in every way a modern Narcissus, a characteristic product of a *fin de siècle* which celebrated the perverse seduction of 'decadence' and dreamed only of slow death, the end of the world and civilisations exhausting themselves in refinement. He wants to turn his life into a decadent work of art, worthy of the hero of Huysmans' *Against Nature*. Whereas Ovid's Narcissus retains his innocence to the end, Wilde's hero undergoes a process of moral degradation which leads him to murder and suicide. For Dorian, 'to become the spectator of one's own life ... is to escape the suffering of life' (128). At first, he hopes to escape both the eyes of others and the law of Time, which ravages and destroys youth. He behaves as an accomplished narcissist before the magic portrait, whose reflection he is happy to adopt: 'Once, in boyish mockery of Narcissus, he had kissed, or feigned to kiss, those painted lips that now smiled so cruelly at him' (123). Every now and then he goes to visit this portrait, armed with a mirror,

> looking now at the evil and ageing face on the canvas, and now at the fair young face that laughed back at him from the polished glass. The very sharpness of the contrast used to quicken his sense of pleasure. He grew more and more enamoured of his own beauty, more and more interested in the corruption of his own soul. (148)

> One day, while looking at beautiful tapestries, he was almost saddened by the reflection of the ruin that Time brought on beautiful and wonderful things. He, at any rate, had escaped that. Summer followed summer, and the yellow jonquils [7] bloomed and died many times and nights of horror repeated the story of their shame, but he was unchanged. (158–9)

At first he is concerned 'to keep for him the curious secret of his life and hide his soul from the eyes of men' (141). He hides the picture so that no one will see it and so that he can freely enjoy his 'eternal youth'. But the portrait he has carefully hidden away soon becomes unbearable to him precisely because it shows him the ravages of time, which he wanted to escape. Sartre's account of anxiety in *Being and Nothingness* is relevant here: 'I flee so that I will not know, but I cannot not know that I am fleeing and the flight from anguish is merely one way of becoming aware of anguish' (1943:82).

Thus in the narcissism of Dorian, who is so profoundly upset at the very idea of growing old, the obsession with death has its own designated place. For Dorian, the self is not a single essence;

as a good *fin de siècle* decadent with his smattering of biological sciences, he thinks of the human being (and thus himself) as 'a complex multiform creature, that bore within itself strange legacies of thought and passion, and whose very flesh was tainted with the monstrous maladies of the dead' (164).

On the one hand, his behaviour is governed by what Freud calls the megalomania of desire, of a manifestly narcissistic nature, on the other, because this desire is always satisfied, it reaches a fatal stage of exhaustion, where once again we find, though for different reasons and in a quite different context, the narcissism of death, in other words the death of desire. Unlike his predecessor, Dorian is mirrored by a Don Juan, but a Don Juan who finally loses his taste for conquest. The confession Dorian makes to Lord Henry is also a statement of failure:

> I wish I could love ... But I seem to have lost the passion, and forgotten the desire. I am too much concentrated on myself. My own personality has become a burden to me. I want to escape, to go away, to forget. (234)

Before fulfilling his destiny, Dorian makes a vain attempt at moral restitution. He tries to play the repentant Don Juan, but it is too late for him to do it properly. His soul remains hardened, despite an increasingly all-pervading feeling of guilt. His despair and self-hatred do the rest, although without driving him to the conversion called for at the last moment by the magic portrait's painter, whom he kills. Nothing can hold Dorian back on the slippery slope on which he gives himself up to the death drive. Ultimately his story is a version of the myth in which Narcissus is driven to suicide. The serenity shown, despite everything, by Ovid's Narcissus has given way to the torments of a modern conscience. In Dorian's story death is no longer a victory over fate, but a defeat which has nothing grand or truly cathartic about it. In wanting to destroy the terrible portrait, Dorian destroys himself. The anguish which eats at him and the symbolic meaning of his final act bring the myth into harmony with the mental universe of the nineteenth century's closing years.

Notes

1. In the light of the criteria set out by Pierre Albouy in his foreword to *Mythes et mythologies dans la littérature française* (1969).
2. See for example Grimal 1991; Brunel 1992; the entry on *Narcissus* in the *Encyclopaedia Universalis* (French edn.). The detail that Narcissus' favours

were sought not only by nymphs such as Echo but also by young men is passed over in most of the summaries I have been able to find, for reasons we can only guess at.
3. See Chemama 1993:31.
4. Grimal refers to a 'Boeotian' version which ends with Narcissus's suicide, which I have been unable to identify and read. At any rate, it is not in Pausanias.
5. *Nox* in some editions of Ovid's text, in the sense of 'death'. See Ovid 1966.
6. *Natural History* 1, II, 9, cited by Picard (1995:58). Narcissus neither repented nor abandoned his love for his own person. He continued with a vengeance, since even when he was received into Hades, he went on looking at himself in the waters of the Styx.
7. The jonquil is a variety of narcissus.

Bibliography

Albouy, P. (1969) *Mythes et mythologies dans la littérature française* (Paris: Armand Colin).
Brunel, P. (ed.) (1992) *Companion to Literary Myths, Heroes and Archetypes*, trans. W. Allatson, J. Hayward and T. Selous (London: Routledge).
Chemama, R. (1993) *La Psychanalyse* (Paris: Larousse).
Green, A. (1983) *Narcissisme de vie, narcissisme de mort* (Paris: Minuit).
Grimal, P. (1991) *Dictionnaire de la mythologie grecque et romaine* (Paris: Presses Universitaires de France).
Ovid (1966) *Metamorphoses*, ed. J. Chamonard (Paris: Garnier Flammarion).
——— (1985) *Metamorphoses*, ed. and trans. D.E. Hill (Warminster: Aris and Phillips and Oak Park, IL: Bolchazy-Carducci).
Picard, Michel (1995) *La Littérature et la mort* (Paris: Presses Universitaires de France).
Sartre, J.-P. (1943) *L'Etre et le néant* (Paris: Gallimard).
Wilde, O. (1994) *The Picture of Dorian Grey* (Harmondsworth: Penguin).

Notes on Contributors

Max Andréoli has been a university lecturer for many years and now holds an associate professorship in French Literature at Kossuth Lajos University, Debrecen, Hungary. He contributes regularly to *L'Année balzacienne*, is the author of *Le Système balzacien*, and is completing a book entitled *Lectures et mythes*.

Patrick Corcoran taught French at London University and Exeter University before taking up a post at ,the University of Surrey, Roehampton. He has published widely on francophone literature.

Gregory N. Eaves studied in Cambridge, London and Davis, California. His background combines Classics, English and Cultural Studies. His research interests focus on Yeats and the occult and on discourse in cultural studies. He describes himself as an 'itinerant academic, guitarist and trickster, currently practising at Kingston University'.

Jas' Elsner is Humfry Payne Senior Research Fellow at Corpus Christi College, Oxford, and was previously Reader in the History of Art at the Courtauld Institute. He is the author of various articles and books on issues in the history, theory and reception of Greek and Roman art, and his most recent book is *Imperial Rome and Christian Triumph: The Art of the Roman Empire AD 100–450* (Oxford: Oxford University Press, 1998).

Wendy Everett is Senior Lecturer in French and Film at the University of Bath. She is the author of *European Identity in Cinema* (Intellect, 1996), and has published essays in *Screen*,

Europa, and the *Literature/Film Review*, as well as in several edited collections. She is currently a member of the Editorial Board of the *Literature/Film Review*.

André Gardies is Professor of film studies at the University of Lyon II. He has published widely on Alain Robbe-Grillet and cinema. His books include *Cinéma d'Afrique noire francophone*, *L'Espace au cinéma*, *Le Récit filmique*, *200 mots-clés de la théorie du cinéma*. His two most recent books are *Le Conteur de l'ombre* (1999) and *Décrire au cinéma* (1999).

Tivadar Gorilovics is Professor of French Literature at Kossuth Lajos University, Debrecen, Hungary, where he was also vice-rector of the University from 1983 to 1986. He specialises in the period 1850–1950 (Renan, Zola, Roger Martin du Gard, Jean-Richard Bloch). His publications include *Recherches sur les origines et les sources de la pensée de Roger Martin du Gard*, *La Légende de Victor Hugo de Paul Lafargue*, *Correspondance de J.-R. Bloch et André Monglond I & II* and a recently published annotated edition of Jean-Richard Bloch's unpublished correspondence, *Lettres du régiment (1902–1903)*. He is general editor of *Studia Romanica*.

Jean-Jacques Hamm, FRSC, is Professor at Queen's University (Canada) and Head of Department of French Studies. His main interest is Stendhal, on whom he has published several books and numerous articles.

Grahame Lock studied in London, Cambridge and Paris. He has worked since 1974 in the Netherlands, at Leiden and Nijmegen Universities, where he is Professor of Political Theory and Philosophy. He was a founding board member of the 'Collège international de philosophie' in Paris and has also taught as a visiting Faculty Fellow in European Philosophy at Oxford University. He is the author of various books and articles on the history of philosophy, political theory and questions of rationality and irrationality.

Xavier Martin is historian of law and Professor at the Faculty of Law, Economics and Social Sciences at Angers University. He has published extensively on the ideology of the French Revolution and on the Civil Code of 1804 and his *Mythologie du Code Napoléon* is forthcoming. Also forthcoming, from Berghahn, is the English translation of his *Nature humaine et revolution française du siècle des lumières au Code Napoléon*.

François Nectoux is Professor of Contemporary European Studies at Kingston University and co-author (with Jill Forbes and Nick Hewlett) of *Contemporary France: Politics, Economics and Society* (1994). He has published widely on French and European economic and environmental matters and his most recent articles have appeared in the *European Union Handbook* and the *Journal of European Social Policy*. He has also written articles and chapters on nationalism and culture and is currently working on a study of social problems in France entitled: *Unemployment and Social Exclusion in Contemporary France*.

Allan H. Pasco is the Hall Professor of Nineteenth-Century Literature at the University of Kansas. His most recent book, *Sick Heroes: French Society and Literature in the Romantic Age, 1760–1850*, was published by the University of Exeter Press in 1997. He is currently occupied with the culture of violence in the last half of the eighteenth century, the first fruits of which will soon appear in *Studies on Early Modern France* and *The Virginia Quarterly*.

Yolande de Pontfarcy is Senior Lecturer in French at University College, Dublin. She has published on courtly and Arthurian literature, visions and other world voyages and Celtic and Indo-European Studies.

Naomi Segal is Professor of French Studies at the University of Reading and the author of numerous articles and eight books, most recently *The 'Adulteress's' Child* (1992), *Scarlet Letters* (co-edited 1997), *Coming Out of Feminism?* (coedited 1998) and *André Gide: Pederasty and Pedagogy* (1998). Her current research projects include the edition in French of a collection of papers on Gide and a co-edition of essays on the indeterminate body.

Trista Selous is Associate Research Fellow at the University of Surrey, Roehampton Institute. She is the author of *The Other Woman: Feminism and Femininity in the work of Marguerite Duras* (Yale University Press, 1988) and numerous articles on Marguerite Duras and on French cinema. She has also published a number of translations and continues to work freelance as a translator and editor.

Lieve Spaas is Professor of French Cultural Studies at Kingston University. She has published articles on Rousseau and the eighteenth century and is part of the CNRS Rousseau research team in Paris. Her books include a sociohistorical analysis of the letters of Catherine de Saint-Pierre to her brother Bernardin, *Lettres de Catherine de Saint-Pierre à son frère Bernardin*, *Paternity and Fatherhood: Myths and Realities* (editor), and *The Francophone Film: a Struggle for Identity*.

Scott M. Sprenger is an Assistant Professor in the Department of French and Italian at Brigham Young University in Utah. He has published articles on Balzac, Mallarmé and Baudelaire and is currently completing a book on Balzac entitled *'Balzac's' Secrets*.

Magda Stroinska is Associate Professor of German and Linguistics at McMaster University in Hamilton, Ontario (Canada). Her research interests focus on sociolinguistics and linguistic relativism, with publications on the theory of prototypes, scientific discourse, cultural stereotyping and the language of propaganda. Since 1996, she also holds a research appointment at Kingston University, UK.

Anna Szabó is Professor of French Literature at Kossuth Lajos University, Debrecen, Hungary. She specialises in George Sand, on whom she has published extensively. She is the author of *L'Accueil critique de Paul Valéry en Hongrie* (1978) and *Le Personnage sandien – constantes et variations* (1991) and has recently published an annotated edition of George Sand's prefaces to her fictional work.

Roger Webster is Professor of Literary Studies and Director of the School of Media, Critical and Creative Arts at Liverpool John Moores University. His interests and publications are in literary theory, the 1930s, and Thomas Hardy on whom he wrote his doctoral thesis.

SELECT BIBLIOGRAPHY

Bachelard, G. (1942) *L'Eau et les rêves*. Paris: Corti.
Balensiefen, L. (1990) *Die Bedeutung des Spiegelbildes als ikonographisches Motiv in der antiken Kunst*. Tübingen: Ernst Wasmuth Verlag.
Braet, H. (1995) 'Narcisse et Pygmalion: mythe et intertexte dans le *Roman de la Rose*, in *Mediaevalia Antiquity*. Leuven: University Press: 237–54.
Bremmer, J. (ed.) (1986), *Interpretations of Greek Mythology*. Totowa, N.J.: Barnes and Noble.
Brenkman, J. (1976) 'Narcissus in the Text', in *Georgia Review* 30:293–327.
Brooks, P. (1987) 'The Idea of a Psychoanalytic Criticism', in S. Rimmon-Kenan (ed.), *Discourse in Psychoanalysis and Literature*. London and New York: Methuen.
Bryson, N. (1988) 'The Gaze in the Expanded Field', in H. Foster (ed.), *Vision and Visuality*. Seattle: Bay Press: 87–114.
Calderón (1963) *Eco y Narciso* [1672], ed. C. Aubrun. Paris: Centre de recherches de l'Institut d'Etudes Hispaniques.
Couloubaritsis, L. (1989) 'Le Schème du miroir chez les philosophes Grecs', in *Figures. Miroirs et Reflets. Cahier du Centre de Recherche sur l'Image, le Symbole et le Mythe* 4. Dijon: Université de Bourgogne: 21–45.
Dalí, S. (1937) *Métamorphose de Narcisse*. Paris: Editions Surréalistes.
Dessuant, P. (1994) *Le Narcissisme*. Paris: Presses Universitaires de France.
Durand, G. (1969) *Les Structures anthropologiques de l'imaginaire*. Paris: Bordas.
Edinger, E.F. (1992) *Ego and Archetype*. Boston and London: Shambhala.
Eitrem, S. (1935) 'Narkissos', in *Realencyclopädie der classischen Altertumswissenschaft* 16:1,721–33.

Eliade, M. (1975) *Traité d'Histoire des Religions*. Paris: Payot.
Elsner, J. (1995) *Art and the Roman Viewer: The Transformation of Art from the Roman World to Christianity*. Cambridge: Cambridge University Press.
––––––– (ed.) (1996) *Art and Text in Roman Culture*. Cambridge: Cambridge University Press.
Fränkel, H. (1945) *Ovid: A Poet Between Two Worlds*. Berkeley and Los Angeles: University of California Press.
Freud, S. (1953–74) *The Standard Edition of the Complete Psychological Works of Sigmund Freud in XXIV Volumes*, trans. J. Strachey et al. London: The Hogarth Press.
Frontisi-Ducroux, F. and J.-P. Vernant (1997) *Dans l'oeil du miroir*. Paris: Odile Jacob.
Gide, A. (1958) 'Le Traité du Narcisse', in *Romans*. Paris: Gallimard, Bibliothèque de la Pléiade.
Goldin, F. (1967) *The Mirror of Narcissus in the Courtly Love Lyric*. Ithaca, NY: Cornell University Press.
Grant, M. (1995) *Myths of the Greeks and Romans*. New York, London, Victoria, Toronto and Auckland: Meridian.
Green, A. (1983) *Narcissisme de vie, narcissisme de mort*. Paris: Minuit.
Grunberger, B. (1970) 'Narcissism in Female Sexuality', in J. Chasseguet-Smirgel (ed.) *Female Sexuality*. London: Maresfield: 68–83.
Hadot, P. (1976) 'Le Mythe de Narcisse et son interprétation par Plotin', in *Nouvelle revue de psychanalyse* 13:81–108.
Hardie, P. (1988) 'Lucretius and the Delusions of Narcissus', in *Materiali e Discussioni per l'Analisi dei Testi Classici* 20–1:71–89.
Hult, D. (1981) 'The Allegorical Fountain: Narcisse in the *Roman de la Rose*', in *Romanic Review* 72:125–248.
Hutcheon, L. (1980) *Narcissistic Narrative: the Metafictional Paradox*. New York and London: Methuen.
Jacoby, M. (1995) *Individuation and Narcissism – The Psychology of Self in Jung & Kohut*. London: Routledge.
Jong, I.J.F. de and J.P. Sullivan (eds) (1994), *Modern Critical Theory and Classical Literature*. Leiden: E.J. Brill.
Kampen, N.B. (ed.) (1996), *Sexuality in Ancient Art*. Cambridge: Cambridge University Press.
Kessler, J. (1982) 'La Quête amoureuse et poétique: la Fontaine de Narcisse dans le *Roman de la Rose*', in *Romanic Review* 73:133–46.
Kohut, H. (1971) *The Analysis of the Self* (New York: International Universities Press).
Lacan, J. (1966) 'Le Stade du miroir comme formateur de la fonction du Je', in *Ecrits 1*. Paris: Éditions du Seuil.
––––––– (1977) *The Four Fundamental Concepts of Psycho-Analysis*, trans. A. Sheridan. Harmondsworth: Penguin.
Laplanche J. & J.-B. Pontalis (1973) *The Language of Psycho-analysis*. London: Hogarth Press.
Lavelle, L. (1939) *L'Erreur de Narcisse*. London: Grasset.

Moreau, P. (1957) *Autour du 'culte du moi'. Essai sur les origines de l'égotisme français.* Paris: Archives des Lettres Modernes.

Ovid (1985) *Metamorphoses* Book 1–4, ed. with translation and notes by D.E. Hill. Warminster : Arris and Phillips.

Pausanius (1971) *Pausanius' Description of Greece*, Boeotia. London: Penguin Books.

Rosati, G. (1983) *Narciso e Pigmalione: Illusione e Spettacolo nelle Metamorfosi di Ovidio.* Florence: Sansoni.

Segal, N. (1988) *Narcissus and Echo: Women in the French* récit. Manchester: Manchester University Press.

Skinner, V. (1965) 'Ovid's Narcissus – An Analysis', in *Classical Bulletin* 41:59–61.

Stemmer, K. (1992) *Haüser in Pompeji 6: Casa dell' Ara Massima.* Munich: Hirmer Verlag.

Stirrup, B.E. (1976) 'Ovid's Narrative Technique: A Study in Duality', in *Latomus* 35:97–107.

Vinge, L. (1967) *The Narcissus Theme in Western European Literature up to the early 19th century*, trans. R. Dewsnap and N. Reeves. Lund: Gleerups.

Wallace-Hadrill, A. (1994) *Houses and Society in Pompeii and Herculaneum.* Princeton: Princeton University Press.

Index

A
Abraham, K., 44, 51, 53
Addison, J., 79, 234
Alberti, L. B., 89–90, 107
Albouy, P., 269–70
Alembert, J. d', 203
Allonville, comte de, 196, 202–03
Allt, P., 176–77
Alspach, R. K., 176–77
Andréoli, M., 3, 13
Apollinaire, G., 159
Apter, E. S., 164
Aristénète, 260–61
Augustine, St, 32, 34
Aulard, F.-A., 196, 203

B
Bacciagaluppi, M., 248, 260
Bachelard, G., 22, 58, 60, 65
Baczko, B., 202–03
Bakhtin, M., 181, 183, 189–90
Balensiefen, L., 92, 104, 107
Balibar, E., 209, 218
Balzac, H. de, 63, 180, 249, 252, 258

Bann, S., 90, 106–07
Barthes, R., 60, 131, 134, 181, 227, 233
Barton, C., 105, 107
Baudelaire, Ch., 79
Beaumarchais, P. A. Caron de, 257, 258
Bec, P., 26, 33
Bek, L., 105, 108
Bentick, S., 199, 203
Benveniste, E., 230, 233
Berger-Doer, G., 98, 108
Bergman, I., 129
Bernard de Ventadour, 3, 25, 32
Bertens, H., 124, 134
Berthier, Ph., 65
Beti, M., 239
Beyle, H., 79, 82
Black Narcissus, 242
Blanchot, M., 83, 85
Bloch, M., 201, 203
Bloom, H., 7, 167–69, 171, 173, 175–77
Boehme, J., 177
Bourne, E. J., 232, 234
Braet, H., 32–33

Bragantini, I., 98, 108
Bremmer, J., 109
Brenkman, J., 107–08
Brilliant, R., 100, 108
Brizard, Abbé, 196, 203
Brooks, P., 143, 149
Brunel, P., 270
Bryson, N., 101, 107–08
Bullen, J. B., 184, 190
Butler, J. (bishop), 51, 53
Byron, G., 81

C
Cabanis, P., 198, 202–03
Caesar, Julius, 8, 197–98, 200, 203
Calderón, P. de, 14, 19–20, 22–23
Callistratus, 91–93, 104, 106–07
Cambacérès, J.-J. Régis de, 202
Caravaggio, M., 90, 92
Carpenter, R. C., 189–90
Caulaincourt, A. A. L., 201, 203
Cecchetto, V., 225, 233
Cephisus, 1, 14, 27, 123, 138, 159
Chamfort, N. de, 202–03
Chamoiseau, P., 241
Chasles, Ph., 252, 260–61
Chasseguet-Smirgel, J., 76
Chateaubriand, F. R. de, 79–80, 84, 139, 202–03, 258
Chemama, R., 270
Chevrier, J., 242–43
Chomsky, N., 230, 233
Chrétien de Troyes, 30–31, 34
Circourt, A. de, 202
Cixous, H., 171, 176–77
Clair, J., 32, 33
Cocteau, J., 145
Coleman, K., 105–06, 108

Coleridge, S. T., 167
Comte, A., 200, 202–03
Conon, 18, 106
Constant, B., 79, 139, 194, 202–03
Cooley, C., 225, 233
Coquillat, M., 78, 85
Corcoran, P., 9, 235, 237, 243
Corneille, P., 81
Cottin, S., 251
Couloubaritsis, L., 26, 33
Courouve, C., 148–49
Crane, H., 167
Crébillon (père), P. J., 256
Cuminal, I., 219

D
Dalí, S., 89–90, 104, 108, 123–24, 128
Dante, 19, 80
Davies, J. C., 164
Delacroix, E., 79
Delay, J., 145, 149, 153, 163–64
Dennett, D. C., 223, 233
Depardieu, G., 76
Derrida, J., 177
Dessuant, P., 65
Dewsnap, R., 35
Diderot, D., 203, 257, 260–61
Didier, B., 63–65
Diop, B., 242–43
Diop, C. A., 236–37, 243
Dodds, E. R., 176
Dortier, J.-F., 218
Dostoevsky, F., 189
Douglas, M., 147, 149
Dover, K. J., 107–08
Dragonetti, R., 31, 33
Drerup, H., 105, 108
Drumont, E., 212
Dubois, P., 32–33
Ducis, J.-F., 256

Ducray-Duminil, F. G. , 251–52
Dufournet, J., 33–34
Dumas (*père*), A. D., 251, 258
Durand, G., 30, 33
Duras, M., 4, 67–76, 79, 251
Durkheim, E., 247

E
Eaves, G., 7, 167
Ebbatson, R., 189–90
Edinger, E. F., 229, 232–33
Edison, T. A., 115
Edwards, J., 233
Eitrem, S., 106, 108
Eliade, M., 30, 33
Eliot, G., 189
Eliot, T. S., 84–85, 89–90, 108
Ellenberger, H., 39, 53
Ellis, H., 39, 231, 233
Ellsworth, P. C., 234
Elsner, J., 5, 7, 89, 105–08
Endymion, 100
Epinay, Mme d', 197, 203
Epstein, R., 232–33
Euripides, 92
Evans, G., 223, 233
Eve, 162
Everett, W., 6, 8, 121, 133–34

F
Fabre d'Eglantine, Ph., 194, 195
Fanon, F., 236, 244
Faye, J.-P., 207, 218
Ferry, J., 8, 215–16
Fiala, P., 208, 218
Flaubert, G., 64–65
Fleming, J. V., 30, 33
Fonvielle, B. F. A., 199, 202–03
Fourier, Ch., 257, 260
Fourrier, A., 30, 33–34
Fowler, D., 106, 108

Fränkel, H., 106, 108
Frappier, J., 25–26, 30, 33
Frazer, J. G., 170
Freud, A., 48
Freud, S., 3, 6–7, 37–49, 51–53, 125, 139, 143–44, 149, 151–52, 161, 164, 167–77, 179–80, 212–14, 218, 257, 266, 269
Friedman, L. J., 31, 33
Fromentin, E., 139
Fromm, E., 248, 259
Frontisi-Ducroux, F., 92, 106–08
Fronto, M. Lucretius, 17, 93, 98, 108–09
Furet, F., 201, 203
Furst, L. R., 259–60

G
Galinsky, K., 106, 108
Gallup, G. G., 223, 233
Garber, F., 259–60
Gardies, A., 5–6, 111, 119, 240, 243
Gaudreault, A., 119
Gautier, Th., 139
Gauvin, A., 241
Gay, P., 152, 164
Geertz, C., 229, 233
Gide, A., 6–7, 15–53, 81–82, 85, 139, 142, 144–49, 151–65
Girard, R., 59, 65
Glover, J., 223, 233
Godard, J.-L., 128–29
Goffman, E., 222–23, 233
Goldhill, S., 106, 108
Goldin, F., 25–28, 32–33
Gollnich, B., 206, 208
Gonzenbach, V. von, 100, 108
Gorilovics, T., 9–10, 61, 65, 263
Goulet, A., 152, 164–65

Graffigny, Mme de, 257
Grant, M., 222, 228, 232–33
Green, A., 40–41, 49, 53, 266, 270
Gregor, I., 189–90
Grimal, P., 270
Grimm, M. de, 197, 203
Grivel, G. , 257, 260
Grunberger, B., 40, 65, 75–76, 151
Grundy, J., 184, 190
Guillaume de Lorris, 3, 19, 28, 30–34
Güntert, G., 33

H
Hamm, J.-J., 4, 5, 77
Hampaté Bâ, A., 239, 242–43
Harari, J. V., 177
Hardie, P., 107, 109
Hardy, B. N., 189–90
Hardy, F. E., 181, 184–86, 190
Hardy, T., 7, 179–90
Harper, G. M., 177
Harré, R., 226, 233
Hastings, M., 210, 218
Hastorf, A. H., 234
Hawkins, D., 189–90
Hawkins, P., 235, 244
Hazlitt, W., 80
Heath, S., 133–34
Heelas, P., 228, 233
Henderson, J., 106, 109
Hertz, N., 171, 177
Hesiod, 17
Hewitt, H., 224, 233
Hill, L., 75–76
Hillman, L., 30, 34
Hirschman, A. O., 53
Hitler, A., 213
Hoffmann, E. T. W. A., 167, 171–72, 176–77
Hofstadter, D. R., 223, 233

Holmes, G., 247, 260
Hood, W. K., 177
Huchet, J.-C., 26, 30, 33–34
Hugo, V., 79, 252
Hult, D., 30, 34
Humphrey, N., 223, 233
Hutcheon, L., 126, 133–34
Huysmans, J.-K., 81, 84–85, 268

J
Jackson, R., 171, 176–77
Jacoby, M., 213, 218
James, H., 180, 189–90
Jashemski, W. F., 99, 109
Jaucourt, L., 196, 203
Jean de Meun, 3, 28, 31–34
Jentsch, E., 171, 176–77
Jong, I. J. F. de, 109
Jouve, P., 207, 211, 218
Jouy, E., 252–53, 255, 258–60
Jung, C. G., 213, 218, 229, 232
Jung, F., 105, 109
Jung, M.-R., 33
Justice, B., 256, 260
Justice, R., 256, 260

K
Kalinka, E., 106, 109
Kamenetz, G., 31, 34
Kampen, N. B., 108
Kant, I., 50
Kaplan, C., 164–65
Karr, A., 252
Kay, S., 26, 34
Kellog, R., 232, 234
Kernberg, O., 40, 255, 261
Kessler, J., 31, 34
Klein, M., 48–49, 51, 53
Klein, W., 105, 109
Klemperer, V., 227, 232, 234
Köhler, E., 30, 34

Kohut, H., 40, 213, 218
Kondoleon, C., 107, 109
Kristeva, J., 23, 151, 183, 188, 190, 214, 218

L

La Fontaine, J. de, 77, 85
Lacan, J., 4–5, 38–40, 47–53, 69, 101–03, 107, 109, 121, 124–26, 134, 151, 183, 188
Laforgue, J., 82, 85
Lamartine, A. de, 79
Lanza, R. P., 233
Laplanche, J., 38, 41–42, 50–53
Lapsley, R., 126, 134
Laqueur, T., 147, 149
Larousse, P., 253, 261
Las Cases, E. A. D. de, 200, 202, 204
Lavelle, L., 17, 23
Lavers, A., 233, 235, 244
Laye, C., 242, 244
Le Pen, J.-M., 8, 205–12, 214–19
Leavis, F. R., 181, 189–90
Lebras, Y., 164–65
Lecoy, F., 28, 34
Lefay-Toury, M.-N., 27–28, 34
Lemaire, A., 47, 50, 53
Levi, D., 107, 109
Levinas, E., 214, 218
LeVine, R. A., 233–34
Litto, V. del, 80, 85
Lock, A., 233
Lock, G., 3–4, 37
Lopes, H., 239, 243
Louvet, L., 260
Luce, L. F., 234
Lucey, M., 163, 165
Lulli, J.-B., 19
Lumière, A. and L., 5, 111–19
Lykes, M. B., 229, 234
Lyotard, J.-F., 133–34

M

Mac Dougall, E. B., 33
Macrobius, 30
Magoudi, A., 207, 211, 218
Maine de Biran, 79
Mallarmé, S., 22–23, 83, 85, 177
Malle, L., 127, 129
Mallet du Pan, J., 202, 204
Manet, E., 187–88
Maréchal, S., 206, 210, 216, 219
Martin, X., 8, 193
Massin, J., 201, 204
Maupertuis, P. L. Moreau de, 199
Maurras, C., 210
Maximus, V., 98
Mayes, P. L. A., 223–24, 234
Mead, G. H., 224, 234
Mégret, B., 206, 210–11, 216–17, 219
Meister, H., 199, 204
Méla, C., 31, 34
Méliès, G., 114, 119
Mercier, L. S., 202, 204
Mérimée, P., 139
Mészáros, M., 129–31
Metz, Ch., 114, 119, 121–22, 124, 127, 131, 134
Michel, D., 104–05, 109
Michelangelo, 80
Mielsch, H., 104, 109
Mill, J. S., 200, 202
Miller, A., 213, 219
Milton, J. 19, 234
Mirabeau, H. G. de, 202
Mitterrand, F., 206
Montaigne, M. de, 22, 77–78, 85
Montesquieu, Ch. de, 196, 198–99, 204
Moreau, P., 81, 85
Musset, A. de, 139

N
Nabokov, V., 53
Näcke, P., 39, 51
Napoleon, 199–204
Nectoux, F., 8, 205
Nerval, G. de, 139, 142, 149
Ngùgì wa Thiong'o, 241, 244
Nietzsche, F., 81
Nodier, Ch., 79
Nogearet, F.-F., see Aristénète
Notz, M.-F., 31, 34

O
O'Keefe, C., 152–53, 164–65
O'Meara, B. E., 201, 202, 204
Osborne, R., 106, 108
Ousmane, S., 239, 241, 244
Ovid, 1–2, 4–5, 7, 10, 14–23, 25, 27, 30–31, 33–34, 37–38, 50, 67–69, 82, 90–93, 98–99, 101, 103–04, 106–10, 123, 131, 137, 139–40, 149, 159, 172–73, 179, 238, 243, 263–70
Oyono, F., 239, 244
Ozouf, M., 201–04

P
Parnell, C., 165
Pasco, A., 9, 247, 249, 254, 261
Pausanias, 1, 9, 18–19, 23, 51, 82, 106, 263, 270
Pellizer, E., 106, 109
Philostratus, 91–93, 100–04, 106–07, 110
Picard, M., 149, 204, 265, 270
Pichois, C., 252, 260–61
Pickens, R. T., 30, 34
Place, J., 260–61
Plato, 26
Pliny the Elder, 265
Plotinus, 23, 106

Poirion, D., 31, 34
Pontalis, J.-B., 38, 41–42, 50–53
Pontfarcy, Y. de, 3–4, 25
Portalis, J. E. M., 202
Poussin, N., 90
Powell, M., 117
Press, A., 26, 34
Prévost, abbé A. F., 139, 141, 149, 255–56
Price, R., 201, 204
Proust, M., 83, 144–45, 181–83, 189–90
Pruner, F., 152–54, 163–65
Pucci, S. R., 260–61

Q
Quarto, D. Octavius, 94
Quérard, J. M., 260
Quinault, Ph., 19

R
Rafn, B., 107, 109
Raynal, abbé G., 199, 204
Reeves, N., 35
Reinhard, M., 194, 204
Restif de la Bretonne, N., 258, 261
Ribard, J., 31, 34
Ricardou, J., 180, 190
Ridge, G. R., 259, 261
Rieff, P., 176, 178
Rimbaud, A., 83, 213
Rimmon-Kenan, S., 149
Ringger, K., 33
Rittaud-Hutinet, J., 119
Rizzo, G. E., 100, 109
Robertson, D. W., 30, 34
Roederer, P. L., 201
Romaine, S., 231, 234
Rosa, S., 80
Rosati, G., 104, 107, 109

Index 285

Rose, J., 106, 109
Rosenfeld, H., 49
Rosset, C., 81–82, 85
Rossum-Guyon, F. van, 65
Roudinesco, E., 52, 53
Rousseau, J.-J., 59, 63, 78, 86, 256, 258, 260
Roussel, 198, 204
Ruano-Borbalan, J. C., 218
Russell, B., 228

S

Sacchini, A. , 256
Sade, D. A. F. de, 81, 257, 261
Samain, A., 79, 86
Sand, G., 4, 57–66, 79, 134, 249, 250, 258, 261
Sankey, M., 76
Sartre, J.-P., 107, 235–36, 243–44, 268, 270
•Schimel, J. L., 254, 259, 261
Schlumberger, J., 148–49
Schnapp, A., 92, 109
Schneider, D. J., 234
Scholes, R., 232, 234
Schönberger, O., 106, 109
Scott, W., 6, 63
Segal, C. P., 109
Segal, H., 48–49
Segal, N., 6, 53, 105, 137, 143–44, 149
Sénac de Meilhan, 202, 204
Senghor, L. S., 235, 244
Shakespeare, W., 23, 53
Shirley, J., 19
Shklovsky, V., 189
Shweder, R., 232–34
Sibony, D., 214, 219
Sieyès, E. J. abbé, 194, 204
Sigelius, 18
Simmons, H., 209, 210, 219
Skinner, B. F., 233
Skinner, V., 106, 109

Smith, E. C., 234
Socrates, 17
Solomon, J., 75–76
Sophocles, 161
Souchard, M., 207–08, 210–11, 214, 219
Soudais, M., 219
Soyinka, W., 236–37, 244
Spencer, H., 170
Spenser, E., 19
Spinoza, B., 15, 23
Sprenger, S., 6–7, 151
Staël, G. de, 79, 194, 202–04
Stemmer, K., 98–99, 109
Stendhal, 5, 80–81, 84–86, 249, 252, 258, 261
Stevens, R., 224, 234
Stevens, W., 167
Stewart, E. C., 228, 234
Stirrup, B. E., 104, 107, 110
Stoughton Hyde, L., 137, 149
Strabo, 18
Strohm, P., 30, 34
Stroinska, M., 8–9, 221, 225, 232–34
Strubel, A., 28, 30, 34
Sue, E., 252, 258
Sullivan, J. P., 109
Szabó, A., 4, 57

T

Tagguieff, P., 207, 219
Talleyrand, Ch. M. de, 227
Talvart, H., 260–61
Tarkovsky, A., 129
Taylor, C., 223, 226, 230, 234
Téchiné, A., 125–26
Thiry-Stassin, M., 27, 34
Thut, M., 31, 34
Tiburtinus, M. L., 94, 99
Tocqueville, Ch. A. C. de, 202, 204
Todorov, T., 213, 219

Tornatore, G., 131
Truffaut, F., 133
Turner, W. M., 7, 184–88
Tyssens, M., 27, 34

V
Valéry, P., 21–23, 78, 81–84, 86
van Eyck, Jan, 187
Vernant, J.-P., 92, 106–08
Vertov, D., 118
Vigny, A. de, 81, 79, 248
Villiers, D. de, 196
Vinge, L., 25–27, 35, 89, 106, 110
Vitz, E. B., 30, 35
Voltaire, 202, 204, 256
Vos, M. de, 99

W
Wagner, R., 185
Wahnich, S., 219
Walker, A., 106, 110
Wallace-Hadrill, A., 99, 110
Wathier, V., 219
Watts, R. J., 223, 234
Weber, S., 171, 178
Webster, R., 7, 179, 184, 190
Werner, K. F., 201, 204
Westlake, M., 126, 134
Wetherall, M., 225–26, 229, 234
Widdowson, P., 181, 189–90
Wilde, O., 10, 67, 144–45, 149, 221, 234,, 263–64, 266–70
Williams, R., 189–90
Wittenstein, I., 209, 218
Wollheim, R., 52–53
Woolf, V., 140, 149, 183
Wunenburger, J.-J., 32, 35

Y
Yeats, W. B., 7, 167–69, 171–74, 176–77
Young, M. de, 260–61

Z
Zanker, P., 99, 107, 110
Zumthor, P., 25, 35

www.ingramcontent.com/pod-product-compliance
Lightning Source LLC
Chambersburg PA
CBHW071151070526
44584CB00019B/2744